STAR WARS REDEEMED

Your Life-Transforming Journey With Jesus and the Jedi

By Bradley Hagan

BIG MERCURY PRESS

Big Mercury Press, LLC
P.O. Box 41782
Mesa, AZ 85274

ISBN 978-0-9971115-1-4

Library of Congress Control Number: 2016918802

CONTENTS

To my wonderful wife

INTRODUCTION

A New Hope! When *Star Wars* first came out in 1977, our world, and especially the United States, comprised a people without much hope. Perhaps it's no coincidence that the 1981 rerelease of the film saw the addition of *Episode IV: A New Hope* to the title. The turbulent 1960s, with Vietnam, racial unrest, and generational discord, as well as the dark 1970s, with its rising crime, energy crisis, and family breakdown, had left millions disillusioned with life and desperate for a brighter future. People looked to all sorts of things for an escape from reality and possibly a little hope, even if for only a couple of hours in a movie theater.

While *Star Wars* may have started off as just another summer movie to help people forget about life's problems, it quickly became much more. Like news of Jesus spreading throughout Judea, not only was everyone talking about *Star Wars,* they were also going to see the space spectacle over and over again. Unable to get enough, some people racked up dozens of trips to this galaxy far, far away, but even that didn't satisfy.

Remarkably, since its release nearly forty years ago, our passion for *Star Wars* has only intensified. Not even George Lucas could have predicted that, well into the 21st century, we would be able to look back and tally not only six additional films but also spin-off novels, video games, T-shirts, toys, lightsabers, lunchboxes, bed sheets, breakfast cereals and more *Star Wars* space stuff than you can shake a Tusken staff at. Now that Disney has acquired Lucasfilm and slated the production of more *Star Wars* movies, it's doubtful we'll be disengaging the hyperdrive any time soon.

But this colossal space opera franchise did so much more than just change the things we buy or entertain ourselves with. It touched us on a very personal, almost spiritual level. Look around. These days, couples get married in *Star Wars*-themed ceremonies. Fans name their children after the characters. And many families make it a tradition to watch Luke and Darth battling it out at special times like Thanksgiving or Christmas. I even named my dog "Vader." You may not go that far, but you picked this book to read over the millions of other choices. Why does *Star Wars* touch people's lives in such a meaningful way that they are willing to camp out for movie tickets, build a life-sized *Millennium Falcon,* or decorate their living spaces with action figures, X-wings, and movie posters?

At some point over the past few decades, *Star Wars* did something few movies do: it transformed from a series of films into a true modern-day myth. This story of strangers in another galaxy, in another time, resonated in the minds, hearts, and souls of people from every walk of life, teaching us about good and evil, love and hate, fall and redemption. It taught us about ourselves, who we were and who we might be. And, like any good myth, the saga conveyed and still conveys the idea of something much grander.

To understand what this might be, we need only examine another cultural phenomenon that was exploding in the years leading up to *Star Wars.* Coincidentally, this movement also took place largely in California, where Lucas was writing his script. Many dubbed this revolution, the "Jesus Movement." Like *Star Wars,* it also represented a retreat from the world, although in this case, people retreated not to movie theaters but to new lives in Christ.

Upon closer examination, both of these exoduses were a response to the same problem, a sense of emptiness that had people looking at the world around them and longing for something better. When Luke Skywalker turns his gaze to the twin sunsets on Tatooine, fearing his life will never matter and yet hoping for a better tomorrow, people could sympathize, as we still do today. At some point we have all felt the same way, because God created us for something more than grinding out a meager existence in the desert. The Bible teaches us that we were meant to live abundant lives with an eternal purpose, lives that glorify the God of the universe, not just ourselves.

About This Book

Some may criticize this book, arguing that I'm forcing Christian themes and symbols into the *Star Wars* galaxy that simply are not there. It's true that the *Star Wars* films are not "Christian" movies per se. In fact, much of the content of *Star Wars* runs completely counter to Christianity, being much closer to an eastern religion like Taoism.[1] In that case, how can I justify this book?

This goes back to the purpose of a myth. C.S. Lewis tells us that a myth is not the truth itself. It is only meant to point us to the truth.[2] *Star Wars* brings up ideas about truth that we can then turn to the Bible to see fleshed out completely. Since Adam and Eve disobeyed God in the Garden of Eden, this world has been under a curse, and people no longer want to bring glory to God. Be that as it may, every person is still made in the image of God, and people who create art, such as movies, continue to have some sense of good and evil. We still see echoes of what was meant for mankind at the beginning. Creation is corrupted, but part of our job as Christians is to detect these echoes, as faint as they may be, and then use them to help turn people's thinking back to God, to his goodness, to his love, to all of his attributes, in order to bring glory and honor to his name.

We're made righteous—that is, accepted by God—by trusting in Jesus Christ's death on the cross alone, but we're made holy here on Earth by learning about God's ethical will for us and then, with the Holy Spirit's help, applying what we learn.

> Do not conform to the pattern of this world, but be transformed by the renewing of your mind. Then you will be able to test and approve what God's will is—his good, pleasing and perfect will. (Romans 12:2)

We learn about God mostly by studying the Bible. But we can also be reminded of him if we know how to watch a movie like *Star Wars*. Therefore, in order to reach this goal, this book will view the entire *Star Wars* saga through the lens of Christianity, consider biblical truths that the movies call to mind, and then rely on the Holy Spirit to use this reflection on Lucas' beloved films to help us love God more and live for him in a more purposeful way.

But is it permissible for Christians to compare secular movies to the Word of God? If so, is it an effective method to help us grow closer to Jesus? These are good questions, and the answer to both of them is "Yes."

In Acts 17, the Apostle Paul chose an amazing and unlikely method of evangelism. While in Athens, he reflected on the pagan culture and statues all around him. As he debated with the Epicurean and

Stoic philosophers, he quoted not one but two of their most popular poets. First, he quoted the Cretan philosopher Epimenides when he said, "For in him we live and move and have our being" (Acts 17:28). Then he quoted a Cilician philosopher named Aratus, "As some of your own poets have said, 'We are his offspring.'" This would not be too earth-shattering if these poets were talking about the God of Abraham, Isaac, and Jacob, but they were not. The lines from these poems originally referred to the Greek god Zeus. Paul realized that the Athenians did not have the biblical categories required to discuss Jesus properly, so he took snippets from their own art in order to point them to Christ. Even though these poets didn't have Jesus in mind when they penned their words, Paul used their writings to make a connection between his audience and the gospel.

In this book, I follow Paul's example and use *Star Wars* as a bridge between readers and Christian theology. However, while Paul's audience in Athens were unbelievers, I wrote *Star Wars Redeemed* primarily for believers. My goal is to use your enjoyment of *Star Wars* to help deepen your love for Jesus. Reading this book won't always be easy. We'll explore some deep theology, and you might have to wrestle with your own beliefs from time to time. Though, the strategy is simple. We love God more when we know him better. And we know him better by studying his Word. The aim here is not to fill your mind with knowledge about the Bible just for the sake of knowledge. My desire is that you knowing the Bible and thus God better will spur you toward a greater love for him and others.

Throughout this book, I also use the term "believer" frequently. By this I don't mean someone who simply believes intellectually in the existence of God or Jesus. If we look to the Bible for our definition, a believer declares that "Jesus is Lord" and believes in his heart that God raised him from the dead (Romans 10:9).[3] A believer confesses his guilt before God and accepts that Jesus' death on the cross fully atoned for the believer's sin. A believer enters into a committed relationship with God, desiring to obey the commands of the Bible (John 14:15). Along the way, I'll also interchange the term "Christian" for "believer." Again, becoming a Christian doesn't happen automatically by being born into the right family or avoiding affiliation with another religious group.

Instead, being a Christian means trusting in Jesus and relying on his grace through faith for salvation (Ephesians 2:8).

By the way, I use the term "redeemed" in the title of this book not because I think *Star Wars* is evil or dangerous but because the films were never intended to bring glory to the God of heaven and Earth. Just like everything else in this fallen world, we need to redeem movies or make them spiritually profitable so that our eyes stay fixed upon Jesus and our lives can count for the King.

One last thing: scattered throughout the book are movie minutiae, extra random information related to the films. Look for the telescope icon to discover things like what the Kessel Run is, how they made a lightsaber, or that Yoda's first name was almost Minch.

I invite you to join me on this journey, not unlike the characters in *Star Wars* who participate in a fantastic adventure. My prayer is that this book will give you a "new hope," which is a greater love for Jesus and his Word. Not only will you learn a lot in these pages, you'll also find a new way to enjoy your study of the Bible and the *Star Wars* movies. I hope you're as excited as I am.

In the words of Han Solo, "Here's where the fun begins!"

PART I

THE FORCE

Many people regard the Force as merely another aspect of George Lucas'
science fiction saga. However, in the final analysis, the Force doesn't have
much to do with science at all (well, except for those pesky midi-chlorians).
Rather, it has more in common with religion. The characters in Star Wars
describe the Force in supernatural terms: sometimes as an impersonal
all-powerful energy, occasionally as a living entity with a will, frequently as a
mystical tool to be used, and, at other times, as an ally or companion.

What's this religious element doing in the middle of a sci-fi tale about a galac-
tic war between rebels fighting an oppressive empire? The answer is that
mankind has frequently looked to religion or the supernatural to solve life's
problems. Therefore, we should see disciples of the Force as religious follow-
ers, striving to learn the ways of this transcendent energy so that, through
their faith, they can deliver themselves and others from life's woes.

Like any good star pilot, let's map out our journey a little before takeoff. In
Chapter 1, we'll examine the Force, searching out the similarities between it
and the God of the Bible. While studying the Christian parallels, I'll point out
the subtle discrepancies as well. We'll explore these differences in further
detail in Chapter 2, "The Dark Side."

THE LIGHT SIDE

●○○○○○○○○○○○○○○○○

The Power of the Force

"Use the Force, Luke" is one of the most famous phrases to come out of the *Star Wars* saga. We love this concept, because, deep down, we know we need some sort of supernatural help in life. Realizing we can't make it on our own, like the Jedi in *Star Wars,* we look to religion. Even Han Solo, who ordinarily puts his trust in his blaster, realizes it's no match for Darth Vader in Cloud City. He needs something—or someone—outside himself if he hopes to survive this ordeal.

In *Episode IV,* Obi-Wan tells Luke, "The Force is what gives a Jedi his power." Indeed, using the Force is the key to power. Power equates to control, and if you have enough control, you can be the god of your world. If your X-wing crash lands in a swamp, no problem; just use the Force and you're back in business. Stormtroopers get in your way? With a wave of the hand, a Jedi mind trick clears your path. The Jedi and the Sith *use* the Force as a helper in times of trouble, an ally in combat, and even as a means to live on after death.

In the *Star Wars* galaxy, the Force is the closest thing to a god, and yet it couldn't be more different from the God of Christianity. Both the Jedi and the Sith can harness the Force, control it, and use it on their terms. In contrast, while the God of the Bible lovingly helps his children in all sorts of ways, the Creator is not a tool for any of his creatures to exploit. Even Jesus would not take advantage of his Father and the incredible power that was at his disposal despite the fact that he was under enormous pressure. While being tempted by Satan in the wilderness, "Jesus answered, 'It is said: "Do not put the Lord your God to the test"'" (Luke 4:12).

This isn't to say we don't have access to God's power, not at all. It simply means that God—not you or me—decides when and how he empowers his people. God's blessings don't give us worldly power; they give us spiritual power over sin. As the Apostle Paul says, "Praise be to the God and Father of our Lord Jesus Christ, who has blessed us in the heavenly realms with every spiritual blessing in Christ" (Ephesians 1:3). (We'll study this important principle more later on.) In contrast, the "prosperity gospel," a popular false teaching, reduces God to nothing but a means to an end—physical comfort and worldly happiness. This type of gospel appeals to the Greedos and the Jabbas of the world, those who want their bank accounts and planetary power increased but have no interest in cleaning up their act in terms of how they treat others.

🔭 Jabba the Hutt ranked #5 on "Forbes Fictional 15" list in 2008. The list ranks the richest fictional characters from films, literature, TV, video games, and comic books. Jabba's wealth was estimated at $8.4 billion.

Even Christians who genuinely love Jesus and haven't fallen prey to a false gospel can misunderstand the power of God. For instance, Philippians 4:13 has become popularized but is often misapplied. The New King James Version translates the verse this way: "I can do all things through Christ who strengthens me." This is a wonderful verse to live by, of course, but only if read and practiced in the intended context. The "strength" in this verse refers not to situations like winning at basketball, passing a test in school, or earning a promotion at work. Instead, this verse and its context teach that God gives his children strength to be content during adverse circumstances. As Paul says in Philippians 4:12,

> I know what it is to be in need, and I know what it is to have plenty. I have learned the secret of being content in any and every situation, whether well fed or hungry, whether living in plenty or in want.

In *Episode IV,* it's a lot more exciting to see Luke use the Force to blow up the Death Star and save the galaxy than it would have been if he had merely learned how to have a better attitude about not going to Tosche Station. Regardless, God desires that we rely on his strength to shun sin. He cares little if we succeed at keeping up with the Joneses or, in this case, the Jabbas.

As Romans 6 says, God gives Christians his awesome power so that they can break free from sin's mastery. Jesus purchased this power for us through his death. This means he not only secured salvation for all who believe and trust in him but also ransomed a life in which we are no longer controlled by our sinful desires. "For by one sacrifice he has made perfect forever those who are being made holy" (Hebrews 10:14).

Will believers ever obey God perfectly? No, not until we're in heaven. Unfortunately, even as new creations in Christ, we still have to contend with sin in our lives. But now, praise God, empowered by the Holy Spirit, we can actually make progress in our fight against sin through his unlimited power!

"One All-Powerful Force"

Similar to God, the Force controls everything. Even though both the Jedi and the Sith respect the Force's sovereignty, Han Solo, the rebel of rebels in *Episode IV,* refuses to submit to its control—and everyone nearly pays the price.

Unlike Han, we have the advantage of being on the outside looking in. For us, it's easy to grasp all the times in the *Star Wars* saga that the Force governs situations and events so that people's destinies are realized and prophecies are fulfilled. As an illustration, in *Episode I,* Qui-Gon and Obi-Wan decide to land on Tatooine for fuel and to repair their ship. They study the star chart and then make the decision. While their actions look completely independent of anything outside of their mental faculties, they're just playing their roles in the Force's larger plan (for lack of a better word). Another instance is when Qui-Gon tells Anakin, "Our meeting was not a coincidence. Nothing happens by accident." This is analogous to how we make our personal decisions. They occur only within the boundaries of what God has determined.

The Force also appears to be like God during moments when bad things happen that seem out of step with the end goal. For example, would it not have been easier for the Force to lead R2-D2 and

C-3PO straight to Ben? Why did they need to be captured by the Jawas first? That could have spelled disaster for the galaxy if Artoo was simply melted down or used for scrap parts, leading to the destruction of the technical read-outs of the Death Star. But if the Jawas hadn't of captured the droids, they never would have wound up in Luke's hands, and Artoo's determination to reach Ben Kenobi at all costs would have never led Luke to pursue his destiny.

This is comparable to the story of Joseph in the Bible. Why did Joseph need to be betrayed by his brothers and sold into slavery? Could God not have accomplished his plan without all this worry, misery, and uncertainty? Only God knows the reason. Nevertheless, his Word gives us a glimpse of one answer in Genesis 50:20 when Joseph says, "You intended to harm me, but God intended it for good to accomplish what is now being done, the saving of many lives." God knew about the coming famine, and he knew he would need someone of Joseph's character in place as an administrator to ensure the people survived. God also knew the only way to build Joseph's character was through a series of trials.

The next time your plans seem to take a dramatic detour from your preferred destination, and you feel like Artoo rolling precariously alone through the rocky, shadowy, Jawa-infested valley of death, remember that sometimes God, like the Force, takes you on a completely different, and often more treacherous, journey than what you were expecting. He does this to build your character, strengthen your faith, and accomplish something of eternal significance, the true measure of which you may only realize much later.

✴ Many fans go on self-guided tours to retrace Artoo's perilous journey through the Tatooine terrain. These scenes from *Episode IV* were filmed on location in California's Death Valley.

As movie watchers, it's obvious that nothing in the *Star Wars* galaxy is more powerful than the Force. But for many characters, this belief does not come easily. Han Solo requires most of *Episode IV* to even acknowledge that the Force exists, and Luke requires much of *Episode V* to put aside his remaining unbelief. It's one thing for a renegade like Solo to thumb his Corellian nose at the Force, but Luke? At times, our hero from Tatooine is as unconvinced of the Force's power as "Doubting Thomas" was of Christ's resurrection. During *Episode V,* Luke dismisses Yoda's instruction to not carry weapons into the cave on Dagobah. Then Yoda's ability to lift an entire X-wing fighter using merely his mind shakes Luke's faith to its very foundation.

As in our world, *Star Wars* characters tend to trust in themselves and technology instead of a higher power. It's true that people have made incredible advancements in fields like engineering, information technology, and space travel, but even this is due to God's grace.

It's also striking how no matter what type of technological advancements we make; death is the one thing we can't control. Our accomplishments in medicine and science are futile Plagueis-like attempts to cheat death, but at best, we can only postpone it.

In *Episode III,* Anakin strives to acquire the power to prevent Padmé from dying. Tragically, he never receives this ability, which he desires so desperately. This is a good reminder that the power of life will always come from Almighty God alone. People may be able to do many wonderful things on Earth, but overcoming sin and death will never be part of those abilities. It's Jesus' authority and power over sin and death that separates him from everyone and everything else.

It's fitting that God has the dominion over death considering he had the power to create the first life. Jesus performed more miraculous signs than anyone else in the Bible, but it's bringing the dead back to life that was the most astounding and most important. This is because the resurrection of Jesus and our own promised resurrection from the dead are crucial to the Christian faith. In fact, Paul says in 1 Corinthians 15:14, "And if Christ has not been raised, our preaching is useless and so is your faith." Similarly, the Jedi see life after death as the ultimate power in the universe. It's the reason Obi-Wan can be struck down, but, in turn, become more powerful than Vader can possibly imagine.

As explained earlier, God gives those who are in Christ power over sin. Paul links this power over sin with the power God will use to raise us from the dead. Paul describes this in Ephesians 1:19–20 when he prays that the Church would know,

His [God's] incomparably great power for us who believe. That power is the same as the mighty strength he exerted when he raised Christ from the dead and seated him at his right hand in the heavenly realms.

For believers, we truly have access to the ultimate power in the universe, both now, and after our own deaths one day, when we are raised to life.

"And A Powerful Ally It Is"

In *Episode V,* when Luke hangs on for dear life from a weather vane beneath Cloud City, we fear this could be the end of our protagonist, especially since Obi-Wan warned him he would not intervene to save him this time. To our surprise and relief, Luke's alliance with the Force saves his life indirectly after he uses the Force to summon Leia to rescue him. This scene is quite fascinating, because even though he didn't pray to the Force, it comes across to us almost like a prayer. Meanwhile, Leia, flying through the clouds in the *Millennium Falcon,* is his liberating angel.

It's not always easy for Luke to trust the Force. His bouts of disbelief are only worsened by the fiery trials he faces throughout *Episode V.* By the end of the movie, however, the dross of his unbelief finally burns away. Luke's confidence in the Force no longer wavers as it did on Dagobah. He realizes that he needn't rely on targeting computers, weapons, or even his Jedi Master. All he needs is his most powerful ally, the Force. The arc Luke travels teaches us that while it's awesome to take down an Imperial walker single-handedly, it's Luke's knowledge and maturity in the Force that is the most inspiring. We'll never be in a position to save the galaxy from an evil Empire, but we will experience uncertainties and difficulties in life. Luke teaches us that we need to have faith in God even when the blast shield is down and we're getting hit from all directions.

Luke experiences the Jedi "Trial of the Spirit" when he confronts Vader in the dark cave on Dagobah. In order to face the dark side within, all Padawans must take on a similar challenge before attaining Knighthood.

Sometimes people present the gospel to unbelievers as a surefire quick fix to solve all of life's problems. Enter into a 50/50 alliance with Jesus, him doing his part and you doing yours, and life will become like strolling through the meadows of Naboo. Sooner or later though, people come to realize that the Christian life is not like that at all. The fact is, as Christians, we are called to take up our cross daily. Jesus promised his followers would suffer all kinds of trials in this life. But the encouraging truth to keep in mind is that our reward will be great in heaven, and our alliance with Christ will last forever.

The Amplified Bible Classic Edition puts Psalm 54:4 this way: "Behold, God is my helper and ally; the Lord is my upholder and is with them who uphold my life." If we are in Christ, we are united with Jesus and receive his spiritual riches. Frequently in life, we're presented with two clear moral choices. One is sinful, and the other is not. These situations test our alliance with Christ, but God helps us so that we can see through Satan's deception. During these trials, it's crucial to recall a verse like 1 Corinthians 10:13, where Paul affirms that,

> No temptation has overtaken you except what is common to mankind. And God is faithful; he will not let you be tempted beyond what you can bear. But when you are tempted, he will also provide a way out so that you can endure it.

The reason for being joined with Jesus isn't so we can accomplish our earthly, material, temporary, and often self-serving goals. Our alliance with Christ achieves God's goal: the refinement of our character so that we radiate the beauty of Jesus in a dark and fallen world.

As easily as God spoke the universe into existence, God can cause anything to occur instantly without our involvement. He doesn't seem to do this for the most part though. Instead, he's patient and uses feeble and fallible people like us to be his instruments to affect those around us. As he works through us, we are also changed. *Star Wars* entertains us, because we enjoy watching the ostensibly weak—like Yoda, Luke, and the Ewoks—overcome obstacles, conquer their enemies, and triumph in the end. It's fulfilling, because we think if they can do it, maybe we can, too. The promising point is that we will come out on top, because Jesus has purchased our victory at the cross. This is God's promise, found in Philippians 1:6, "being confident of this, that he who began a good work in you will carry it on to completion until the day of Christ Jesus."

"Size Matters Not"

Most *Star Wars* characters who are able to manipulate the Force are unremarkable; they don't possess any special abilities outside the use of the mystical energy field. Jedi Master Yoda is no exception. When he first encounters Luke in *Episode V,* Yoda humbly tolerates Luke's impatience and condescending attitude. Indeed, after Luke discovers Yoda's true identity and his training begins, Yoda comments about his own less-than-imposing stature. Yoda knows that others judge him by his appearance and write him off as ineffective and worthless, but he points out that his ally is the Force, which renders his physical size immaterial.

Star Wars has a recurring theme of goodness coming from simple, everyday folk (even if they are diminutive, green-skinned aliens) and triumphing over the seemingly bigger and more powerful evils of the universe. Luke Skywalker, the central figure in the original trilogy, is an unassuming farm boy from the godforsaken, hick planet of Tatooine. He overcomes a multitude of adversities to save the galaxy from tyrannical scum and villainy. But he couldn't have done any of this without the help of his all-powerful ally, the Force. In *Episode V,* when Luke's feet are stuck in the wampa's icy cave ceiling, there's no way his hand can reach his lightsaber. It's not until he stops straining physically and calls on the help of the Force that he breaks free.

🔭 Several scenes involving a wampa were shot for *Episode V*. The Rebels had imprisoned a wampa in a pen in their base on Hoth. One deleted scene shows C-3PO tearing the warning label off the pen door, leading a snowtrooper to open the door and be attacked.

This is not unlike how things are with believers and the Holy Spirit. As Paul says, God purposely chooses the weak of this world to become his followers so that his mighty power is displayed clearly.

> Brothers and sisters, think of what you were when you were called. Not many of you were wise by human standards; not many were influential; not many were of noble birth. But God chose the foolish things of the world to shame the wise; God chose the weak things of the world to shame the strong. God chose the lowly things of this world and the despised things and the things that are not to nullify the things that are, so that no one may boast before him. (1 Corinthians 1:26–29)

As in *Star Wars,* the God of the Bible almost exclusively uses the least likely of men to become heroes in the faith. One of the best illustrations is when he chose simple fishermen to be some of the apostles, men upon whom he would build his Church. In the world's eyes, the sensible choice would have been charismatic leaders or people with wealth and influence. That's not the way God operates though. He doesn't want us to rely on our own resources no matter how awesome they may seem, because doing so only leads to pride or despair. In *Episode VI,* Han Solo's pride goes before his fall when he steps on a twig, alerting the Imperial scouts of their presence. Later, he boasts that breaking into the control bunker on Endor won't be a problem. But it's actually the little Ewok Paploo who plays the most pivotal role by luring three of the scouts away.

Regrettably, those without Christ aren't the only ones who look down their nose at the meek of society. Christians can fall into this same trap of putting a person's appearance, talents, or accomplishments ahead of his heart. For instance, many of us might think it's wise to pick successful businessmen to be elders and deacons. In spite of this, when the Bible gives instructions for choosing leaders, it puts no premium on such qualities. That's because God views the Church not as a business for men to run but as a body of believers from all walks of life who work together for God's glory. God's qualifications for who will lead his people are much "smaller" in the world's eyes, qualities such as gentleness, sincerity, and self-control. Han Solo would never have picked Paploo to launch the surprise attack on the control bunker, because from a cursory scan, the "little furball" doesn't pack the punch needed to defeat the Imperial scouts. Unfortunately, we tend to write off people for similar reasons, overlooking their God-given gifts and abilities because they don't meet our physical standards. In the process, we forget the words of Yoda, "Size matters not. Look at me. Judge me by my size, do you?"

Before the attack on the Death Star in *Episode IV*, Gold Leader asks, "What good are snub fighters going to be against that?"

"The Empire doesn't consider a small one-man fighter to be any threat, or they'd have a tighter defense," Dodonna replies.

The Empire's miscalculation of how effective a small, one-man fighter can be, when empowered by the Force, has devastating ramifications for them. Fortunately, we can learn from their short-sightedness to avoid underestimating ourselves, others, or, worst of all, God.

"I Don't Believe It"

The use of the Force clearly causes divisions between the Jedi and the Sith, but it's actually skepticism of the Force that causes mock-ery, confusion, and persecution from the common observer. For Admiral Motti, the Force is a sham and its followers a nuisance. He's not shy about pointing out Darth Vader's "sad devotion to an ancient religion." In response, Vader adopts a more intense version of apologetics and "forces" Motti into believing his religion is real by choking him.

Many who are not ashamed to take the name of Christ may face the same sort of hostility Motti displays, whether in the halls of a junior high school, by the water cooler at work, or during a family dinner. How should we respond to such challenges?

Let's set aside Vader's chokehold approach and look at how Luke and Obi-Wan handle a mild case of ridicule from Han Solo. After Han laughs at Luke during his exercise with the training device on board the *Millennium Falcon,* Luke gets irritated, calling him out on his unbelief. But Luke's annoyance does little to change Han's mind about the Force. It's interesting how Obi-Wan takes the opposite approach, not trying to prove the existence of the Force at all. He actually smiles rather than get offended at Han's aspersions.

While we should always be ready to give an answer for the hope that we have, there is something to be said for Obi-Wan's approach. Perhaps he knew that attempting to argue Han into having faith was pointless. Maybe he was simply so secure in his knowledge of the

Force that he didn't feel the need to defend himself. The point is, unbelievers will cross our paths constantly, and we shouldn't be surprised if, like Han, they laugh at our faith. Rather than get angry at them, we need to think more like Ben Kenobi and also pray that God might enlighten them in time, perhaps in part through our example.

Sometimes the characters believe in the Force but don't think they have the ability to understand or control it. In *Episode VI,* Princess Leia tells Luke, "You have a power that I don't understand and could never have." Luke goes on to explain that she has the Force, too. She just needs to learn how to use it.

In real life, some people hold to an intellectual belief in God and that one can even be saved by accepting Jesus. Their problem is similar to Leia's. They are reluctant to step out in faith for any number of reasons. They may feel like their sin is too great to be forgiven or that they can earn righteousness by improving their behavior. Both of these attitudes are simply different forms of pride. The reason could also be laziness, intimidation, confusion, or any combination of the above.

Hebrews 3:12 contains a warning for professing believers against unbelief: "See to it, brothers and sisters, that none of you has a sinful, unbelieving heart that turns away from the living God." Just as there are moments when a Christian's faith gets shaken, when he sins and turns away from his Lord temporarily, there are times when someone who normally believes in the Force has a moment of doubt. Luke, who believes in the Force most of the time and defends its existence, struggles to have faith during his training with Yoda on Dagobah. When Yoda implies that Luke can use the Force to lift his X-wing out of the bog, Luke's first reaction is disbelief. Then, at Yoda's persistence, he gives it a half-hearted shot—and fails. Afterward, he retorts, "You want the impossible."

In response, Yoda uses the Force to lift the X-wing out of the wet, muddy swamp. Luke exclaims, "I don't believe it!" to which Yoda replies, "That is why you fail." If there's one exchange that sums up life, this is it. Whether you are a Christian or not, the fact you don't believe God's Word is the reason you fail. It might be a failure that causes you to sin, or it could be the great failure that leads to hell. This ultimate failure is rejecting the only way to salvation, which is through the person and work of Jesus. During the times when our faith is shaken, we need to ask God to strengthen our confidence in him so we can believe his promise of forgiveness, trust wholly in his power over sin, and know absolutely we will be with him after we die.

🔭 In 2007, the Diego Area Rocket Team (DART) built a 23-foot-long model X-wing propelled by four rockets engines. The model cost $7,000 and exploded seconds after takeoff.

"A Great Disturbance"

Those who learn the ways of the Force are very sensitive to any disturbance within it. In *Episode V*, the Emperor and Darth Vader feel the awakening of Luke Skywalker into the knowledge and use of the Force. Obi-Wan also senses a great disturbance when the inhabitants of Alderaan are murdered, and on Dagobah, Luke can hardly concentrate on his training because of the visions of Han and Leia in pain. These are all cases of how the Force invades the minds of both Jedi and Sith alike.

For Christians, the Holy Spirit takes the role of "disturbing" us by agitating our hearts and minds so that we, like Luke, ask, "What's wrong?" To understand this process better, let's look at John 16:8, which reads, "When he [the Holy Spirit] comes, he will prove the world to be in the wrong about sin and righteousness and judgment." Theologian and pastor R.C. Sproul says that before we are saved, the Holy Spirit acts somewhat like the prosecuting lawyer for God in his heavenly court.[4] He convinces us of our wretchedness and that God's wrath looms over us. This is how people become aware of their sin and need for salvation, similar to how God convicted Paul (then Saul) of his sin while on the road to Damascus (Acts 9). The *Millennium Falcon* has a red warning light that flashes when the deflector shield weakens and the ship is in danger. The Holy Spirit, while not as obvious, graciously warns people to reconcile with God before it's too late.

Akin to the Force, the Holy Spirit also causes a disturbance in the life of every believer when he remains in a rut of sin. In these times, God's Spirit convicts believers of the truth of Scripture and that their thoughts or actions are contrary. Webster's dictionary defines conviction as "the state of being convinced of error or compelled to admit the truth."[5] The Spirit does this by making the unrepentant person miserable. Paul explains in 2 Corinthians 7:10 that "Godly sorrow brings repentance that leads to salvation and leaves no regret, but worldly sorrow brings death." God loves his children so much that he won't let them live in willful disobedience. The Spirit will produce godly sorrow. That is, he will disturb them to the core of their being so that they'll turn away from their sin and obey God.

In contrast, unbelievers experience worldly sorrow when they are bothered by their guilty conscience. This is the type of sorrow that leads to death, because they never truly repent and turn to Jesus to be saved. In *Episode V,* both Han Solo and Lando Calrissian utter the phrase, "It's not my fault," and C-3PO tells Artoo, "Don't blame me" when misfortune happens. Unbelievers will always find a way to blame someone or something else for their own mistakes and shortcomings.

In another manner, Christians can be discouraged by their own thoughts or false guilt, apart from the Spirit. Therefore, we need to know the Bible well enough to distinguish if we're in sin by breaking God's commands or if we're simply making up rules for ourselves that God never intended. This is another reason for the heavy emphasis on doctrine in this book. We need to know what the Bible says not only so that we bring glory to God but also so that we are not beaten down by a false sense of God's disapproval for failing to keep laws he never decreed we should keep.

In *Episode II,* Anakin promises Padmé that they will find out who is trying to kill her. Obi-Wan scolds him and says they will not exceed their mandate. This is comparable to our relationship with God. God has given us laws that we are to obey, and yet our tendency is to add to them and thus exceed our mandate. In later chapters, we'll discuss more about the concepts of God's grace, the laws we are to follow, the reasons for obeying, and the role of the Holy Spirit in the midst of it all. For now, understand that the Holy Spirit will not let us remain comfortable if we are living in stubborn disobedience to what God requires of us.

Second only to the commandment to love God with all of our heart, soul, and mind is God's commandment to love our neighbor as ourselves (Matthew 22:36–40). In fact, when it comes to loving other believers, the Holy Spirit unsettles us when they suffer. Paul sums it up well in 1 Corinthians 12:26: "If one part of the body of Christ suffers, every part suffers with it; if one part is honored, every part rejoices with it." Similarly, Obi-Wan falters as he feels the deaths of millions of people on Alderaan. This makes sense for a Jedi, seeing as they're so interconnected with every living creature. If people who make up part of the Force die, the Jedi feel the deathblow.

Thinking about this should spark in us a desire to love others in the body of Christ so that when we hear about folks in our church family going through hard times, we have compassion for them, pray for them, and meet their needs, if we can. The point is, Christians aren't to live their lives in isolation from other believers, not sharing, not investing in each other's lives, and not caring what happens to them. We're to love one another to the point that when a member of the body of Christ suffers, we feel it as deeply as Obi-Wan felt the suffering and death of his fellow Alliance members on Alderaan.

Conclusion

It's always encouraging to see God's truth reflected in our fallen world, even if it's an unintended, smudged reflection. Now that we've looked at some of the similarities between the Force in *Star Wars* and the God of the Bible, the next chapter will uncover the dark side of the Force that runs antithetical to the Christian faith. We'll dive deeper into the differences between the Force and God and help believers hone their ability to discern between Christianity and other religions and worldviews.

2

THE DARK SIDE

○ ● ○ ○ ○ ○ ○ ○ ○ ○ ○ ○ ○ ○ ○ ○ ○ ○

Luke: "I'm Not Afraid"
Yoda: "You Will Be"

When *Star Wars* originally invaded our galaxy, it shook our world in what we now consider typical pop culture ways. At first, the film left its mark on relatively meaningless things like birthday party themes, disco moves, and Pez dispensers. It wasn't long though before no realm of society was spared from the movie's influence. Even America's proposed missile-defense program, to which people would trust their very lives, co-opted the "Star Wars" moniker. For good or bad, the *Star Wars* phenomenon seemed poised to conquer everything and anything.

Today, the popularity of *Star Wars* is greater than ever, thanks to a generational snowball effect. Like their parents, children of the children who first saw *Star Wars* in theaters are growing up steeped to their Boba Fett Underoos in all things *Star Wars*. I don't think this is anything to be alarmed about. In fact, May the 4th is always recognized at our house, where you'll find even our one-year-old promoting X-wing fighters on his onesie.

When children watch a *Star Wars* movie, usually they're too entranced by all of the action to notice the underpinning philosophies. If you ask kids about the corruption in the Senate, the motivation behind Lando's betrayal, or the dark doctrines of the Sith, they'll look at you like you're crazy. All they know is *Star Wars* is a lot of fun!

Problems occur, however, when the stakes are raised beyond whether or not children have the latest *Star Wars* Lego set. Over the last several decades, *Star Wars* has so captivated the minds and hearts of its fans—many of whom are now professors, politicians, and pastors—that the Jedi philosophical and religious views tend to impact our world whether we realize it or not. Some enthusiasts are so passionate about wanting the Jedi influence in our world that they actually consider themselves members of the Jedi Church. While "Jediism" is not recognized as an official religion by any government at the moment, it's probably only a matter of time.

🔭 The Temple of the Jedi Order refers to "real people that live or lived their lives according to the principles of Jediism, the real Jedi religion or philosophy."[6]

On the surface, this seems not only harmless but also possibly good. After all, Jedi ideals are virtuous. Who wouldn't want more peace, justice, and benevolence in our society? Still, it's one thing to put a "May the Force be with you" sticker on your car window. But if watching the movies shapes your ideas about the weightier issues in life, such as good, evil, love, hate, revenge, redemption, the afterlife, and God, then it's easy for people to be led astray. We need to constantly sift the ideas promoted in *Star Wars* through a biblical grid, letting only the grains of truth remain. At some point, we need to ask, what does all this have to do with my journey with Jesus?

Since the attitudes and ideas purveyed by pop culture can often sway Christians in ways they don't realize, this chapter describes a number of principles that will help you take hold of the biblical truths in *Star Wars* without unwittingly allowing unbiblical notions to gain a foothold in your mind. As Paul warns us in Colossians 2:8, "See to it that no one takes you captive through hollow and deceptive philosophy, which depends on human tradition and the elemental spiritual forces of this world rather than on Christ."

Like many pop culture phenomena, *Star Wars* presents its ideas from a philosophical viewpoint that runs counter to Christianity. Therefore, we obey God's command found in the above verse by not falling prey to this way of thinking. To avoid being duped, we must learn not only the truth of Scripture but also verse ourselves in these counterfeit philosophies. As we study the ethics, beliefs, and ideologies found in *Star Wars,* we'll determine what opposes the Christian worldview so that we can, as Paul also explains in Colossians 2, have the full riches of complete understanding, in order that we may know the mystery of God, namely, Christ.

"A Long Time Ago..."

Ecclesiastes 1:9 tells us, "What has been will be again, what has been done will be done again; there is nothing new under the sun." Solomon's wise words, written so long ago, still hold true today, especially when we consider current religions and spiritual movements.

Most, if not all, postmodern faiths might appear relatively new. One such movement is actually called "New Age." But, in actuality, we can find the seeds of such philosophies, attitudes, and beliefs far into the past. As we continue to examine the religious aspects of *Star Wars,* it's beneficial to ponder how ancient philosophies inspired Lucas to develop the concept of the Force, and, in turn, how these philosophies continue to impact our world today. Who were the philosophical forefathers who influenced the world (and Lucas), and what did they think about ultimate reality? If we can grasp these intellectual concepts, we'll be in a better position to defend against assaults on biblical truth when pagan ideas creep from the movie theater into our churches.

Looking back at world history, we see elements similar to Jedi beliefs germinating from both the east and the west. Let's start by going back to Greece in about 500 BC, even before Socrates arrived on the scene. Philosophers were starting to ask certain ontological questions, such as what exists in the world, why we are here, and the ultimate nature of reality. God tells us in Ecclesiastes 3:11 that he has set eternity in the human heart, and Romans 1:20 says, through nature, God's invisible qualities, his eternal power and divine nature, are revealed to man. Problems happen, though, when humans distort God's truth.

Early Greek philosophers examined the world around them and hypothesized that different elements were responsible for the origin or the ultimate reality of everything. The Greek philosopher Thales thought water was the single material substance from which all other things came into existence. For Heraclitus, fire was the most fundamental element.[7] Similarly, for the Jedi, energy is the essence of the galaxy, an energy *created by* all living things. This leaves no room for an all-powerful, intelligent creator, i.e., God, starting and sustaining life. It turns the biblical model on its head.

Under this design, creation doesn't emanate from a personal being. Instead, an impersonal power wells up from the natural world, a power that glorifies created things rather than the Creator. Most importantly, this ultimate power doesn't hold its followers account-able for sin, a concept fundamentally different from Christianity. The Force cooperates with the will of the Jedi and partly obeys the Jedi's commands. True reality is that God created man, man rebelled, and now man looks to Creation, rather than to the Creator, to answer the big questions of life, questions that God himself put into man's heart.

In addition to Greek philosophy, many other ideas, philosophies, and faiths shaped Lucas' idea of the mystical energy field that con-trols all things. For instance, all sorts of people speak of a universal life force. Hindus call it *prana,* the Japanese teach *Ki,* Taoists refer to the *Chi,* Native Americans name it *ni,* and so on.

These different cultures provide for themselves a seemingly viable substitute for God. They reject the God of Scripture with his moral demands and replace him with a pseudo-spiritual religion that gives them everything they feel they need to transcend this life of suffer-ing. This is simply a working out of Romans 1:25, where Paul states, "They exchanged the truth about God for a lie, and worshiped and served created things rather than the Creator—who is forever praised. Amen."

God is Not an Energy Field

Obi-wan offers a concise definition of the Force in *Episode IV:* "It's an energy field created by all living things. It surrounds us and pen-etrates us; it binds the galaxy together." In a similar fashion, some New Agers believe everything in the universe, including people, is made of and gives off energy. Knowing how to manage this energy can have huge positive effects on a person's health and happiness. Some individuals believe this energy can even give them powers like telekinesis, telepathy, and clairvoyance, similar to the Jedi and the Sith.

The main problem with this concept is that energy is talked about like it is some sort of entity containing spiritual qualities. Somehow, the collective energy from everything in the universe morphs into a living presence that has the same properties found in other living creatures. The truth is, energy is not a conscious being. Sproul rightly makes the point that you might hear it defined as the capacity to do work or the equivalent of mass times the speed of light squared, but it has no personal characteristics like those found in people, and it definitely has nothing in common with the God of the Bible.[8]

The New Age movement teaches that divine energy is already within us. We just need to open the door to this energy to experience its benefits. The movement also teaches that the whole universe is God, and since we are part of the universe, we're also divine. We are gods (and goddesses), but past life experiences or negative energy is blocking the channels, preventing this positive energy from flowing freely. All we need to do is figure out how to open it up, and we can achieve our godly potential.

Star Wars characters speak of this energy in comparable ways. Obi-Wan instructs Luke that a Jedi can feel the Force flowing through him. Learning how to control this Force can give him great powers. George Lucas simply took the same New Age thought found here on Earth and injected it into *Star Wars*.

🔭 Lucas was influenced by Native American religion, which teaches that everything has a spirit or energy. The name "Skywalker" falls in line with a typical Native American naming convention, setting up an allegory with something in nature.

Some people who think that energy created the universe point to the Big Bang theory as proof. Many scientists say that, billions of years ago, there was an extremely tiny collection of matter. This matter exploded and expanded, creating our universe. They postulate that energy was the main cause of this expansion, and energy continues to cause the universe to grow.

God has characteristics that could not possibly be used to describe energy. For example, Micah 7:18 reads,

> Who is a God like you, who pardons sin and forgives the transgression of the remnant of his inheritance? You do not stay angry forever but delight to show mercy. You will again have compassion on us; you will tread our sins underfoot and hurl all our iniquities into the depths of the sea.

Micah is anthropomorphizing God in a way that is not literally accurate. God's anger is just and controlled, not like our frequent, impetuous tempers. He also doesn't literally stomp out sins with his foot or throw our iniquities into the sea. However, on a metaphorical level, everything Micah says is true.

The bottom line is that God is a personal living being. He's a Spirit who controls everything. He sacrificed his only Son to purchase a people so they could share in an eternal paradise of fellowship with him. The scientists who hypothesize the Big Bang theory or any other approach that seeks to explain the origin of the universe as coming from an impersonal energy fail to explain love, faith, sin, suffering, death, and all the other pieces of life's puzzle. If you're going to describe the creation of the universe, it's only logical that you must provide solid answers for everything that exists. Otherwise, your theory is simply a guess, and not a very good one at that.

Yoda tries to convince Luke that we are luminous beings and not crude matter. On this point, New Agers are really no different from scientists. Even though they want to be luminous beings practicing spirituality, they ignore being made in the image of God and trade it in for being nothing more than crude matter that evolved out of the primeval sludge. As we unpack the beliefs of the various religions, philosophies, and scientific theories man has invented, we'll better understand how nothing but Christianity truly gives us the reasonable and solid foundation upon which a faith can be built.

Darkness and Light

Many New Agers think energy holds the key to unlocking the power over one's life. If we can understand and control this energy, we can rise to a greater level of consciousness. Like the Jedi, they start by trying to understand the good and the bad energy of the universe. In the *Star Wars* galaxy, the two sides of the Force, light (good) and dark (evil), are opposed to each other yet need each other in order to keep life in balance. This belief is straight from Taoism, but it is similar to New Age thought as well.

Let's pause and define how New Age received its name. It refers to the new era that will be ushered in when certain planets and stars align. Astrologers claim we've been in the Age of Pisces for the last 2,100 years or so, and we're on the cusp of the Age of Aquarius. New Age thought tells us the universe is made up of two different types of energy, male and female. Like Taoism and *Star Wars,* these two energies are in conflict with each other, but they also need each other to achieve balance. Like Yin and Yang, there are traces of female attributes like emotion and compassion in the male energy and a small amount of male attributes like logic and ambition in the female energy.

 The traditional Yin-Yang symbol is shown here. If you image search online for "Star Wars Yin Yang," you will see many variations on the symbol incorporating the good and bad elements of *Star Wars*.

Once we find out that Darth Vader is Luke's father, we realize that our hero has a little of his father's evil inside him, fulfilling the Yin-Yang principle. Luke and Vader are in conflict with each other yet, in a strange way, they need each other. To demonstrate this relationship, Luke starts off wearing all white in *Episode IV,* but by *Episode VI,* he wears all black. This is a great visual for how Luke is in the middle of his own moral war between the light and dark energy of the Force.

The problem, according to New Agers, occurs when the male energy of the universe wants to dominate the female energy. This patriarchal, oppressive type of energy causes wars, violence, and injustice in the world. Some New Agers think Christianity is a masculine, rigid, controlling system. This is why they pray and give devotion to Mother Earth, Mother Nature, and the Divine Mother. The concept of a Father—indeed, the connotation of the word "father"—alarms the New Ager immediately, putting him at odds with Jesus. In New Age thought, improving one's individual life and the earth as a whole depends on each person thinking positively in order to attract more feminine energy and restore balance to the universe.

As Christians, sometimes we struggle to think of God as a real being with whom we can have an actual relationship. It's not surprising when you consider God's nature in light of ours. Though, all of the barriers that once separated us from him are removed in Christ. In the past, humans thought of God like they might consider energy: invisible, far away, and unknowable. But now, as Ephesians 2:13 tells us, the blood of Christ has brought believers near.

It's supposed to be comforting to Luke when Obi-Wan tells him that the Force will always be with him. In reality, how reassuring is it to have an impersonal, unknowable energy be with you, especially considering that this energy has a dark side that could lead you into destruction? Thankfully, unlike energy, not only will God never leave us; he is personal, knowable, and good.

God is Light

"This is the message we have heard from him and declare to you: God is light; in him there is no darkness at all" (1 John 1:5). In the Bible and in *Star Wars,* light is a metaphor for goodness just as dark is a symbol for evil. In fact, dozens of Bible verses use the word "light" in place of Christ. This is why it's blasphemy to suggest that God, who is infinitely holy, has even a smidgen of darkness.

In contrast, as I mentioned above, *Star Wars* characters believe that the Force has both a light side and a dark side. Moreover, the Jedi never seem concerned with snuffing out evil permanently. Jesus' goal, on the other hand, is not to keep good and bad in balance; his mission is to eradicate evil once and for all. He has already defeated sin and death at the cross, and when he comes back a second time, he will take his followers to heaven where evil and darkness will finally and permanently cease to exist: "The city does not need the sun or the moon to shine on it, for the glory of God gives it light, and the Lamb is its lamp" (Revelation 21:23).

In Taoism, as well as in *Star Wars,* there's no holy God in the Christian sense, only a moral conflict between two sides of the living Force. People apply the same dualistic principle when they think there's both good and bad energy in the world. This goes back to why the Yin-Yang symbol is so popular. People like to think their sin is natural and justified, that even the "good" of the universe has a little bit of evil and vice versa.

Even though we endeavor to radiate God's light, we will never be completely without sin until we reach heaven. In fact, as we grow in Christ, we become more sensitive to our sin and see it all the more. Nevertheless, we are called to strive continually for the light, for holiness, and not accept even the smallest trace of sin, rejecting the New Age movement and the Jedi's view of existence.

"It Surrounds Us and Binds Us"

If we want to split hairs, the notion of the Force is more panentheistic than pantheistic. What's the difference? Pantheism is the belief that God is everything and cannot be distinguished from the natural world. The word pantheism is made from the Greek word *pan,* which means "all," and *theos,* which means "God," resulting in the notion that all is God. Panentheism is the belief that God is in everything but still separate from nature. For the casual *Star Wars* fan, it's difficult to draw a distinction between the two views. When we hear that the Force is everywhere, in everything, and binds everything together, we interpret that as meaning that everything in the universe, including the ultimate power, is one and the same. That's pantheism. It's not until we understand that the Force is separate from everything that the designation of panentheism can be made.

Sometimes, we can also subconsciously invoke the transitive property of equality when thinking about the Force. Meaning, if a) the Force is everywhere, including people, and b) the Force is considered spiritual, then c) people, in a certain sense, are presumed to be spiritual, too. This goes back to Yoda's point of being luminous creatures. If everything and everyone is, from this point of view, god, then this satisfies the sinner's desire to be the god of his own life. Furthermore, since energy is not personal, sovereign, or holy, there's no real authority over the individual, and relativism is the natural outcome. This desire to be the ruler of our personal world is what humanity has always wanted, and this belief seduces us with a framework to try to achieve it.

God's Word teaches that God is omnipresent, meaning he is everywhere. But, God is not "in" everything like he is fused somehow into Creation. He is still separate from Creation. A cursory scan of Scripture reveals Bible verses advocating that God literally fills all things. For instance, Jeremiah 23:24 states, "'Who can hide in secret places so that I cannot see them?' declares the Lord. 'Do not I fill heaven and earth?' declares the Lord."

God filling heaven and Earth should not be understood in a spatial way, as water filling a glass, but rather that there's nowhere we can go to escape God. He even peers into our hearts and minds to know our thoughts. This should be comforting for the believer and terrifying for the unbeliever. Paul declares in Colossians 1:17, "He [Jesus] is before all things, and in him all things hold together." This sounds similar to the description of the Force Yoda gives when he tells Luke that the Force flows through everything: himself, a rock, a tree. However, considering the context of this passage, this verse is describing the supremacy of Christ and that all of Creation is dependent upon him for its very existence.

The Force Will Be With You... Maybe

The Force is all around Luke Skywalker, yet his Jedi Masters instruct him to reach out to the light side, ally with it, and not be duped by the dark side, which is always trying to lure him away. This is a daunting and lonesome proposition. Even though this powerful Force practically engulfs Luke, it's up to him to figure out how to ally with it in order to receive any benefit. Like a person trying to make his way in the world without God, everything depends on him. Even if Luke succeeds in cooperating with the Force, there's no guarantee it will stay with him. In fact, if something is with you, it usually implies that you or it must do something to preserve the relationship. The real power and comfort for Christians comes from the Holy Spirit, who is not "with" us but "in" us—and he's always "for" us. Even if our assurance wavers at times, our right relationship with God and his Holy Spirit is permanent.

In *Episode II,* Obi-Wan rebukes Anakin for losing his lightsaber. He tells Anakin that the weapon is his life, and he must keep it with him at all times. Anakin's physical life may have depended on his lightsaber, but his spiritual life depended on whether or not the light side of the Force stayed with him. Sadly, as we know, it did not. This shouldn't surprise us, because the light side of the Force, like the dark side, has no allegiance to anyone. Without a guarantee that one will not leave a relationship, no one can have hope. Christianity is the one religion that offers such hope; because we have a God who promises that he will never leave us or forsake us (Hebrews 13:5).

🚀 Jedi lightsabers were traditionally either blue or green until Samuel L. Jackson asked George Lucas if his character, Mace Windu, could wield a purple one.

Sometimes, well-intentioned believers pray that God would be with their loved ones as they travel or be with them during some other sort of trying situation. This equates to those in *Star Wars* who wish the Force to be with their companions. Christians don't need to pray that God will be *with* a person, because, as I've already established, he's omnipresent. But, if our friends and family are not believers, we need to pray that God would be with them as their Lord and Savior. In other words, we need to pray that God will change their hearts and minds to trust in the gospel.

Finally, God does not base his commitment to us on our accomplishments, even our spiritual ones. He has taken up residence in our hearts forever and will never abandon us, because we are his children. In Christ, we can't do anything to increase his love for us, and we can't do anything to diminish his approval. It's important we understand that the Holy Spirit will never leave us, because God makes a connection between his Spirit and our final promise of heaven. "When you believed, you were marked in him with a seal, the promised Holy Spirit, who is a deposit guaranteeing our inheritance until the redemption of those who are God's possession— to the praise of his glory" (Ephesians 1:13b–14).

A Taoist, a Jedi, or anyone else, who looks to the energy of the universe for his religion can never have the assurance provided through the father-child relationship of Christianity. In Romans 8, Paul teaches that God has adopted us as sons and daughters. We are not only children but also co-heirs with Christ. God has done everything possible to ensure that we will be in a relationship with him forever. This truth is one of the many that separate Christianity from all other faiths—including Jediism—and is why Christians are the only people who can know for certain that their Father will be with them always.

One of the reasons there's no guarantee that the Force will always be with a Jedi is that the Force is merely energy in a state of flux. With every change in the universe, the Force vacillates between light and darkness. If the Rebel Alliance wins a battle, the light side might wax, if they lose, the light side might wane. Granted, these cases are usually not very measurable or clear. In fact, since the Jedi don't know all the happenings in the universe, the Force's fluctuations seem downright arbitrary.

Unfortunately, the Force's inconsistency does not relieve a Jedi from his responsibilities. He's supposed to reach out, often through meditation, in an attempt to connect with this ever-changing Force.

In one of his wiser moments, Luke asks Yoda, "But how am I to know the good side from the bad?" Yoda's answer, "You will know. When you are calm, at peace," does not satisfy Luke's uneasiness, and well it should not. Any religion that incorporates impersonal energy as its main cornerstone builds on a precarious foundation. Why would you ever trust your life, especially your eternal life, to such an impersonal, irregular force? Luke is anxious during his training on Dagobah, because he knows the danger of the dark side; he just doesn't know how to defend against it.

It's comforting that we don't have to fear uncertainty in our Christian walk. Unlike changes in the Force, God doesn't change. "Jesus Christ is the same yesterday and today and forever" (Hebrews 13:8). He has always been perfectly good in all his attributes from eternity past: perfect wisdom, perfect power, perfect love, perfect justice, and perfect motives. God doesn't try to balance his qualities to a more preferred state, because there isn't one. Since God doesn't change, unlike the Jedi, we do not need to be slaves of our worry, that is, our "bad feelings" about future events.

🔭 Six different characters in *Star Wars* say, "I have a bad feeling about this" or a variation of it. Harrison Ford, as Indiana Jones, also said it in 2008's *Indiana Jones and the Kingdom of the Crystal Skull.*

Considering that the Force is described as living and changing, the Jedi must learn about the Force constantly in order to control it and discern its will. Some Christians have a tendency to view God's will as living and changing, too. We ask questions about God's will for our lives and then wait for how God might answer. Does he want me to take that job? Does he want me to marry that person? Does he want me to go on a mission trip? If God were fickle, like the Force, then who could ever have peace about any decision? But, fortunately, God remains the same, and his *ethical* will remains unchanged in the pages of the Bible.

Since God's ethical will is not a moving or hidden target, we needn't turn inward to discover it, focusing on our emotions or trying to sense what he wants. This is such a large and misunderstood topic that I have devoted an entire chapter to the Holy Spirit's role in our decision-making to learn if we are responsible to find not only God's ethical will but also his "controlling will."

The Unfriendly Force

The Force is incapable of love, loyalty, or sacrifice. When Alderaan is destroyed, Obi-Wan senses a disturbance in the Force. Sadly, the perfunctory energy to which Obi-Wan has devoted his life can give him no comfort. When he needs hope desperately, the Force can offer none. All it can do is make Obi-Wan aware of the horrible occurrence. Obi-Wan is still alone. Not only can the Force not offer support like a friend, from our perspective, it appears to withhold so much more. The Force is indifferent to the Rebels' plight, Alderaan's destruction, and Obi-Wan's grief. Indifference is even worse than hatred. At least with hatred, someone cares enough to put forth effort to think about you. In contrast, the Force's indifference demonstrates its inability to be concerned about its followers.

Not being a friend, the best the Force can be is an ally. In the context of war, one side's only hope is to gain and keep support from its ally.

🔭 The Empire in *Star Wars* mirrors the Nazis, just as the Rebel Alliance echoes the Allied powers of World War II. Russia was America's ally against Hitler in WWII but targeted the USA as an enemy in the Cold War.

In practice, the Jedi can only depend on the Force if they have a strong enough belief and do everything correctly to control the power. Ironically, even though the Jedi are absolutely devoted to the Force and are a part of it, they constantly have to be on guard, so that the dark side doesn't seduce them like Satan did to Eve in the Garden of Eden. The Force can actually be so "unfriendly" as to become the means of their spiral into destruction.

In addition, the more sensitive to the Force a Jedi becomes, the wider the door to heartache opens during times when the dark side prevails. For example, in *Episode V,* Luke cannot keep the vision of Han and Leia in pain out of his head. He has no peace about the situation, especially when he feels like it's up to him to rectify their predicament.

Similarly, in the Garden of Gethsemane, Jesus knew he had to die to reconcile us with God. He was so distraught about the coming ordeal that he sweated drops of blood. Unlike Luke, who only had Yoda and Obi-Wan, neither of whom could help him, Jesus had a loving Father to talk to in his time of great need. God sent an angel to strengthen Jesus. He didn't leave him alone in his misery feeling powerless and forsaken.

Thankfully, in contrast to the Jedi, we have a personal God to whom we can pray at any time for help. God probably won't send us an angel when we go through trials. But he has given us every- thing we need in the Bible and the Holy Spirit. Peter sums it up best in 1 Peter 5:7, "Cast all your anxiety on him because he cares for you." Believers should not feel tossed to and fro by life's circum- stances. When we build our lives on the solid foundation of Jesus Christ, we are comforted knowing that God, who only wants our ultimate good, will never let us slip through his fingers. We always have access to the Father, because Jesus bridged the chasm that once separated us.

Jesus Christ is so much more than a powerful ally with which we can unite to better ourselves. Simply put, Jesus is a friend to believers. He's not the pushover type of friend to be taken advantage of. He's not the kind who smirks at our offenses. He's not the sort without the backbone to speak out against our sin. Most of all, he doesn't only befriend us when we deserve it. On the contrary, he is the best friend possible, because he laid down his life for us when we were his enemies.

> Greater love has no one than this: to lay down one's life for one's friends. You are my friends if you do what I command. I no longer call you servants, because a servant does not know his master's business. Instead, I have called you friends, for everything that I learned from my Father I have made known to you. (John 15:13-15)

Christ died so the penalty for our sin would be paid. His death has made us acceptable to God and freed us from the slavery of sin and death. Jesus said we are his friends if we do what he commands. The amazing thing is his commands are not burdensome, because, as Ezekiel prophesied, Jesus purchased a new heart for us (Ezekiel 36:26). Metaphorically speaking, this heart of flesh replaces our heart of stone and gives us a new spirit that desires to serve God. As Ephesians 2 says, God even prepared our good works in advance for us to do. God is sovereign and loves us so deeply that he has done everything possible to give us life to the full, even at a great cost to himself, making him the most wonderful and faithful friend possible. That's a lot more than we can say for the Force!

"Partially, But It Also Obeys Your Commands"

In *Episode IV,* Luke asks Ben if the Force controls his actions. Ben says it does partially, but it also obeys his commands. Some of us, likewise, think praying is a means to coerce God into doing our will. In Genesis 18, Abraham tries to talk God into saving Sodom and Gomorrah from destruction. Some people interpret this passage as a sort of negotiation with God and a model for how we should pray. However, this conversation was a specific occurrence in history.

If we take all of Scripture into account, this particular prayer should not be the blueprint for how we talk to God. From our perspective, he only controls us partially, because we make decisions throughout our day—many of which go against his will. While we do not fully understand how prayer works, it's evident from Scripture that God is in no way obligated to obey us or give us what we want. Incidentally, just because God closes the first door does not mean we should automatically give up our responsibility to try again.

🔭 United Artists and Universal Studios both turned down *Star Wars*. Despite setbacks, Lucas pressed on and found a way to make his film.

There's another difference between God's sovereignty and the Force's control. When C-3PO walks through the desert wasteland of Tatooine, he says, "We must be made to suffer. It's our lot in life." Threepio's fatalistic comment sounds similar to people of other faiths when they use words such as *lot, luck, destiny, serendipity,* and *chance* to describe the mystical power that seems to dictate one's outcome and is beyond the individual's control. This power or force is not a personal supreme being, and it is definitely not a father who loves his children intensely. It is simply a cold, indifferent fate figuratively rolling the dice to determine how we end up.

As described in Romans 1:18, God designs situations for punishments, not blessing, for those who reject him. "The wrath of God is being revealed from heaven against all the godlessness and wickedness of people, who suppress the truth by their wickedness." So if C-3PO represents one who denies God, his bleak assessment is not without warrant or accuracy.

God mercifully causes the sun to shine on the evil and the good and sends rain on the righteous and the unrighteous. Even though this is true, unless it's God's will, an unbeliever will not be able to improve his situation regardless of his desire or effort. God's sovereignty always overrules man's ability. With every step C-3PO takes to find refuge from the desert wastelands, he journeys closer to even worse suffering, his capture by the Jawas. Sometimes God orchestrates terrible situations for those who do not accept him, yet he is still kind and gracious to them in countless ways. Mainly, the unbeliever with breath in his lungs still has the opportunity to repent and believe the gospel. As Paul says in Romans 2, God's kindness is meant to lead us to repentance.

God controls believers' situations with the opposite purpose in mind. He carefully crafts all of life's events for the good of the person who loves Christ. "And we know that in all things God works for the good of those who love him, who have been called according to his purpose" (Romans 8:28).

Christians can be comforted knowing the power and person behind this sovereign force is good. We can relax knowing someone greater, wiser, and more loving than ourselves is controlling the universe and our own personal circumstances. This knowledge helps us at a very basic level. When going through difficult trials, sometimes a person's only question is, "Why is this happening to me?" The first thing Leia says to Han after being taken prisoner by the Empire in *Episode V* is "Why are they doing this?" Han doesn't have an answer.

Believers can have peace knowing there are good reasons for the trials we endure. The overarching reasons are to bring glory to God and to sanctify (make holy) our character. Moreover, we are not like random asteroids ricocheting around the universe, waiting to be pulverized. Therefore, we should be thankful and not frustrated that God does not obey our commands, because we don't have the complete picture, the divine wisdom, or the pure motive to discern what is best. It's usually only after the fact that we can look back and see the wisdom and goodness in God's sovereignty. Only Christianity and the supernatural work of the Holy Spirit can give us the assurance of God's control and peace regarding our lack of control in the midst of life's storms.

PART II

THE DARK PATH

During the first conversation Obi-Wan has with Luke about the Force, the wise Jedi Master explains to Luke about the dark side. Likewise, we will spend a large portion of the beginning chapters of this book doing the same. Just as you only have to turn a couple of pages in your Bible before learning of Satan and sin, this part of the book will help you understand how easy it is to walk the dark path in this life. More importantly, it will give you biblical precepts to help you avoid following in the footsteps of Anakin.

In Chapter 3, we'll consider fundamental principles to make sure you are starting on the right path. In Chapter 4, we'll answer the long debated question: Is Christianity a religion or a relationship? In Chapter 5, we'll explore how deception is a key part in Satan's strategy, just as it was for Palpatine. In Chapter 6, you'll learn how Yoda's wise counsel to Luke can help you keep your emotions serving God and not the devil. Finally, in Chapter 7, you'll see how the Emperor used tactics right out of Satan's playbook to deceive Anakin and turn him to the dark side.

3

AVOIDING THE FIRST STEPS

○○●○○○○○○○○○○○○○○○○

"Once You Start Down the Dark Path"

I n *Episode V,* Yoda cautions Luke, "Once you start down the dark path, forever will it dominate your destiny." Yoda admonishes Luke, because his young Padawan knows little of the Force and next to nothing about the dangers of the dark side. During Luke's training on Dagobah, Yoda warns that the dark side is quicker, easier, and more seductive. In the prequels, we see how correct Yoda is as we watch Anakin's tragic transformation into a Dark Lord of the Sith. Even though Anakin's journey to the dark side is inevitable, almost half of the *Star Wars* saga is aimed at showing Anakin's gradual turn to evil. This gives us the opportunity to pick apart Anakin's choices to see how he fell from the light side of the Force.

For us, God's Word is similar to Yoda's warning to Luke. It tells us how dangerous and tempting the darkness is. While conversion to Christianity often involves a dramatic change from a dark lifestyle to one of light, the opposite is rarely true. The descent from light into darkness is often a series of small steps, much like in Anakin's life. This means we must do everything possible to ensure not only that we're on the right path but also to guarantee that we remain on it. This is why Proverbs 4:26–27 urges us to, "Give careful thought to the paths for your feet and be steadfast in all your ways. Do not turn to the right or the left; keep your foot from evil."

Incidentally, when I use the phrases "dark path" and "dark side" in reference to believers, I use them the way Paul, John, and Peter use the term "darkness." When these apostles use this term, it's often in the context of believers sinning. When we sin, we're committing deeds of darkness (acts of disobedience) that are inconsistent with whom we are as Christians. Believers are new creations in Christ. Our hearts are no longer dominated by darkness as they once were, but we still struggle with sin, for which we must repent continually. The gospel promises that those in Christ will stay on the narrow path forever, in other words, our salvation is guaranteed. And yet we're still commanded to evaluate our thoughts, words, and actions regularly to make sure we're living as children of light. As Paul says in Romans 13:2, "The night is nearly over; the day is almost here. So let us put aside the deeds of darkness and put on the armor of light."

Jesus warns us in Matthew 7:13 that the road to destruction is broad, and many travel upon it. It's obvious that unbelievers are on this road, and unless they repent, they will continue down it until the day God judges them. What is not so apparent is that God's Word also commands believers (who are already on the narrow path) to ensure that their lifestyle is representative of their profession, i.e., not like those on the dark path. This is another biblical truth that, from our vantage point, is paradoxical. It seems illogical that if our salvation is assured, why are we told to make sure we remain on the straight and narrow?

Think of it like Luke and the others escaping from the Death Star in *Episode IV.* From one perspective, the Empire let them go so that the *Millennium Falcon,* which had been fixed with a tracking device, would lead them to the Rebel hidden base. So, their escape was guaranteed. From Luke, Leia, and Han's point of view, however, they had to do everything in their power to escape. We will explore this fascinating concept of God's sovereignty in relation to man's responsibility later. For now, we can rest knowing that this enigma is part of God's Word and is therefore true, even if we can't quite wrap our minds around the notion.

🔭 Mark Hamill and Carrie Fisher gave their stunt doubles the day off and swung across the Death Star's central core shaft on their own. This classic stunt was shot in one take!

Admittedly, keeping on the right path is a precarious tightrope walk. If we slip too far to one side so as to become legalistic, we might think our salvation is by works, which it is not. If we lean too far to the other side so as to disobey, we misunderstand and abuse God's grace, a serious infraction that Paul warns about in Romans 6. Since the bulk of the New Testament teaches us how to say *no* to sin and *yes* to righteousness, we'll explore several situations when we can inadvertently stray from the path of light. A good verse to take to heart going forward is Ephesians 5:8: "For you were once darkness, but now you are light in the Lord. Live as children of light."

Holy Spirit in a Blood Test?

So far we've learned that God gives all believers power through his Holy Spirit so that we can make progress in our war against sin. That's why it's so crucial to make certain we are true believers. Indeed, if this isn't the case, then the problem is much bigger. Not only are we still enslaved to sin; we are also under the wrath of God. So, how can someone think he is a Christian but not really be one? Let's reexamine the Jedi and the Sith to see if drawing comparisons between our faiths can help us answer this important question.

How does one start his journey to learning the ways of the Force? How does he become a Jedi or a Sith? It starts at a biological level. Both the Jedi and the Sith are strong in the Force because of a high count of midi-chlorians, microscopic life forms that exist inside the cells of all living beings. This count can be determined with a simple blood test. This is how Qui-Gon confirms that Anakin is strong in the Force. Just like children might have a genetic makeup similar to their parents, younglings in *Star Wars* may have a high level of midi-chlorians depending on their parents' genes. Hence, Luke and Leia inherit Anakin's sensitivity to the Force. They have the Force not because they wanted it or chose it; they have it due to their biological relation with their father.

A large number of those who would call themselves Christian usually do so because of an association with their parents or family. Particularly in the more religious or conservative parts of America, many folks say they were raised in a "Christian home." Often, this means their parents had some semblance of Christianity. Maybe they attended church, prayed before meals, or celebrated religious holidays. Close friendships also influence our religious identity. Luke became strong in the Force not only because of his bloodline but also due to the powerful sway Obi-Wan and Yoda had in his life. Intimate relationships like these impact our ideas of God and religion just as much if not more than our immediate family does.

Like a misreading of a midi-chlorian count, comparing ourselves with others or associating with something else can give us a false sense of our standing with God. For instance, many assume that if someone is a theist and an American, he is automatically a Christian. This was especially true before the 1960s when the cultural norm was to attend church on Sundays. Currently in some particularly religious pockets of America, people still succumb to societal pressure to attend church even though they would rather stay home. Polls continue to reflect that a vast majority of people call themselves Christians even though they bear worldly fruit. In the end, whether it's because of their family, friends, or tradition they have inherited not a relationship with God but merely a superficial religion at best.

🗡 Little blood is spilled in *Star Wars* because the high heat of laser blasts and lightsabers cauterizes the wounds immediately.

All of this is not without biblical precedent. God made a covenant with the nation of Israel in the Old Testament. He set his favor upon a group of people comprised of families. Like Luke and Leia, the Israelite children did not make a decision to have the Lord in their lives. Sons and daughters were identified as God's people, because they were born to Israelite parents. They simply inherited the position. A good illustration of this is when Joshua says, "But as for me and my household, we will serve the Lord" (Joshua 24:15). In the same way, parents today either assume their children are Christians, make their children's decision to follow Christ for them, or pressure them to do so. This commonly results in the younger generation acquiring a false sense of righteousness, a fictitious relationship with the Lord, and zero power against the sin that dominates their lives. Many churches find it acceptable to baptize infants. The Bible, however, reserves baptism as a practice only for those who have made an outward profession of their internal reconciliation with God. Children, due to their sinful nature in Adam, need to reach a place of genuine belief and repentance just like adults do.

That said, it's still far better for children to be raised and influenced by Christian parents who are living out their faith. This is a wonderful witness that God may use down the road in a child's life to help draw him or her to faith. In *Star Wars,* the opposite happens. Qui-Gon decides he needs to take Anakin away from his mom, Shmi, because she knows nothing about teaching her son the ways of the Force. Qui-Gon sees the importance of shepherding Anakin through his journey. Likewise, in our world, if moms and dads parent in light of the gospel, hopefully they will teach their children about who God is and their desperate need to trust in Jesus for salvation. Without someone to train them, children will grow up oblivious to their need for Jesus.

Problems can arise though if parents muddy the waters by teaching God's Word inaccurately. Parents should teach their kids that they cannot gain God's favor without Christ, and definitely not by riding on their parents' spiritual coattails. Just because parents might think the mischief their child causes is endearing, God views his actions as rebellion and justifiable reason for punishment.

Even though a child in *Star Wars* can inherit sensitivity to the Force, in real life, becoming a believer requires a decision to make Jesus the King of your life. We'll study more of these concepts later, building on what we have touched on here. For now, it's important to understand and accept that we can never be righteous because of an association to a family, a nation, or a church but only through a personal faith in Jesus Christ.

"A Strong Influence on the Weak-Minded"

Previously, we studied the beliefs of the Jedi and how they are similar to many New Age and eastern beliefs. Much like how Luke learns to guard against the subtle influences of the dark side, we need to protect ourselves from all sorts of bad doctrines that can creep into our churches. Studying Luke and Anakin's experiences, as well as how other Jedi and Sith live out their faith, will strengthen our Christian mindset so that we mature spiritually, bring glory to God, and avoid the influence of not only other belief systems but also the world.

In *Episode IV,* Luke declares in astonishment, "I don't know how we got past those troops. I thought we were dead." To which Obi-Wan responds, "The Force can have a strong influence on the weak-minded." The goal for us is to be "strong-minded." I don't use the term "weak-minded" here to describe a lack of intelligence but to portray the person who has given a backseat to learning and meditating on the Word of God.

Like the Bible, the Jedi Code is given to the Jedi for their own good. Disregarding the authority of the Jedi laws and the Jedi High Council usually leads to great loss. Part of Anakin's terrible downfall is that he ignores the Jedi Code as well as the other Jedi rules regarding behavior.

The Jedi Code:

There is no emotion, there is peace.
There is no ignorance, there is knowledge.
There is no passion, there is serenity.
There is no chaos, there is harmony.
There is no death, there is the Force.

By the time we reach *Episode II,* Anakin's infatuation with Padmé has long since taken first place in his heart, mind, and soul. He tells Jar Jar that he has thought about her every day since they parted. Knowing full well that the Jedi forbid attachment, Anakin blows off the rule that he finds so restrictive and does whatever feels right to him.

Later in the movie, Padmé confronts Anakin with the law that forbids him to love. Just like so many in our world who twist the Word of God for their own purposes, Anakin perverts the true intention of the law so he is free to pursue Padmé romantically. Anakin allows his mind to become confused. He fails to discern the good of the Jedi teaching and the wise guidance from the Jedi Council from the evil of the dark side, including the Emperor's manipulation. The result is Anakin's turn to the dark side and his enslavement to Palpatine, giving an all-too-literal connotation to his addressing the Emperor as "Master."

Many elements in *Star Wars* can pose risks to us when we fail to discern the good from the bad. This applies to the behaviors of the characters, the overall themes, *and* the philosophical messages (both intentional and unintentional) that the movie conveys to its audience. But, you may ask, "How can a fictional movie present problems to real world faith?" It's not that *Star Wars* introduces ideas counter to Christianity. Instead, it reinforces certain worldviews that have already infested our culture.

More than ever, churchgoers are trying to be like the world in the areas of dress, speech, and interests. They do this for good reasons sometimes, such as wanting to be more relatable to unbelievers in the hope of sharing the gospel. Unfortunately, they can also strive to be similar to the world, because they love it in the way the Bible bans. "Do not love the world or anything in the world. If anyone loves the world, love for the Father is not in them" (1 John 2:15). Peter Sprigg, senior fellow for policy studies at the Family Research Council says, "Christians are perhaps more influenced by the culture than they are by the teachings of Scripture or the Church."[9]

Like Anakin wanting both the Force's power and Padmé's love, professing believers want God's approval *plus* the pleasures of the world. While doing this, they seek after money, career, possessions, sex, reputation, entertainment, comfort, health, or improved physical appearance more than God. They invest in romantic relationships, friendships, and even family more than companionship with the Lord. Like Jesus' explanation of the "Parable of the Sower," they allow their worldly ambitions, worries, and pride to snuff out what's left of their faith. As a result, some professing Christians fail to stand out from their unbelieving neighbors. Their light has become dim and almost unnoticeable. The behaviors listed below stem from their underlying weak-minded beliefs.

> The acts of the flesh are obvious: sexual immorality, impurity and debauchery; idolatry and witchcraft; hatred, discord, jealousy, fits of rage, selfish ambition, dissensions, factions and envy; drunkenness, orgies, and the like. I warn you, as I did before, that those who live like this will not inherit the kingdom of God. (Galatians 5:19–21)

While it's true that Satan can have a negative influence on us when we are weak-minded like Anakin, the flip side is also true: God can have a positive influence on us and protect us from Satan's attacks when we apply our minds to the Bible. In Ephesians 6, Paul emphasizes the importance of this when he commands believers to ward off Satan's attacks by learning the Bible. "Finally, be strong in the Lord and in his mighty power. Put on the full armor of God, so that you can take your stand against the devil's schemes" (Ephesians 6:10–11).

Paul, in Ephesians 6:17, commands to take up the sword of the Spirit, which is the Word of God. We can resist the tactics of the devil by remembering who we are in Christ and knowing and living out Scripture. If we believe God's Word and obey his commands, we will bear good spiritual fruit. If our core beliefs have been influenced heavily by the world, we'll produce the worldly fruit described above. Like Obi-Wan telling Luke to "learn about the Force" early on in his journey, we need to learn more about God. We do this by studying his Word. Jesus is God incarnate. Jesus is the way God showed who he is to man. Like God revealing himself through Jesus, he reveals himself to people through his written Word. Therefore, when we learn about and obey the Bible, we learn about and obey Jesus. When we do that, we improve our relationship with him.

As we proceed through this book, I'll use many examples from *Star Wars* to show you how we might misinterpret, neglect, or miss out on significant biblical teachings that we should be following. You'll see how we can deliberately ignore the rules that God has given us, just like Anakin ignores the Jedi Code. Studying all of this will help you appreciate the great harm that can come from not having a solid theological foundation. And we'll see how knowing and applying God's Word makes our lives look more like the light of Christ and less like the darkness of the world.

"Feel, Don't Think"

When Luke trains with his lightsaber on board the *Millennium Falcon* using the laser-firing seeker ball, Obi-Wan gives him a helmet with the blast shield down, covering his eyes completely. Obi-Wan tells him, "Let go your conscious self and act on instinct." Luke realizes the absurdity of this immediately and asks how he can fight if he can't see. Obi-Wan replies, "Your eyes can deceive you. Don't trust them." This is a great teaching when your pupil is learning about the Force. Unfortunately, the admonition to let go and act on instinct is a horrible instruction if the goal is to avoid sin, misery, and spiritual death.

As evidenced in Genesis 3, when we fail to discern the devil's schemes and choose instead to "act on instinct," we sin. Knowing God's will isn't as hard as we make it sometimes. Even though God doesn't talk to us audibly like he did to certain people in biblical times, through the Bible he tells us everything we need to know. The problem occurs when we forget or neglect to learn what the Bible teaches.

The Jedi seek to unplug their minds. They attempt to stretch out with their feelings. In many of these situations, it seems they often discard the ethical standards of the Jedi in lieu of gaining what they want, whether that be a hyperdrive, getting past stormtroopers, or marrying Padmé (in Anakin's case). Since we are faced with a similar kind of dilemma, to obey God or follow our selfish desires, we should think through our circumstances carefully to determine the right path. Unlike the Jedi, we shouldn't let our feelings trump God's ethical standard, which is laid out in the Bible.

If we think the above Jedi instruction is an isolated exchange between Obi-Wan and Luke, we need only recall Qui-Gon's final words to Anakin before the big pod race in *Episode I*. The Jedi tells the young boy, "Remember, concentrate on the moment. Feel.

Don't think. Trust your instincts." To understand the danger of this, let's consider the real world example of premarital sex. Sex outside the God-sanctioned covenant of marriage is rampant in our world. Sadly, many Christians participate in it just like unbelievers. If two believers are in a dating situation and they really want to honor the Lord, what's the best strategy to avoid sexual sin? Should they put themselves in a situation where they're alone, focusing on the moment, feeling, not thinking, and trusting their instincts? We all know where that can lead.

There are reasons why this sort of thing happens among professing believers, why we hear about scandals where pastors sleep with women in their churches. It's not a mystery why people sin, not only sexually but also in every area of life. The answer is plain: We forget God. We neglect the study and application of his Word. We let the culture tell us it's okay to unplug our minds, to trust our instincts, to do what feels right or makes us happy. Even from the pulpit, we hear, "Let go and let God." I know this well-intentioned phrase is meant to encourage believers to stop worrying and trust God. Unfortunately, sometimes we let go of our discernment instead of our worries. I don't mean to judge the persons who use this expression. They may truly love the Lord and want to honor him. However, we need more than platitudes in our fierce battles with Satan. We need to mature as much as we can in the knowledge of the Bible. Contrary to Qui-Gon Jinn's advice, we need to stop feeling and start thinking. We need to strive with everything we have to renew our minds by the Word of God, as Paul commands us in Romans 12:2, "Do not conform to the pattern of this world, but be transformed by the renewing of your mind. Then you will be able to test and approve what God's will is—his good, pleasing and perfect will."

> ⚔ Qui-Gon's name is derived from "qigong," an age-old Chinese healing practice comprising breathing, meditation, and body movements intended to control the flow of the life force.

Scripture uses the eyes as symbols of finding the truth. Take Isaiah 44:18, "They know nothing, they understand nothing; their eyes are plastered over so they cannot see, and their minds closed so they cannot understand." When Paul was converted, Acts 9:18 recounts that "something like scales fell from his eyes and he could see again. He got up and was baptized." And let's not forget the miracles when Jesus healed blind men. Mark 10 recounts how Bartimaeus followed Jesus immediately after the Lord restored his sight. Somewhere along the way, people have lowered the blast shield and tried to maneuver through the Christian life without spiritual eyes. We think we can go it alone, coasting on the little bit of biblical information we've picked up from Sunday mornings. That power does not last though. God has designed us so that we need to renew our minds regularly with his Word so that we can think through and make God-honoring, biblically responsible decisions. When we do this, we'll choose to serve, love, and sacrifice more, because we won't be waiting until we "feel" like doing it.

Summary

In this chapter, we learned the importance of ensuring our faith is really ours and not simply inherited from someone else. We also learned how vital it is to know and apply God's Word and not to rely on our feelings to guide our walk with the Lord. If these principles are true for you, then your feet are ready to continue on the path of light. While these doctrines are a great starting place, I wish it were that easy to avoid the dark side. But there is still much to learn if we hope to resist the devil and his schemes. Like Princess Leia understood before the attack on the Death Star, "It's not over yet."

4

RELATIONSHIP OR RELIGION?

○○○●○○○○○○○○○○○○○○

The Padawan Legalist

When I was a young believer, I became very discouraged with my walk with the Lord. I was confused, because it seemed like I was doing everything I was supposed to do. I was told to study the Bible, so I did. I was told I should pray often to God, so I did. I was told to attend church faithfully, serve others graciously, fast occasionally, tithe regularly, and throw in a mission trip or two to round things out. I did it all, but the formula I had created for a good Christian life still failed to deliver. I needed to be moving at light speed to accomplish it all, but it felt like my hyperdrive was broken, Satan was firing laser blasts at me, and my deflector shields were just about gone. Fortunately, before my hope was totally blown away, a Christian brother was wise enough to see that I had stepped onto the path of legalism and loved me enough to help me get back on track.

The disciplines I listed above can be spiritually profitable, if done with the right attitude. In my case, though, something—or, rather, someone—was missing from my Christian life. Ironically, that person was Christ! During my busyness, I had lost sight of my relationship with the Lord. I had exchanged him for a schedule packed with religious activities, programs, and to-do lists. This chapter will help you to avoid this mistake and a host of similar errors.

Since Christians should keep their minds fully engaged, willing to wrestle through complicated biblical topics in order to grow closer to God, let's consider and answer an important and often divisive question: Is the Christian faith a relationship or a religion? Determining this will help us avoid stumbling down the dark path of legalism, antinomianism, or fear of man. In this chapter, we'll study the religious and relational aspects of the Jedi and Christian faiths and point out the common convictions drawn from each perspective.

Hokey Relationship?

As I have already established, in *Star Wars,* following the ways of the Force is, first and foremost, a religion. Han Solo calls it a "hokey religion," and Admiral Motti describes Vader's devotion to his religion as "sad." In our world, people seem to have the same scorn for religion. While being spiritual might be viewed positively, being religious is not, except in certain social circles. It all depends on who (usually a celebrity) endorses a particular faith. The right endorsement can make any religion seem less hokey and perhaps even hip.

🎯 "I love the idea of God, but it's not stylistically in keeping with the way I function. I would describe myself as an enthusiastic agnostic who would be happy to be shown that there is a God. I can see that people who believe in God are happier." — Carrie Fisher[10]

Even though spirituality can be trendy, Christianity has rarely been seen as cool or something to be admired. In fact, going back to the first century, we see the disdain the world had for the religion that taught about a crucified Messiah. "Jews demand signs and Greeks look for wisdom, but we preach Christ crucified: a stumbling block to Jews and foolishness to Gentiles" (1 Corinthians 1:22–23). Today, people still view Christianity as a foolish religion and use a variety of derogatory terms such as *Bible thumpers, Jesus freaks,* and *holy rollers* to describe its followers. By and large, unbelievers view Christians as hypocritical, annoying, judgmental, narrow-minded, gullible, or stupid.

I believe Christians attract animosity from the world partly because Christianity incorporates a relationship aspect that is foreign to other faiths. Perhaps, you've heard believers use the phrase "personal relationship with Jesus" to describe how they view their life in Christ. Maybe you describe your faith in these terms. Christianity teaches that some will continue this personal relationship in heaven while those who do not have this relationship will suffer eternal punishment in hell. This causes many to look down on Christians with, if not disgust, at least confusion.

The world's hostility toward Christians can cause a lot of fear. But, Jesus warns us, "Do not be afraid of those who kill the body but cannot kill the soul. Rather, be afraid of the One who can destroy both soul and body in hell" (Matthew 10:28). God has given Christians incredible boldness and courage, so much so that many have willingly died as martyrs. Unfortunately, in America we have become so used to our way of life that we cower at even the smallest threats to our reputation, comfort, or safety.

By the time we reach *Episode IV,* the Jedi light has all but gone out of the universe. In fact, Governor Tarkin tells Vader he is "all that's left of their religion." Imagine that. You are the only Christian left on Earth. Would you have the boldness to defend your faith in a room full of the most powerful political and military men in the galaxy, many of whom are hostile to your beliefs? Whereas we shouldn't applaud the way Vader defended his beliefs while aboard the Death Star, we ought to admire and imitate the confidence he has in his faith.

Adding to Christianity's stigma, the world sees those who worship Jesus as people who need a crutch to get through life. Even worse, people think this crutch is attached to a ball and chain, preventing them from doing what they really want. And, as Han Solo would say, why would you ever give up your freedom to be ordered around by someone else? The space renegade sums up his view on life, including his opinion of the controlling power of the Force, with the statement, "Let's get one thing straight! I take orders from one person! Me!" Solo recognizes that the Force puts the Jedi into just enough of a subservient role that he wants nothing to do with it. He wants his individuality, his freedom. In a spiritual sense, he wants to fly, well… solo.

The promising fact for Christians is that Jesus tells us in Matthew 11:30 that his yoke is easy and his burden is light. It's not a ball and chain at all. Unfortunately, unbelievers never discover this truth. If they do choose a religion, they choose one without the complications of a relationship. They know all too well from their experiences that relationships require work and sacrifice.

🔭 Mark Hamill never let the hard work of marriage lead to divorce. He looked outside Hollywood and married Marilou York, a dental hygienist, in 1978.

Relationships add unwanted drama, annoying troubles, and painful trials to our lives. Indeed, the Han Solos of our day seem fairly content on their own. Because of this, unbelievers think their independence is freedom. Yet, they are not free from sin's control and can never be truly free without Jesus. They have no power or motivation to change their wicked ways.

Unbelievers may choose to follow a religion other than Christianity, but it'll still be only that, a religion. There's no secure relationship in which they can rest. There's no loving God from whom they can draw strength. There's no atonement through which they can receive unconditional acceptance. When there's only religion, ultimately, there's no reason for the heart to want to follow any rules, and the Han Solo effect kicks in. In fact, rules in the heart of an unbeliever will only stir up his sin all the more. "For when we were in the realm of the flesh, the sinful passions aroused by the law were at work in us, so that we bore fruit for death" (Romans 7:5).

In contrast, it's actually the love Christians have for God that causes his decrees to be not burdensome but a joy. This is what motivated David when he wrote the following words in Psalm 119:47–48: "For I delight in your commands because I love them. I reach out for your commands, which I love, that I may meditate on your decrees." David made the connection that we need to make. He loved God and, therefore, loved God's law. This mindset, along with the transforming work of the Holy Spirit, gives us the desire to obey God.

God designed our hearts for a relationship, not simply a religion. Consider Anakin Skywalker. It's not enough for Anakin to have a religion. He needs a relationship, specifically his marriage to Padmé. He needs Padmé so badly that he's willing to trade his religion to protect his relationship with her. Regrettably, Christians can also trade what they have with God for a human relationship.

In college, I became romantically involved with a young woman who was not a believer. Over and over again, I compromised my Christian convictions in order to maintain the relationship. I finally came to my senses and ended things with her, but my sin had already caused a lot of spiritual damage. God says he is the only relationship we need, and he cautions us to never start down the wrong path by putting our loved ones before him in our hearts. We need to be on guard that we don't, like Anakin, misplace our affections. "Anyone who loves their father or mother more than me is not worthy of me; anyone who loves their son or daughter more than me is not worthy of me" (Matthew 10:37).

God knows we are most fulfilled when he's first in our lives. This is why he demands our total devotion, humility, and obedience, so that we are not seduced by the world's deceptive offer of something better. From day one of our walk with God, we must accept him as our only Master. When we submit to him, we protect our hearts from the worldly things that vie for our worship.

In *Episode II*, Anakin talks back to Obi-Wan regarding the Council and Obi-Wan's authority over him. "You will pay attention to my lead," Obi-Wan responds. "You will learn your place, young one." Interestingly, later in the saga, Obi-Wan calls Anakin his friend. This emphasizes that such a relationship (including our relationship with God) can become an intimate friendship, but only if the foundation is built upon us submitting to the one in authority.

To illustrate this point, Paul uses marriage as a picture of our relationship with God. In this model, the husband ought to love his wife as Christ loves his Church and the wife should submit to her husband like the Church submits to the Lord. Marriage is a beautiful picture of Christ and the Church, but only when the husband and wife act out their roles properly. Anakin twists this design when he puts Padmé above his religion and no longer submits to those over him. Anakin's religion can never fill the void in his heart, but he hopes a relationship can. Therefore, he renounces the Jedi faith, because to him, saving Padmé is more important. Tragically, Palpatine, like the serpent in the Garden, tricks Anakin into turning to the dark side. When this happens, the Emperor takes Padmé's place, becoming the only one to whom Anakin can turn. Anakin inadvertently exchanges his relationship with an "angel," as he once described Padmé, for one with a shadowy figure surrounded by red and black; colors we normally associate with Satan.

As followers of Christ, we enter into a wonderful relationship with a God who is faultless in every way. It's a relationship that will never disappoint us. Unlike an earthly spouse, Jesus gives us everything we need for life and godliness. We don't need to look elsewhere for something more like Anakin does in his quest for power.

Paul tells us in his letters that incredible things happen when God adopts us into his family. In Ephesians 1, he says we have redemption through his blood and that we are guaranteed the inheritance of heaven. Likewise, he tells us in Romans 8 that our adoption leads to sharing in God's glory. Galatians 4:5 says that God sent his Son "to redeem those under the law, that we might receive adoption to sonship." Anakin did not have a father. Obi-Wan steps in though and acts not only as Anakin's Master but eventually as his father as well, as evidenced by Padmé's comment that Obi-Wan loves him like a son. It took years for their relationship to reach that point, but God loves us this intimately from day one. The above verse from Galatians addresses the terrible predicament of religious people who are under the law and without hope, but it also teaches us that God treats us like sons and daughters when we're adopted in Christ. In short, God rescues us from a faulty religion and gives us a perfect relationship.

Devotion to an Ancient Religion

Okay, so we understand that Christianity is a relationship. Great. And nothing could be bad about viewing our walk without any religious entanglements, right? Well, that depends. New Testament writers James and Paul use the term "religion" to describe our allegiance to God. Hence, religion isn't bad by definition. So, how should we understand our religion in the context of our relationship with God? In the first part of this chapter, we learned the potential pitfalls when we add our "good works" to our relationship with the Lord. Now we'll see how neglecting our religious duties can have a negative effect on our relationship.

Christianity differentiates itself from other religions by being a system of faith and worship established by God through his Word. In contrast, all other religions are manmade, which is why so many end up being antithetical to the Christian faith. This is not to say we can't learn a thing or two from the disciples of other religions. Even though Buddhism, Hinduism, and Jediism are strikingly different from Christianity, they all have traditions, practices, ceremonies, rituals, and spiritual disciplines designed to help their followers mature in the faith.

We see examples of this in *Star Wars*. Through the rigorous training Luke undergoes on Dagobah, he heightens his sensitivity to the Force. However, when he wants to leave to rescue Han and Leia, Yoda and Obi-Wan urge him to stay and finish his training instead. They know that Luke is walking right into battle with an enemy he's not prepared to face. "Only a fully trained Jedi Knight with the Force as his ally will conquer Vader and his Emperor," Yoda warns him. "If you end your training now, if you choose the quick and easy path, as Vader did, you will become an agent of evil." For Luke, feeling the Force is not enough. He must learn how to control it through training.

🔭 Disney Parks offer a "Jedi Training Academy," where a Jedi Master trains young children. The Padawans wear brown robes, take the Jedi oath, and learn to use their powers for good as they practice ancient Jedi skills, such as brandishing a lightsaber.

As the rest of *Episode V* plays out, Luke fails to stop Vader and needs to be rescued by Leia, the very person he went there to save. Similar to Luke, we should not neglect our spiritual training or we'll be ill prepared for the trials of life. Hebrews 5:14 teaches us that those who have learned about God's righteousness and the truths of his Word have "trained themselves to distinguish good from evil," the critical objective Yoda and Obi-Wan fear Luke will never achieve.

As we think about our religious training, let's pause and remember how our sanctification relates to how God judges us. When we give our lives to Christ, God declares us righteous at a precise moment in time. We are declared holy, because Jesus satisfied God's justice for us, and there's nothing we can add to our good standing. Yet, even though we are holy in God's sight, he doesn't take us up to heaven at the moment of conversion. Instead, we begin a lifelong journey of learning about God in order to love and serve him here.

Practicing spiritual disciplines like praying, connecting with other believers, and meditating on Scripture helps us grow closer to God. But, similar to the story I shared earlier about my foray into legalism, such disciplines can also do more harm than good. The difference depends on our attitude. Do we pray with selfish motives? Do we reach out to only the Christians with whom we click? Do we study the Bible only to show off our knowledge? Do we rush into situations, like Anakin's first lightsaber fight with Count Dooku, without training ourselves in righteousness, only to be slammed against the wall by our sin? "Have nothing to do with godless myths and old wives' tales; rather, train yourself to be godly. For physical training is of some value, but godliness has value for all things, holding promise for both the present life and the life to come" (1 Timothy 4:7–8).

How to be Disciplined Like a Jedi

Even though Jediism is a far cry from Christianity, believers can be motivated to be spiritually disciplined by watching how the Jedi practice their religion. For instance, in the *Star Wars* prequels, we see how disciplined Yoda is when he meditates. He spends hours a day by himself strengthening his connection to the Force.

We see this same level of commitment on the dark side. Darth Vader is a busy Sith Lord. I imagine it takes a lot of time to conquer a galaxy. But even in the midst of his daily regimen of choking people, hunting down Rebel scum, and intimidating everyone around him, Vader knows the importance of keeping in tune with the Force. Therefore, he orders a meditation chamber be built aboard his Star Destroyer, *Executor,* so he can retreat and reconnect with the source of his power.

🔭 Vader's meditation chamber uses hyperbaric oxygen therapy. Inside the pod, the air pressure is increased so that his lungs can gather more oxygen. This explains why he can remove his mask and helmet once inside.

Back in the real world, it's easy to neglect studying the Bible or praying to God on a regular basis. If only we could push a button to close off the world the way Vader does, we might stand a chance. But while we don't have pods like Vader's, many of us do have iPods. And when they're turned on, things like Facebook, Twitter, and YouTube can be major time sucks. Our TVs, video games, smartphones, tablets, and other devices can certainly be used for God's glory, but too often all they give us is a practically unlimited number of choices to distract ourselves from our main purpose in life, which is to make our time count for our King. If we are looking for an easy button, all these devices have one. It's the one that turns them off. And if Darth Vader can have the discipline to find a place of solitude, surely we can do the same in order to spend time with our Father.

Let's consider another spiritual discipline of the Jedi. For them, practicing asceticism helps them to avoid attachments that are forbidden in the Jedi Order.[11] It's Anakin's attachment to his mother and to Padmé that the Jedi Council senses—and dreads—in him. On Dagobah, Yoda, in classic Buddhist fashion, tells Luke to "train yourself to let go of everything you fear to lose." We find a biblical parallel in Matthew 6. In this portion of the Sermon on the Mount, Jesus starts off teaching on three spiritual activities: giving, prayer, and fasting, thereby instructing us on how to let go of our money, our control, and our physical sustenance. But the overarching attachment common to all three, the one we most fear to lose, is the attachment to our own righteousness.

Again, it's hard to talk about religious disciplines without the warning of legalism. The Christian life is not just about doing the right things; it's about why and how we do them. Jesus' point is not to give so much money that we go broke or eat so little that we starve ourselves for the sake of self-denial. Of course, like the Jedi, it's always good for us to train our hearts to resist being put into bondage by the temporary physical things of life. However, more important than this caveat is Jesus' instruction for us to let go of our own righteousness in the midst of our religious activity, because it's only then that we can relax in his righteousness on our behalf.

The Jedi are not original in their strict adherence to abstinence in many areas of life. Followers of several different religions deny themselves the physical pleasures of this world. In their minds, they exchange physical comforts for righteousness or enlightenment. They don't consider their sacrifices as a weakness but rather as a source of strength. From the world's perspective, this is a more logical, pull-yourself-up-by-your-spiritual-bootstraps approach versus relying on the death of a Jewish carpenter from the first century.

Along the lines of denying ourselves certain things for a time, Jesus' command to store up spiritual treasures in heaven resembles the Jedi regulation against loving carnal things. This rule teaches us to value nothing (material or otherwise) above the Lord. Unfortunately, even treasuring our own good works can fall into this category. Knowing this, Jesus says that if the religious act with the wrong motives, they forfeit their heavenly reward (Matthew 6). In reference to believers serving the body of Christ, Paul elaborates on a similar point in 1 Corinthians 3:13, "Their work will be shown for what it is, because the Day will bring it to light. It will be revealed with fire, and the fire will test the quality of each person's work."

We should be thoughtful when working for God's kingdom. As much as we might strive to do good deeds in this area, the eternal fruits of our efforts will be burned up if our works were not done to bring glory to God.

In the Bible, fire usually represents judgment. Hence, it's fitting that Anakin's physical body burns in the lava on Mustafar. By this point, he has already plummeted headlong into the dark side. Anything that represents what good he may have done in the past might as well be burned away along with his spiritual goodness. On that day, he appropriately loses his blue lightsaber, too, the final symbol of what he used to uphold for the good of the galaxy.

Flowing out of Jesus' teaching on giving, prayer, fasting, and storing up treasures in heaven, he says this,

> The eye is the lamp of the body. If your eyes are healthy, your whole body will be full of light. But if your eyes are unhealthy, your whole body will be full of darkness. If then the light within you is darkness, how great is that darkness! No one can serve two masters. Either you will hate the one and love the other, or you will be devoted to the one and despise the other. (Matthew 6:22–24)

Obi-Wan or Yoda could have just as easily given this remarkable warning to Luke or Anakin. It serves as a good reminder that we should focus on why we do what we do and not let the darkness of sin get in our way of serving the Lord.

After one of Luke's failures during his training, Yoda scolds him with the words, "Control, control, you must learn control!" Yoda doesn't say anything about feelings in this rebuke. For Luke, control is something he must learn through the knowledge of the Force. In fact, everything else in his journey hinges on him being able to accomplish this. It's the reason Obi-Wan urges Luke not to leave Dagobah before learning how to control the Force. Later, during their duel, Vader remarks that Luke has been taught to control his fear and encourages him to release his anger and hate. Vader knows Luke's training has not been completed and that he can be swayed easily if he loses control of his emotions.

In Paul's letter to Titus, he says, "Similarly, encourage the young men to be self-controlled." Sounds a lot like Yoda. The New Testament is replete with commands to have self-control, to be disciplined.

> For this very reason, make every effort to add to your faith goodness; and to goodness, knowledge; and to knowledge, self-control; and to self-control, perseverance; and to perseverance, godliness; and to godliness, mutual affection; and to mutual affection, love. For if you possess these qualities in increasing measure, they will keep you from being ineffective and unproductive in your knowledge of our Lord Jesus Christ. (2 Peter 1:5–8)

We must also learn self-control. It's not something that will just happen. The verses in 2 Peter give us a chain with self-control being an important link right in the middle. The requirement we are to add before self-control is knowledge of God's Word. When we learn the Bible, we are in a position to learn self-control. Indeed, the Holy Spirit uses this knowledge to transform us from the inside out. Like Luke, everything else in our journey (perseverance, godliness, mutual affection, and love) hinges on this.

Keeping the Balance

It's helpful to think of Christianity as covering a spectrum. On one end is relationship, and on the other end is religion. If we swing too far to the relationship side, we might neglect profitable things like studying the Bible or repenting of sin. On the other hand, if we fall too far on the religious side, we may forget that our Father accepts us unconditionally because of Jesus, not because of what we do for him. Paul addresses this constant balancing act in Romans 6. He explains how some will want to take advantage of God's grace and thus fail to take sin seriously. This will happen to us, too, if we abandon the religious aspect of Christianity.

"Antinomian" is a fancy theological term that Webster's dictionary defines as "one who holds that under the gospel dispensation of grace, the moral law is of no use or obligation because faith alone is necessary to salvation."[12] Even though our good works don't save us, God commands us to do them. Our religious obedience is how we show that God is really the one in charge of our lives. He also commands us to follow his laws, because that is how his Spirit transforms us into the people he wants us to be.

In the past, I've also swung too far to the other side of the spectrum, away from the legalistic side to a "God is all grace" approach. I found this to be even worse than legalism. Why? Because it is Satan's craftier attack. We hear frequently about the dangers of trying to earn God's favor, but we don't hear much about any impending trouble with his grace. Let me explain what I mean.

During this period of my life, I reasoned that I should stop trying so hard to change. Instead, I ought to just "believe" in God more, and then he would remove more sin from my life. This is comparable to Obi-Wan and Yoda urging Luke to unlearn what he had learned, let go of his conscious self, and simply become a channel for the Force.

Surprisingly, I found that after years of this strategy, little changed in regards to my sanctification. It's not that I fell deeper into sin; I just sort of plateaued. I also felt distant from God and wondered why he wasn't rooting out the sin in my life. I began to understand, though, that a balance must be struck. I realized that resisting sin is not easy, and I started to understand that God and I are in this fight together until the day he takes me to heaven. When he commands us to do our part in our spiritual battles, we need to obey. We never have an excuse to surrender to sin. As Paul says in 1 Corinthians 10:13, "No temptation has overtaken you except what is common to mankind. And God is faithful; he will not let you be tempted beyond what you can bear. But when you are tempted, he will also provide a way out so that you can endure it."

To reiterate, God is gracious beyond our comprehension, and our ethical efforts do not earn favor with him. That being said, we ought not throw in the towel and simply take advantage of his grace. To do so is neither "right nor safe" (to borrow a phrase from Martin Luther). But that is exactly what can happen if we forget the religious side of our faith and think we can coast on God's mercy and a prayer we spoke twenty years ago.

The Jedi strive to grow continually in their knowledge of the Force. Even when they are in exile, Yoda and Obi-Wan still put their Jedi beliefs into practice. It is actually during this time that Qui-Gon teaches Obi-Wan the path to immortality. The Jedi also battle constantly against the seduction of the dark side. They can never take a vacation from their religious disciplines, and neither can we. Doing so leads us to participate in what we might perceive as the peccadilloes of everyday life, such as gossip, laziness, impatience, jealousy, anger, or worry with a "God will forgive me" attitude in the back of our minds. Instead, we need to take the opposite approach. Taking every thought captive for Christ helps us resist the sin that so easily creeps in.

🔭 Lucas initially gave Yoda the first name "Minch." Then he (thankfully) decided that simply calling him "Yoda" added more mystery to his character.

Sometimes it feels like we're just using human effort when we wage war against sin and that nothing supernatural is happening. However, God gives us the spiritual strength to overcome sin even if we don't realize it. More than that, he has actually planned our good works from eternity past (Ephesians 2:10). Recognizing God's hand in the behind-the-scenes work of the Holy Spirit helps us to remain humble in our victories over sin. In addition, remembering that God gets the credit when we grow in holiness helps us turn our gratitude back to him. Our relationship with him is strengthened, and we appreciate him all the more.

Christianity is definitely a religion in the sense that we have a responsibility to live a life worthy of the calling we have received. Every so often, living the Christian life can become overwhelming. During such times, we need to pause, take a deep breath, and know that God accepts us unconditionally. When we do, it's much easier to view our good works with the right perspective, not as burdens to overcome but as opportunities to show our love for God. This is why it's encouraging for believers to gather together and "spur one another on toward love and good deeds" (Hebrews 10:24). We can be inspired to live for God more when we see each other doing it.

A Fine Balance

The beginning of this chapter asked if the Christian faith is a relationship or a religion. The answer? It's both. Because of this, living the Christian life is a daunting venture. We must avoid becoming legalistic in our religion and avoid becoming antinomian in our relationship. To make matters worse, sin and Satan will always push us to err on one side or the other.

Like us, Anakin and Luke must balance relying on the power outside themselves and exercising their own abilities. If they forget that the Force is the source of their powers, they become prideful and ineffective. If they don't discipline themselves to learn all they can about the Force, they become weak and can accomplish little. Anakin's pride leads to his ruin in *Episode III* when he decides to have his religion and his relationship on his own terms. In *Episode VI,*

Luke starts to turn in the same direction and must rein in his anger, fear, and pride so he can reject the same path that consumed his father.

Feeling isolated in our journey only makes the dark days darker. We will feel alone at times, and the world will give us no refuge. We might have a Han Solo at work, an Admiral Motti for a neighbor, and General Grievous for a father-in-law, all of whom say that Christianity is only for nerfherders. When this happens, we can't let the fear of man tempt us to choose a false, religious version of Christianity or a compromised, surface relationship with Christ. Other people might find such an approach acceptable, but God does not. "But rejoice inasmuch as you participate in the sufferings of Christ, so that you may be overjoyed when his glory is revealed. If you are insulted because of the name of Christ, you are blessed, for the Spirit of glory and of God rests on you" (1 Peter 4:13–14).

The Jedi are in the minority compared to the rest of the galaxy, just like Christians are a minority in the world. But they press on through all the abuse and, in the end, defeat the dark side and bring balance to the Force. Of course, our lives will look different than the characters in *Star Wars,* but the essence of the spiritual dilemmas we encounter is the same.

When we face certain decisions in life, will we rob God's glory by trying to earn salvation through religion, or will we scorn his character by wanting only his grace and not his lordship? Our answers to these questions will determine if we veer to the dark side, the path that leads away from God, or remain in the light and enjoy fellowship with God and other believers forever.

5

THE LIES WE CLING TO

○○○○●○○○○○○○○○○○○

"So, You've Accepted the Truth?"

The Jedi do such a good job of clearing their minds that they often clear out their scruples along with it. In fact, they ignore their principles on such a regular basis that one begins to wonder if they have any allegiance to the light side, to other people, or to truth and justice. Maybe clearing their minds (along with any laws about being truthful) is how they ignore their guilty conscience. Since their religion has no savior to take away their guilt, they have to find a way to deal with it on their own.

We've already seen that eradicating evil, including dishonesty, is not at the top of the Jedi's to-do list. Qui-Gon, Yoda, Obi-Wan, Anakin, and Luke all lie, deceive, and act unethically when it suits them. Going forward, we'll consider how compromising on the truth in everyday life eventually causes you to relax your stance on the importance of a true view of yourself, the world, and Christ. This gives the evil one fertile ground to cultivate the seeds of distrust in the God of the Bible.

Palpatine—The Father of Lies

George Lucas modeled much of Palpatine's manipulation of the government on Adolph Hitler. Like the former Nazi leader, the Senator of Naboo crafts his rise to authority, the way a medical droid might perform surgery on a robotic hand, carefully putting each piece into position until it all worked as a single unit ready to grip a deadly weapon.

✈ DEKA Research and Development have developed the most advanced prosthesis to date. They named their FDA-approved bionic body part the "Luke Arm," paying homage to the one Luke receives at the end of *Episode V*.

Palpatine's ruse harkens back to the Garden of Eden, where a sly serpent saw an unsuspecting victim, planted a seed of distrust, watered it with pride, and waited for his lethal harvest. "You belong to your father, the devil, and you want to carry out your father's desires. He was a murderer from the beginning, not holding to the truth, for there is no truth in him. When he lies, he speaks his native language, for he is a liar and the father of lies" (John 8:44).

Palpatine's conquest happens on a galactic scale, but to reach his objectives, he starts with an individual, paralleling the strategy of Satan with Eve and the lasting repercussions for the entire human race. For his takeover of the Republic, Palpatine targets Padmé, telling her that Chancellor Valorum will do nothing to save her planet and that she needs to take matters into her own hands. He follows this pattern to a "T" when he sets his sights on Anakin, telling him that the Jedi cannot be trusted, that Anakin should become a Master, and eventually manipulating him to play a major role in murdering the other Jedi.

Anakin's relationship with the Emperor and mankind's relationship with Satan are both built on a foundation of lies. When we fail to acknowledge the truth, we allow Satan to capitalize on our weaknesses. When we, like the characters in *Star Wars*, fail to put a premium on truth in the mundane aspects of life, how can we expect to discern truth in the eternal?

Impersonating a Deity

When the Ewoks come to regard C-3PO as a god, Luke wants him to use his "divine influence" to get them out of the mess they are in, notably, the fact they are about to become the main course at a banquet. Threepio refuses at first, saying it's not proper to impersonate a deity. In fact, it's against his programming. But he finally capitulates to his master's command and lies to the Ewoks about having magic. At least C-3PO has more of a conscience than the Jedi—which isn't saying much. Regardless, he goes against his conscience when he pretends to be a god.

> ✈ Anthony Daniels had this to say regarding the computer-gener-ated C-3PO in the prequels' action scenes: "With me [in the suit], he's always going to move the same way and have the same reac-tions, timing, and so on. With CG, you're working with some brilliant person on the keyboard who is trying to pretend to be me."[13]

When we deceive, we impersonate Satan. In essence, we're saying we know better than God and we'll try to control things on our own. The Serpent in the Garden is the Father of Lies, because even though he wasn't really God, his pretense was enough to impact the destiny of the human race to the point where we attempted to be our own god. The devil impersonated God, claiming to know the reality that God was hiding from Eve. Satan knew Eve was unpre-pared to have her trust in God challenged. His lie pertained to the fruit, but the unspoken, underlying lie was, "serve me, and you'll like my rules better." This is what Eve's heart really wanted to hear, and Satan was the "deity" she wanted to serve.

Even though it turns out okay for Luke and the others, the oppo-site is usually true when we distort, ignore, or nullify the truth. The reason God's wrath is upon humanity is that people suppress the truth by their wickedness. God has made the truth of him-self plain to them, but they still reject him (Romans 1:18–19). The Bible makes the connection between wickedness and deception. "You who practice deceit your tongue plots destruction; it is like a sharpened razor. You love evil rather than good, falsehood rather than speaking the truth. You love every harmful word, you deceitful tongue!" (Psalm 52:2–4).

Think about the story of Ananias and Sapphira in Acts 5. They sold a piece of property but kept back part of the money for themselves.

Then Peter said, "Ananias, how is it that Satan has so filled your heart that you have lied to the Holy Spirit and have kept for your-self some of the money you received for the land? Didn't it belong to you before it was sold? And after it was sold, wasn't the money at your disposal? What made you think of doing such a thing? You have not lied just to human beings but to God." (Acts 5:3-4)

When we lie to people, we really lie to God. That puts things in their proper perspective and shows why we must take the sin of lying seriously. It would have been fine for Ananias to have sold his property and kept a hundred percent of the profits for himself. But he lied about how much he received and pretended to give it all away. This is so serious that it's one of the rare times in the New Testament when God strikes a man and a woman dead because of their sin.

These Aren't the Truths You're Looking For

Lies pave the way to the dark side. Let's look at more examples of when the characters in *Star Wars* deceive so we can be sure not to follow in their footsteps. The following few verses are good ones to commit to memory in this regard:

> Everyone who does evil hates the light, and will not come into the light for fear that their deeds will be exposed. But whoever lives by the truth comes into the light, so that it may be seen plainly that what they have done has been done in the sight of God. (John 3:20-22)

When it helps his situation, Qui-Gon ignores the Jedi teaching about compassion for others and chooses instead to lie, cheat, and manipulate anyone who stands in his way. He attempts a Jedi mind trick on Watto to accept his Republic credits. In the process, he uses Watto's weakness (greed) to his advantage. In addition, he lies by saying he won the pod in a game of chance. Referring to the need to trust Anakin with their fate, Qui-Gon tells Padmé, "The Queen does not need to know," deliberately hiding the truth from someone who should be involved in this major decision. And the list goes on.

🔭 Lucas worked on the script for *Episode IV* during the Watergate scandal. As in *Star Wars*, America was getting accustomed to lies even from the "good guys" like President Nixon.

Yoda and Obi-Wan are no better. Both deceive Luke when they feel it's "right" to do so. When *Episode VI* came out in 1983, relativism had already been defining how people regarded truth. The following exchange when Luke asks Obi-Wan why he didn't tell him that Vader was his father represents the popular "that's true for you, just not for me" attitude:

Obi-Wan: So what I have told you was true…
from a certain point of view.

Luke: A certain point of view?

Obi-Wan: Luke, you're going to find that many of the truths we cling to depend greatly on our own point of view.

Even before Luke is born, Obi-Wan tells Anakin, "Only a Sith Lord deals in absolutes." Obi-Wan's words exemplify the relativism of our postmodern society, which prompts people to not only question what truth is but also to reinvent it. In doing so, people redefine the biblical view of marriage, which leads to same-sex unions; the biblical view of sexuality, which leads to rampant perversion; and even the biblical view of life itself, leading to roughly 125,000 murders of unborn babies worldwide each day.[14]

We also see this moral relativism in an exchange between Obi-Wan and Anakin in *Episode III* when they argue about who is evil. In response to Obi-Wan's declaration that Palpatine is evil (an absolute statement, by the way), Anakin says, "From the Jedi point of view! From my point of view, the Jedi are evil."

Like the Jedi, so many in our culture avoid dealing in absolute truths. But if the Bible and Jesus are true, then every other path that claims to lead to God is false. Not only that, the Bible states that the lifestyle unbelievers want to lead is evil and grounds for punishment. Therefore, they will choose a belief system that allows for their sin and gladly lose Christianity in the sea of hundreds of other worldviews.

Relativism is widespread in the 21st century, but it's certainly not new. Even the Serpent in the Garden prompted Eve to question if God really said what he said. Consider also this dialogue between Jesus and Pontius Pilate. "'You are a king, then!' said Pilate.

Jesus answered, 'You say that I am a king. In fact, the reason I was born and came into the world is to testify to the truth. Everyone on the side of truth listens to me.' 'What is truth?' retorted Pilate" (John 18:37–38a).

Obi-Wan's answer regarding perspective irritates Luke, because, like us, he knows deep down that truth is objective, and he wants it. Everyone searches for truth and meaning in life. God has implanted this desire in our hearts. That's why it's so powerful, because, as Jesus tells us in John 14:6, he *is* the truth. Unfortunately, few people accept Jesus and exchange the truth for a lie. Similar to Anakin's gradual descent into more fear, anger, and hate, God tells us in Romans 1 that he gives people over to their sin after they make this dreadful exchange.

Starting at the end of *Episode II,* Anakin lives a life of deception, concealing his marriage to Padmé. His Masters have unwittingly taught him that it's acceptable to lie in certain situations, and now they are the ones being deceived. Anakin, along with everyone else, views deception as useful weapon in his arsenal, and he doesn't distinguish between his victims. At one point he does say to Padmé that he's "tired of all this deception," but his next statement is, "I've given my life to the Jedi order, but I'd only give up my life, for you." Do you see the subtle twist of words? It's a mark of relativism where words and phrases take on different meanings or lose their meanings altogether. The truth, according to the Jedi, is that Anakin has committed his life to their Order and no one else, but when no one is looking, he's really dedicated not to the Jedi or even to Padmé, as he claims, only to himself.

"No! That's Not It!"

Regrettably, we all dishonor God at some point through our deceitfulness. Maybe we obey the speed limit only when the police are around. Maybe we accept someone's "thank you" for praying for him or her even though we didn't. Maybe we unintentionally blurt out an inaccurate answer to a question that catches us off guard. Unfortunately, other times, we know full well that we're not being truthful, but we do it anyway. Paul, like James, knows the evil that can come from our lips. Thus, he commands our words to be honest, helpful, and clean at all times.

> Therefore each of you must put off falsehood and speak truthfully to your neighbor, for we are all members of one body. Do not let any unwholesome talk come out of your mouths, but only what is helpful for building others up according to their needs, that it may benefit those who listen. (Ephesians 4:25, 29)

Satan will also tempt us to lie when doing so might accomplish what we see as the greater good. Because they're trying to defeat the evil Empire, the Jedi justify their duplicity. They think stopping the biggest evil is grounds for perpetrating smaller offenses. In your life, what sorts of things qualify as the greater good? Do you ever feel that reaching those good goals should supersede God's commands to be honest?

Those of us who are husbands often put providing for our families in this category. What do you do if your boss, who has the forgiving nature of Jabba the Hutt, tells you to lie in the hope of landing a lucrative deal? The office can already be a place where we compartmentalize our Christian life and leave our values at home. But it's even worse if we feel like our job, reputation, or financial security is at stake. During these circumstances, we may be tempted or easily pressured by others to be less than upfront. Again, think of how Han intimidates C-3PO when the droid refuses to lie for them on Endor. When it comes to their career, guys can feel the same kind of pressure from bosses, coworkers, customers, society, or even their family members to do the wrong thing. If we're coerced to act unethically, we might assume that since God wants us to provide for our families, we should do whatever it takes even if that means telling an occasional lie.

Much of the Ewok forest was shot near Skywalker Ranch in California. Incidentally, Endor is a Canaanite city that is named a few times in the Old Testament.

It doesn't take much prodding before a job intended to meet our families' needs becomes a job to fulfill our selfish wants. Whether it's Jabba buying Chewbacca from Boushh (Princess Leia in disguise),

Qui-Gon negotiating with Watto for a hyperdrive, or Han Solo selling his ship's services to Obi-Wan and Luke, introducing money to the equation frequently causes people to be sinfully shrewd. It certainly did for Ananias and Sapphira. In 1 Timothy 6, Paul warns about the dangers of the love of money. He closes his council saying, "Some people, eager for money, have wandered from the faith and pierced themselves with many griefs" (1 Timothy 10b).

Once Han hears that Obi-Wan and Luke have never heard of the *Millennium Falcon,* he feels it's time to embellish in order to earn a bigger paycheck. When more money is to be had, Han lies through his Corellian teeth by saying his ship made the Kessel run in less than twelve parsecs. Judging by Obi-Wan's reaction, he doesn't fall for Han's used car salesman tactic for a second. Nevertheless, Han acts selfishly throughout most of *Episode IV,* and his lying is just more evidence of this.

These ethical forks in the road don't exist only in the workplace. Often, we are tempted to forgo being honest in our personal relationships, too. At the beginning of *Episode V,* Han wants Leia to tell the truth about how she feels about him. Leia skirts the issue, giving him a line about him being a help to the Rebels. Her statement is true, but it's false in the sense that she's not giving Han a straight answer. It's comparable to when we are angry at someone but say "nothing" when he or she asks what's wrong. Not surprisingly, Han responds angrily, "No! That's not it!" and demands the "real" truth. Even if it requires us being vulnerable and humble, our relationships will deepen the way God intends if we're always honest with one another.

✸ Harrison Ford described Han Solo as "The great rapscallion of the universe."

When it comes to relationships though, we should still be judicious about when and how we tell the truth. Obi-Wan, as Luke's surrogate father, lies to Luke to protect him. Regarding this, Yoda says later that Luke was not ready for the burden of the truth. In the same way, it's not good for us to weigh down our children with information that they're not emotionally, intellectually, or spiritually prepared to handle. However, it's one thing to withhold details for these reasons; it's another thing to lie outright. This is one more circumstance when we might think the ends justify the means. When we reason that God's way is usually right except for particular situations, we're basically saying that we are wiser than God.

"Why, You Slimy, Double-crossing, No Good Swindler!"

Many of us are not tempted to lie and deceive the way some the Jedi do. Of course, the lack of the Jedi mind trick does factor into this a bit. Personally, one of the main reasons Satan doesn't go after me in this area too much is that I'm a terrible liar! Just ask my wife. She can spot a half-truth from a mile away. But the wrath of my wife, the government, my employer, or any authority God has set up over my life shouldn't be my motivation for being honest. Fear of earthly repercussions is what motivates unbelievers. Our love for God should be the incentive for our honesty.

Even though I may not go through life weaving a web of lies the way Qui-Gon does, I can look back and see how I have been deceptive in other ways. For instance, during my single days I manipulated social situations so that I could talk with an attractive young woman in our church group. I would change my plans in order to be someplace when she was. Instead of being upfront and simply asking her out on a date, I sinfully (and rather cowardly) behaved in an underhanded way. I didn't tell bold-faced lies like Palpatine, but compared to God's standard, I did no better.

Unfortunately, it has become very easy for all of us to get away with being dishonest. Technology has revolutionized how we conduct business and how we engage socially. Consequently, computers and the Internet provide the anonymity to perpetrate all kinds of sinful deeds that people would have never had the courage to do in the past. The digital age also gives us a mindset that if something is not tangible, then it's not real, and God's laws against stealing no longer apply. Consider using your neighbor's wireless network for your Internet without his permission, for example, or downloading copyrighted music, movies, or video games for free. Many people will say there's nothing wrong with these activities. But, from a legal and divine standpoint, it's theft and therefore sinful.

Just as we receive mixed messages from the Jedi when they preach respect and compassion for others and yet at the same time lie to them, we send mixed messages when we aren't consistently law-abiding. Not only do we have a duty to God to repent of dishonesty, we also have an obligation to those around us who are watching what we do at every turn in the road.

The Worst Mind Trick

The Christian life should be characterized by trustworthiness. It's a life that Anakin and the rest of the Jedi could never obtain. Their deceit dulled their integrity so much that they were oblivious to the Emperor's lies until it was too late. Obi-Wan tells Padmé that "He [Anakin] was deceived by a lie. We all were." Anakin is definitely not honest with others, but that isn't the primary cause of his spiritual demise. The main problem with Anakin is that he lies to himself. He inaccurately views himself as an amazing, unstoppable "force" all on his own. But in actuality, he's a weak person filled with so much pride that he's defeated by mere words.

I've written a lot about deceiving others, of which we should strive to repent, but deceiving others is really only the symptom of something much worse. The most dangerous thing you can do is deceive yourself. Like Anakin, it's when we think we're better than we are that we're in the most jeopardy. As John says, "If we claim to be without sin, we deceive ourselves and the truth is not in us" (1 John 1:8). James also warns, "Those who consider themselves religious and yet do not keep a tight rein on their tongues deceive themselves, and their religion is worthless" (James 1:26).

There's something a lot more sinister going on in our hearts when we deceive ourselves. The context of Paul's argument in Romans 1 is that unbelievers suppress the truth because of their wickedness. Any time we believe a lie rather than God, it's sin. Anakin repeatedly refuses to take an honest look at his faults and hates whenever someone else points them out. Padmé kindly tells him, "Mentors have a way of seeing more of our faults than we would like. It's the only way we grow." If we want to mature as Christians and not remain as spiritual infants, we must be honest with ourselves when it comes to the deep, nasty sin that resides in our hearts, the sin that causes us not only to lie but also to disobey God by thinking untrue thoughts (Philippians 4:8).

Even though there are two distinct paths in this world, one leading to life and the other to destruction, the light path is not completely illuminated. We must still traverse shadowy areas. These areas are not so much on the metaphorical road we're on but in the dark, decayed regions of our heart. It's the remaining sin that we have to deal with every day.

So, how can we honor God and defend against Satan's lies? We must be honest with ourselves. We need to be like the tax collector in Luke 18:13 who said, "God have mercy on me, a sinner." When we honestly embrace the bottomless aspect of our sin, we can flee to the cross and receive the forgiveness we long for and need so desperately. Only then can we live the life that Jesus promised when he said, "If you hold to my teaching, you are really my disciples. Then you will know the truth, and the truth will set you free" (John 8:31b–32).

6

THE DARK CHAIN

○ ○ ○ ○ ○ ● ○ ○ ○ ○ ○ ○ ○ ○ ○ ○ ○ ○

"Everything You Fear to Lose"

By recruiting future Padawans while they're young, the Jedi acquire the children free of any preconceived fears or cares. That's why when Anakin shows up as a "seasoned" nine-year-old, Yoda, Mace, and many on the Jedi Council refuse to train him. Unlike Jesus, who specializes in dealing with the worst of us, the Jedi Council regards Anakin as "damaged goods" because of his fear and anger. After they refuse to train Anakin, he demands to know what being afraid of losing his mom has to do with anything. "Everything," Yoda says. "Fear is the path to the dark side. Fear leads to anger. Anger leads to hate. Hate leads to suffering."

If lies are the foundation upon which Palpatine and Satan build, then fear, anger, and hate serve as the brick and mortar. In this chapter, we'll explore how Anakin and Luke deal with these emotions, how they make both good and bad decisions, and yet how only Luke manages to avoid succumbing to the dark side. As you study their decisions and behavior, you'll learn how to handle your fear, anger, hate, and suffering in appropriate, biblical ways so that you can reduce the darkness of sin in your life.

During their lightsaber duel, Count Dooku taunts Anakin, telling him he senses fear in him. "You have hate, you have anger, but you don't use them." Unlike the Jedi, the Sith aren't afraid of these emotions. For them, the more they stir up their evil passions, the stronger they become. And the more the Emperor can arouse these feelings in Anakin and Luke, the closer they get to the dark side. This is why the Jedi avoid attachments in the first place, because they lead to fear. In fact, it's Anakin's devotion to his mother and Padmé that make him an easy target for Palpatine.

Like the Emperor with Anakin, Satan also knows how to exploit our fears. We can usually distill our anxieties down to the fear of getting hurt, either physically or emotionally. The characters in *Star Wars* wrestle through their own anxieties. Lando fears the Empire will take away everything he's built. Obi-Wan experiences fear when he senses the voices of Alderaan crying out in terror. Mace fears Anakin's judgment is clouded. Han fears a bounty hunter will kill him. C-3PO fears he will get melted down. Luke fears his loved ones will die. Honorable as some of these concerns might be, Yoda still warns that fear of loss is the path to the dark side.

🔭 "Fear. Fear attracts the fearful, the strong, the weak, the innocent, the corrupt. Fear. Fear is my ally." — Darth Maul, from a TV advertisement for *The Phantom Menace*

If we go back to Matthew 6, Jesus makes a link between what we treasure in our hearts and what we worry about. God commands us not to worry about the things in this life. We should love and care for people but not to the point where we fear losing them. Comparable to Anakin, the fear of losing something—or someone—we cherish can actually cause us to do great evil in an attempt to hold onto it.

Fortunately, God doesn't discriminate like the Jedi Council. He also doesn't intend for our new life in Christ to be weighed down with fear and worry. Our problem is that we still have bad habits and incorrect thinking ingrained from when we lived our lives without God. Paul commands us to be transformed by the renewing of our minds. We need to identify not only what we worry about but also why we worry. If we can do that, we can replace those fears with God-honoring thoughts. In doing so, we'll prevent our fear from leading us to the more dangerous areas of anger and hate.

Commanded to Fear

Anakin ignores his Masters' counsel to fear the dark side. In *Episode III*, he tells Obi-Wan, "I do not fear the dark side as you do." At a point when Anakin should be very concerned about what the dark side may do to him, he hopes instead that the dark side will give him greater powers.

This lackadaisical attitude flourishes in our modern culture. Many people go through their day without much thought about the ramifications of their choices. They smoke cigarettes, drive recklessly, drink excessively, and eat unhealthy foods. From the outside looking in, these folks have a good thing going; no mental burdens whatsoever. They live for the moment, not even valuing self-preservation. But it's not that these persons don't have fears. They have just found ways to suppress them. They're caught up in living from one busy day to the next without giving much thought to the one most important fear that they should have: the fear of God. They rarely wonder if the Bible is true, if there will be a final judgment, or if only those who love Jesus will be saved.

Luke and Anakin's paths begin to separate over this fear of the dark side. Anakin is concerned not about the dark side's dangers, only its benefits. With this perspective, he craves that which makes him feel secure, loved, and powerful, eventually leading him to care only about his "new empire." Solomon experimented with this sort of personal worship, i.e., focusing only on himself. He tried filling his life with pleasures, riches, work, wisdom, and anything else he could devise. But afterwards, he deemed everything meaningless. Not only that, pursuing all of these worldly things only led him to fear because "No one knows what is coming—who can tell someone else what will happen after them?" (Ecclesiastes 10:14).

Solomon packs the entire book of Ecclesiastes with the dread and uncertainty of life. Remarkably, his solution to all of this is to replace those fears with the fear of God. He ends the book with these words: "Now all has been heard; here is the conclusion of the matter: Fear God and keep his commandments, for this is the duty of all mankind. For God will bring every deed into judgment, including every hidden thing, whether it is good or evil" (Ecclesiastes 12:13–14).

Sometimes we misunderstand the fear of God. The problem occurs when we think all fear is sinful. Many Christians, in an effort to preserve God's reputation of being loving, dismiss the notion that we should fear God. But there is a difference between fearing God and being fearful of God.

Similar to Luke, it's good to control our fear, like he does during his first lightsaber duel with Darth Vader. We obey God when we block out worry. Although, the Bible continually affirms the fact that we should fear God. How do we reconcile the two?

From one perspective, unless you are in Christ, you should fear God, because his holiness demands that your sin be atoned for. You should worry that at any moment God could take your next breath and judge you for your sin. On the other hand, if you are in Christ, you are no longer under condemnation. As David says, "If you, Lord, kept a record of sins, Lord, who could stand? But with you there is forgiveness, so that we can, with reverence, serve you" (Psalm 130:3–4). The key in verse 4 is the words "forgiveness" and "reverence." A believer's fear of condemnation should be replaced by a reverent fear: a deep respect and awe for the Maker of heaven and Earth who redeems us. In Christ, we shouldn't fear God striking us down like he did Ananias and Sapphira. And yet, we should still work out our salvation with fear and trembling. This means we don't allow a misunderstanding of God's grace to cause us to disobey him. As the writer of Hebrews warns, "If we deliberately keep on sinning after we have received the knowledge of the truth, no sacrifice for sins is left, but only a fearful expectation of judgment and of raging fire that will consume the enemies of God (Hebrews 10:26–27).

Since you are reading this book, you probably understand that you needed to be saved and have submitted to Jesus as Lord. But even though we've dealt with the fear of God's judgment, we still need to tackle two other fears common to believers: 1) fear of trials and 2) fear that we are still not good enough. Let's take a look at the first one.

"In You Must Go"

Prior to Yoda sending Luke into the cave on Dagobah to experience the "Trial of the Spirit," Luke says he feels cold and death. Yoda "reassures him," saying that the place is "strong with the dark side of the Force. A domain of evil it is. In you must go."

If I was Luke, I would think, "Um, yeah, no thanks." Talk about fear! But isn't this exactly the picture of the Christian life? Doesn't God call us to undergo all kinds of scary trials? Yoda was not simply concocting some sort of sadist trap for his unsuspecting Padawan. Rather, he gave Luke this test so that Luke could examine his own heart, to see the darkness within, in order to overcome it. In a similar way, God puts trials in our lives to test our faith and force us to deal with our sin. For this reason, we don't need to fear adversity or that God will not be with us. Not only does he customize our difficulties to help us achieve spiritual maturity, he gives us the strength we need to be victorious.

While it's true that Obi-Wan requires Luke to face Darth Vader alone in *Episode V,* earlier in Luke's journey, Obi-Wan gives his naïve apprentice much needed help in precarious situations. Right before walking into the cantina in *Episode IV,* Obi-Wan tells Luke to watch his step because of the riffraff in the bar. Luke responds arrogantly. "I'm ready for anything."

In Lucas' early drafts of *Episode IV*, Mos Eisley was the spaceport "Gordon" on the planet "Aquilae." This was most likely a gesture to the "Flash Gordon" serials that inspired the director.

Like Luke, the Apostle Peter frequently and arrogantly thought he was ready, too. In Matthew 14, when Jesus walks out on the water to the disciples, they are terrified and cry out in fear. "But Jesus immediately said to them: 'Take courage! It is I. Don't be afraid'" (Matthew 7:27). When Peter walks out on the lake and sees the wind and begins to sink, he doubts. *Immediately,* Jesus reaches out his hand and catches him, just like Obi-Wan promptly steps in to save Luke from the two who try to kill him in the cantina. God warns us to not be haughty like Luke at Mos Eisley, but he also promises to help us by providing a way to escape from sinning during our trials.

So, if you think you are standing firm, be careful that you don't fall! No temptation has overtaken you except what is common to mankind. And God is faithful; he will not let you be tempted beyond what you can bear. But when you are tempted, he will also provide a way out so that you can endure it. (1 Corinthians 10:12-13)

As believers, we can rest knowing that even if we're not in control, God is. More than that, God orchestrates everything for the good of those who love him (Romans 8:28). When we forget this, all kinds of fears creep in. Luke makes a classic hero, because he replaces fear with self-control, courage, and sacrifice. His adventure is one daunting ordeal after another, but all of this drives him to trust the Force even more, and ultimately, he conquers his fears. It's when we act like Anakin, who doesn't trust in the light side to provide for his needs, that we lose sight of God's care and give way to fear.

Unfortunately, it's probably harder than ever for people in our society to control their fears. Maybe it's because we're drowning in information and much of it frightens us. All you have to do is go online for two minutes, and you'll walk away dreading a new product that causes cancer or a massive storm that's heading right for your home town. However, being cautious of dangers doesn't necessarily lead to the dark side. In fact, God gives us the knowledge and a healthy respect for these things in order to protect us. If we walked through life oblivious to the hazards of fire, guns, and speeding cars, many might not make it past childhood. But God does not give us this awareness so it can turn prudence into anxiety. Rather, every fear provides the opportunity to trust God in the midst of upsetting situations. Comparable to Peter walking on the water, we need only to keep our eyes on Jesus, not our circumstances, so that fear doesn't rob us of our faith that Jesus' care is more than sufficient in every situation.

Pride Leads to Fear

Often, it's difficult to tell when someone is feeling fearful. We might notice certain body language, such as pacing the floor or biting fingernails, but this is entirely subjective. When anger takes over though, it's plain for all to see. People raise their voices, say cruel things, and slam doors. Interestingly, the wisdom of Yoda and the Bible prompts us to trace behavior back to the heart. If we follow the dark chain back even further, we discover that beneath every fear is pride.

Fearing that people might not appreciate his talents, Luke wastes no time defending his skills as a star pilot in the cantina. We can't see Luke's insecurities or his fear, but we can see the outburst to which they lead. Deep down, all of us feel we are not good enough. It's the reason self-help books are so popular. It's why some people exercise, earn master's degrees, or climb Mount Everest. No matter their station in life, most people try to excel at what they do so they can provide for their family, receive accolades, and feel good about themselves. Of course, when you become a Christian, you learn how little our earthly accomplishments matter to God. That being said, we still have a tough time letting go of the self-righteousness we spent so many years developing. In short, we are afraid to let go of being good in the world's eyes and trust that Christ's righteousness is enough.

When Yoda tells Luke that he's not ready to be trained, Luke's fears rise to the surface, giving way to anger. "I am ready... I can be a Jedi. Ben, tell him I'm ready!" Luke faces the uncertainty of not becoming a Jedi, the one thing he wants more than anything. When he sees this slipping away, he lashes out. Yoda has seen Luke's father go down this same path of pride leading to fear and fear leading to anger. He knows what may follow and wants nothing to do with another's journey to the dark side.

Even though we lay down our self-righteousness when we trust in Christ, it doesn't take long before we fear that people or even God won't see the value of what we offer. When we fear disapproval, we instinctively tighten the grip on our own record and performance. Similar to Anakin, we become more concerned about defending our worthiness than we are at doing the right thing with a God-honoring attitude. That leads us to spending our time and energy developing our worldly self. This lofty view of ourselves might be tied to physical appearance, health, IQ, bank account, possessions, work reputation, obedient children, religious prominence, or whatever we feel will make us a success. We invest so much time crafting and nurturing our righteousness that we become scared of losing to the point that we lash out at anyone who tries to take it away.

"Fear Leads to Anger"

When I watch *Episode IV* with others, it's inevitable that someone will laugh when Luke starts whining about not getting to go to Tosche Station with his friends. Soon after, he says, "Oh, Biggs is right. I'm never gonna get out of here!" eliciting the same amused response from the audience. At times, he acts like a spoiled brat, not a likely candidate for the hero of the galaxy. But when we watch what Anakin's anger leads to, things aren't so funny.

When the Jedi Council does not choose Anakin to become a Jedi Master, he explodes in anger. "This is outrageous! It's unfair!" Yoda and Mace sense not only anger but also pride in his powers. When *Episode III* draws to a close, Palpatine tells Anakin (now Darth Vader) that, "In your anger, you killed her [Padmé]," which is not entirely untrue. It's Anakin's anger that drove him to the dark side and caused Padmé to lose the will to live.

🔭 The Darth Vader suit Hayden Christensen wore at the end of *Episode III* was extra heavy and uncomfortable (at Lucas' request) so that it would be more believable that Anakin was wearing it for the first time.

Why does fear lead so often to anger not only in *Star Wars* but in real life, too? For Luke, his fear turns to anger most often when people dear to him are hurt, threatened, or killed, such as when the Empire murders his uncle and aunt, when Han refuses to help rescue Leia, when Vader kills Obi-Wan, when Han and Leia are in pain at Cloud City, when the Rebels fall into the Emperor's trap, and when Vader threatens to go after Leia. Luke's anger represents the righteous anger found in the Bible and almost always happens when goodness is endangered in some way.

The Silver Lining of Furious Wrath

God is the holy King of the universe. Therefore, he must punish those who do not honor him. God can no more resist doing this than Luke can resist destroying the Death Star. Luke must assault evil, and so must God. But God is graciously slow to anger, as Numbers 14:18 states, enduring man's sinfulness for millennia and waiting patiently until the Day of Judgment. Nevertheless, Paul warns that this day will come, "But for those who are self-seeking and who reject the truth and follow evil, there will be wrath and anger" (Romans 2:8).

Lamentations 2:1 speaks of a dark cloud of God's anger. Can there possibly be any sort of silver lining? Christians can find the encouragement in Paul's letter to the Romans.

What if God, although choosing to show his wrath and make his power known, bore with great patience the objects of his wrath prepared for destruction? What if he did this to make the riches of his glory known to the objects of his mercy, whom he prepared in advance for glory. (Romans 9:22–23)

These verses highlight the silver lining of grace in God's wrath. It's grace, because "all have sinned and fall short of the glory of God" (Romans 3:23) and deserve wrath. In *Star Wars*, the good guys defy the Empire, because it's evil. But from the perspective of the Empire, its wrath is just. The Rebels have broken the law. That's why they're called "Rebels." It's the other way around for us, though we are still rebels. Humanity, at its core, has rebelled by refusing to align with God's jurisdiction, and no one deserves mercy. Not only that, whereas the Emperor fights for evil, wanting to dominate others in order to increase his kingdom, God fights for good, punishing the wicked because of their unbelief and rebellion and taking back the personal kingdoms each unbeliever has stolen from him.

While the Sith's wrath during Order 66 is a terrible holocaust wiping out almost all of the Jedi, it lasts for only a short time. People hope that God's wrath might be transitory as well. Yet, the Bible doesn't teach about any sort of place like purgatory where a sinful person, over time, may atone for crimes against an eternal, holy God. Therefore, knowing our terrible predicament and how he could not compromise his justice, God sent his Son to take the infinite punishment for us. In this, God's anger was directed away from those who trust in Christ and towards Jesus. God's anger doesn't simply dissipate by itself. Jesus' death appeases God's anger, because it satisfies his need for justice. Jesus, being in nature God, took the full brunt of the Father's wrath and, unlike us, did not need to be punished for eternity.

As dreadful as God's wrath is for the unbeliever, it actually show-cases God's holiness, patience, and mercy. Paul spends more time in the book of Romans talking about God's wrath than he does in any other letter. Towards the end, he even uses the knowledge of God's wrath to actually spur love for our enemies.

> Do not repay anyone evil for evil. Be careful to do what is right in the eyes of everyone. If it is possible, as far as it depends on you, live at peace with everyone. Do not take revenge, my dear friends, but leave room for God's wrath, for it is written: "It is mine to avenge; I will repay," says the Lord. (Romans 12:17–19)

Paul goes on to say, "If your enemy is hungry, feed him; if he is thirsty, give him something to drink... do not be overcome by evil, but overcome evil with good" (20a–21). At the end of *Episode VI*, Luke has the opportunity to pour out his wrath on Vader, but he doesn't. Instead, he shows love and mercy. Just like Paul describes in these verses, Luke's love and goodness overcomes Vader's hatred and evil. Vader is so moved by Luke's love that he repents of his wicked-ness and returns to the light.

🔭 In the Return of the Jedi Blu-Ray edition, Darth Vader screams out "No!" right before he stops the Emperor from attacking Luke with Force lightning.

God's wrath teaches us that we don't need to seek revenge against our enemies, even if it's the mental revenge of hating them. When we let God be God and obey his command to love our enemies, we can overcome evil with good.

"In Your Anger, Do Not Sin"[15]

God makes a distinction in his Word between righteous and sinful anger. Some believers think they are supposed to absorb every injustice life throws at them with a big smile on their face. But that's not how Jesus did it, and it's not what the Bible teaches. For example, when Jesus saw that the people had made his Father's house into a den of robbers, he made a whip and drove the animals and moneylenders out of the temple. Part of our responsibility as

Christians is to know where we have license to be biblically angry and where we do not.

Throughout the ages, man has wrongfully used the Bible to justify all kinds of evil in God's name. Those involved in the Crusades, the Irish Protestant/Catholic conflict, the Spanish Inquisition, and the Ku Klux Klan perverted God's laws, anger, and wrath, stealing an authority reserved only for him and used it as a platform for their evil agendas. Today, many people protest abortions and homosexuality in the name of God but act despicably towards others in the process. For all these groups, pride led to fear, fear led to anger, and anger led to hate. Yoda warns Luke that anger, fear, and aggression flow easily, quickly joining you in a fight. Similar to the Jedi and the Sith, anger flows easily into men and women's hearts. And once that anger is in us, we, like the groups mentioned above, want the Bible to justify our thoughts and actions.

Anakin feels his anger is justified when the Sand People take Shmi. His anger rises slowly from the time he first dreams about her. Fear and worry spiral his emotions downward until his anger and frustration over not knowing where she is become unbearable. All along, he views himself as the innocent victim and that something foreign and evil invaded his life to cause this trouble. Every thought leads him closer to betraying the Jedi way. His anger doesn't just cause him to try to rescue his mother, which would be a noble act. Rather, it's the catalyst for his barbaric revenge against her abductors.

Balancing Anakin's unbridled anger, Padmé usually shows no animosity towards anyone, wanting diplomacy to prevail in every situation. But even she must take up a blaster gun when the Geonosians sentence her and her friends to be executed. Anakin, surprised by her actions, asks, "You call this a diplomatic solution?"

"No," she responds, "I call it aggressive negotiations."

Like the good guys in *Star Wars,* there are times for us to use our God-given anger to combat evil not in a sinful way or with guns but in a manner that honors Christ.

🔭 Natalie Portman wore a T-shirt with the words "Stop Wars" in classic *Star Wars* font on Saturday Night Live, making a political statement in line with her famous character, Padmé Amidala.

Palpatine tells Anakin in *Episode III,* "I can feel your anger. It gives you focus, makes you stronger." Unlike Luke using his anger to save, Anakin uses his anger to destroy. This raises good questions for us. Do we use our anger to defend God's honor or our own? Do we use it to build people up or tear them down? Does our anger lead to justice or hate? The answers to these questions will determine if our anger is righteous or sinful.

God designed anger as part of our emotional makeup, but like all of his gifts, we can use it for his glory or our own. There are indicators to decide if my anger is sinful. Usually, a situation starts off by someone aggravating me. Maybe the person spoke unkindly, cut me off in traffic, or just made me look bad. In the short term, if I retaliate by being unloving, either through my thoughts, words, or actions, then it's clear that I've sinned.

Nevertheless, there are appropriate times for believers to become angry. When people insult our God, it should rouse righteous anger within us. When we see people made in the image of God treated unjustly, it should anger us. And during the times when Satan entices us with the next promised delight, we should let our anger lead to hating him and the sin he dangles before us. We will need wisdom from God to know how to manage this area of our lives, because if we fail to obey Christ in this area, the path upon which we stumble will only darken.

"Anger Leads to Hate"
God's Holy Hate

During a Bible study many years ago, a new acquaintance exclaimed, "God doesn't hate anything." His response was to a statement I had made about God hating evil. I walked away questioning myself. But after studying Scripture, it was undeniable. God does hate.

Unlike the Sith, God's hate is not sinful. In fact, it would be wrong for him not to hate evil. It would be a deficiency in his justice and holiness if he overlooked or rewarded evil with any sort of benefit.

There are six things the Lord hates, seven that are detestable to him: haughty eyes, a lying tongue, hands that shed innocent blood, a heart that devises wicked schemes, feet that are quick to rush into evil, a false witness who pours out lies and a person who stirs up conflict in the community. (Proverbs 6:16-19)

God doesn't just hate evil behavior; he hates the people who do the evil. Psalm 5:5 is short and to the point. "The arrogant cannot stand in your presence. You hate all who do wrong."

Hate is part of God's character. But how can this be so? Isn't God love? Some, like my friend from the Bible study, think it's practically blasphemy to suggest that God has an ounce of hate in him.

To examine this argument, consider Luke Skywalker. Early in *Episode IV,* he's the epitome of innocence but proves he hates when he says, "It's not that I like the Empire. I hate it." This doesn't startle or offend us. Instead, we admire him for it. As the audience, we already know enough about the Empire to know it's evil. And something that's evil should be hated. The problem is when we apply hating evil to ourselves or to those around us. We don't want to believe that God might curse our children, our friends, or our sweet grandmother who never did anything wrong except maybe bake us too many cookies. Unfortunately for them, they inherited a sinful record from Adam and commit their own sins. Because of this, God detests both the sin and the sinner.

Hate is a big part of the problem that separates us from God. He despises evildoers, and evildoers despise him. Hate also keeps people from accepting Christ, their only hope. But when a person trusts in Jesus, God's hate not only turns away from the believer, God's favor actually turns towards him. In Christ, we are no longer rejected but accepted. This is a profound mystery, but it's the heart of the gospel. It's why we can desire God, because he showed such great compassion to us, his enemies, by sacrificing his only Son.

Luke doesn't shock us when he says he hates the Empire. But what does surprise us is when he forgoes the chance to destroy Darth Vader, the person who has caused him and others to suffer so much. Instead, Luke throws away his lightsaber, preferring to be martyred by the Emperor than kill his father. At a time when it would have been very easy to hate, Luke chooses to love sacrificially like God's Son did for us.

Hate Leads to Murder

Let's reflect on how Simeon and Levi's anger led to hate in Genesis 34. In this account, Shechem raped Dinah but then wanted to marry her. As a result, Dinah's brothers were furious and devised a scheme of revenge. They tricked Shechem by saying that in order for him to marry Dinah, he, along with every male in the city, had to be circumcised.

> Three days later, while all of them were still in pain, two of Jacob's sons, Simeon and Levi, Dinah's brothers, took their swords and attacked the unsuspecting city, killing every male. They put Hamor and his son Shechem to the sword and took Dinah from Shechem's house and left. The sons of Jacob came upon the dead bodies and looted the city where their sister had been defiled. They seized their flocks and herds and donkeys and everything else of theirs in the city and out in the fields. They carried off all their wealth and all their women and children, taking as plunder everything in the houses. (Genesis 34:25-29)

Simeon and Levi let their anger control them to the point of doing wicked acts. Instead of forgiving Shechem, they betrayed and killed him. And the text says they didn't stop there but killed every man, kidnapped the women and children, and stole everything of value. Some would say their anger and actions were justified. However, Jacob, their father, didn't think so. As he passed out blessings to his sons, he said,

> Simeon and Levi are brothers—their swords are weapons of violence. Let me not enter their council, let me not join their assembly, for they have killed men in their anger and hamstrung oxen as they pleased. Cursed be their anger, so fierce, and their fury, so cruel! I will scatter them in Jacob and disperse them in Israel. (Genesis 49:5-7)

As Palpatine says, anger can give us a focus that we wouldn't have normally. God gives us this emotion to use for good not evil. Too often though, we use that focus to sin and inflict pain on those around us, as Simeon and Levi did to the Hivites. There are consequences for our anger and hate, either immediately, later in life, or during God's final judgment. For instance, even though Simeon and Levi were in line to receive the blessing of the kingdom, Jacob passed them over because of their evil actions, giving their inheritance to Judah instead. Hence, Jacob gave each person the blessing or curse he deserved.

Anakin has the same choice to allow his anger to lead to hate when he falls victim to the Tusken Raiders' horrific kidnapping and eventual murder of his mother, Shmi. Nightmares plant the worry in Anakin's heart, but it's not until he confirms his fears on Tatooine that his anger takes over. As he rides the speeder bike in search of his mother, we can all relate to what he may be thinking: "What have those monsters been doing to her for all these weeks? This is so unfair." Most likely he's also fantasizing about what he'll do to the Sand People once he finds them. He'll be able to finally carry out the revenge he wants so badly. And yet, riding on his speeder bike is the only time that he has a chance to think things through. This is probably the last opportunity to decide if he should follow the Jedi way or kill with his sword, just like Simeon and Levi.

Anakin finds his mom with only enough time remaining for her to say a few words before she dies. When she passes, Anakin's eyes show his anger transform into a powerful hate. When Anakin returns to Padmé, he tells her, "I killed them. I killed them all. They're dead, every single one of them. And not just the men, but the women and the children, too. They're like animals, and I slaughtered them like animals. I hate them!"

🔭 As the scene cuts from Anakin slaying the Sand People, we hear Qui-Gon's Force ghost yelling, "Anakin, Anakin... No!" They used the audio from *Episode I* when Qui-Gon warned Anakin of Darth Maul's approach.

An extremely small percentage of us will actually let our anger and hatred lead to murder, but it's striking how God's Word associates hatred with murder. "Anyone who hates a brother or sister is a murderer, and you know that no murderer has eternal life residing in him" (1 John 3:15). The Christian life is not just about avoiding the wrong things. For instance, 1 John teaches it's not good enough to simply not hate your brother or sister. We must actually love them. And not just superficial love either. John defines love as laying down our lives for our brothers and sisters, considering that Jesus Christ laid down his life for us. This is the radical sign of true belief. This is the type of love Anakin never found, not even with Padmé. In reality, it's Anakin's son, Luke, who demonstrates this self-sacrificing love to underserving Anakin and gives us the good example to follow.

Turning Back to the Good Side

As we study the entire chain of emotions about which Yoda warns, each one gets increasingly harder to rein in. It's easier to repent of anger than hate. It's easier to repent of fear than anger and so on. But what happens if you're angry with someone? How can we prevent it from turning into hate? For starters, we need to be aware of how anger works. Usually, if someone hurts us, we can either forgive him or try to hurt the person back. Since most of us will not try to avenge ourselves in any meaningful way, we'll just sit quietly by and stew. Instead of taking any sort of action to reconcile, we mentally replay how we were wronged, becoming angrier each time. If we're not careful to take our thoughts captive, bitterness will set in and we will hate the person, wishing animosity towards him.

John says, "Whoever claims to love God yet hates a brother or sister is a liar. For whoever does not love their brother and sister, whom they have seen, cannot love God, whom they have not seen" (1 John 4:20). John makes it clear that those who hate will not inherit eternal life with Christ. That means they are not even believers! John isn't talking about the passing seasons of life when we are so angry at someone that hate develops. All believers fall into this state at some point, but the Holy Spirit will convict them of their sin and cause repentance. John refers to the persons who have such bitterness and hatred in their hearts that they are not willing to forgive. They would rather hold onto their hate. It's these people who, while they may profess Christ, were never believers in the first place.

Luke repents of his anger and hate, forgives Darth Vader, and refuses to kill him and the Emperor. He would rather die as a martyr to the Jedi way than deny it by killing the two villains. Unlike his father, Luke chooses to control his fear, anger, and hate. Luke has many reasons to hate Darth Vader. Vader indirectly murdered his uncle and aunt, imprisoned his sister, killed his mentor, tortured his best friend, cut off Luke's hand, tried to turn him to the dark side, and threatened to turn his sister to the dark side, too. The easy move for Luke would have been to leave Vader to wallow in his own miserable existence. This is basically what Leia encourages him to do when she urges him to run far away and not face him. But Luke refuses to be indifferent to Vader. Instead, he embarks on a mission to "save him," to "turn him back to the good side." This is another picture of Christ and those he saves. We give God every reason to hate us instead of love us, yet he chooses to seek us out at a great cost to himself.

Throughout life, we will encounter difficult people whom we would rather not love. While we might not hate them, we would rather resign them to a place of unimportance in our hearts. The Bible doesn't give us this option though. Not only are we to put off hate; we are to put on love.

I have heard of cases where a believer visits a criminal in prison who murdered the believer's loved one. The believer brings the murderer meals, prays for him, shares the gospel, and becomes his friend. How is this possible? Most would, if not seek the death penalty for the perpetrator, at least want nothing to do with the person. But that's not the love of Christ. The love of God specifically loves enemies. This is the sort of love that causes our light to burn bright for the Lord that he may be glorified in heaven and on Earth.

Before Luke rescues him, Vader is in his own private prison, his own personal hell. His fear has led him to be consumed by both anger and hate, and now a metal shell encases him like a jail cell incarcerates a murderer. But Luke, like Christ did for us, breaks Vader out of his bondage to the dark side. He removes Vader's helmet so that Anakin can finally see with his own eyes, like God removing the scales from our eyes to see our Redeemer. Luke shows us that no matter how far we go down the dark path of fear, anger, and hate, we can always turn back. This is the hope that all believers have. But, sadly, we don't always make the right choice.

"Hate Leads to Suffering"

Walking in Darkness

The Jawas' thievery, Lando's betrayal, the Tusken Raiders' savagery, Sebulba's cheating, Jabba's debauchery, Palpatine's dishonesty, Vader's bloodthirstiness—the list goes on, and in every case, these characters' horrible actions cause others to suffer, sometimes unto death.

Hatred usually develops after one party causes pain to another, as in the cases of Threepio hating the Jawas, Luke hating the Empire, Vader hating the Rebels, Jabba hating Han Solo, and Palpatine hating the Jedi. Incidentally, this hatred almost always begins with some sort of fear that leads to anger. Even though the side that hates wants the other to suffer, the hating backfires and causes the worst suffering to happen in the hater's heart.

The Bible teaches, "But anyone who hates a brother or sister is in the darkness and walks around in the darkness. They do not know where they are going, because the darkness has blinded them (1 John 2:11). When Anakin turns to the dark side, he, for all intents and purposes, is blind. Not only has the Emperor blinded him, Anakin chooses to cover his own eyes from any good that still remains in him. The Sith teach people to stir up their hatred, because if it burns hot enough, it can sear any remaining goodness in the heart.

When Vader slaughters the Jedi during Order 66, he sheds a tear. Not only does the Emperor cause Vader to hate the Jedi, he causes him to hate himself. Satan knows that if we are busy hating others, God, and even ourselves, that hatred will grow and fester. Our conscience will become calloused and immune to the conviction of the Holy Spirit. If God doesn't show mercy, we'll spiral deeper into hatred until all hope is lost. Like the Emperor, the devil promises that hating someone who has wronged us will make us feel better. But the opposite is true. Analogous to the Sith, the hate swells, the hate flows, and before we know it, we are slaves to it.

There's much fan speculation as to the significance of the number 66 in Palpatine's executive order. Some say it's a reference to FDR's order 9066, an assassination attempt on Hitler, or the number of the beast in Revelation 13:18.

The thirty pieces of silver seemed so good to Judas before he betrayed Jesus. But after seeing Jesus condemned, Judas was seized with such remorse that he could not stand being in his own skin anymore and hanged himself. While Judas thought that killing himself would end his self-inflicted suffering, death doesn't end the suffering for any unbeliever. In fact, it's only the beginning. If one does not repent of hating his neighbor, it will be grounds for God to punish the offender for all eternity. When Yoda speaks of suffering, it's only in this lifetime. There is hope that the suffering will end at least when this life does. This is not the case for someone who sins against an eternal, holy God. Like being thrown into the Sarlacc, they will find "a new definition of pain and suffering."

Suffering Leads to Joy

Few people experience as much suffering as Luke Skywalker. As mentioned earlier, Darth Vader is the primary cause. To add to the list, Luke grows up not knowing his real mom and dad, laboring tediously on a planet that he despises, and sees his best friend Biggs Darklighter killed in war. It seems every time Luke begins to care for someone, something takes that person away. These trials cause him to have a bad attitude and lose his ability to rejoice. Given the path his father takes, we are unsure as the story goes on if he will also succumb to the dark side.

However, to borrow a line from Darth Vader, Obi-Wan has taught Luke well. For the most part, Luke controls his fear. He reins in his anger quickly. He doesn't allow hatred to take up residence in his heart. Moreover, with so many reasons to seek revenge, Luke chooses to show love and grace to his biggest nemesis, Darth Vader. In *Episode VI*, Luke, lightsaber in hand, stands over the unarmed Sith Lord. One final strike will finally put an end to the monster that has caused so many to suffer unjustly. But, Luke stops and thinks things through. He looks at what's left of where Vader's hand used to be and understands that if he strikes Vader down in hate, he will suffer the same awful fate as his father. Luke could have easily killed Vader, but he throws his lightsaber away, leaving himself defenseless as he defies the Emperor.

The love and mercy that Luke shows to Vader strips away the cold, hard heart of the Dark Lord. He responds to Luke's amazing grace by sacrificing himself. Vader knows that if he steps into the Emperor's lightning, it will fry his life-support suit, but he does it anyway. This is another picture of Christ and his Church. First, the Son saves us, his enemies. But then, because of the Holy Spirit working in us, stirring up love for God, we seek to reciprocate this love by becoming living sacrifices, as Romans 12:1 says, "Therefore, I urge you, brothers and sisters, in view of God's mercy, to offer your bodies as a living sacrifice, holy and pleasing to God—this is your true and proper worship." Only then are we willing to turn back and "step into the lightning" for our Lord. This is why James can tell us to count it joy when we suffer trials. This is the reason why the apostles could rejoice after being flogged (Acts 5) because they had been counted worthy of suffering disgrace for the name of Jesus.

Suffering Leads to Hope

At the end of *Episode VI,* good conquers evil. Light triumphs over darkness. Contentment replaces fear. Compassion displaces anger. Love wins over hate. Joy overcomes suffering. Not only is Luke able to avoid falling prey to the dark side of the Force, he rescues his father from it. Luke provides a path back to the light side, causing his father to finally be free of the internal suffering he has undergone for so much of his life. Through sacrifice, through suffering, they reach a place where it was all worth it. All of the painful trials they endured were needed to produce the crop of virtue, to bring them to this point in their spiritual journey. As Han Solo would say, "Not a bad bit of rescuing, huh?"

The Jedi, Buddhists, Hindus, and even many Christians want to avoid suffering at all costs and generally consider it more of a curse than a blessing. Many reason that if you are suffering, then you must have done something evil to deserve it. This was the question to Jesus in John 9 regarding the man born blind. "'Neither this man nor his parents sinned,' said Jesus, 'but this happened so that the works of God might be displayed in him'" (v. 3).

The Miraluka, a human-like species in the *Star Wars* universe, are born without eyes. They use Force sight to perceive their environment.

Jesus also responded to this sort of thinking in Luke 13: "Jesus answered, 'Do you think that these Galileans were worse sinners than all the other Galileans because they suffered this way? I tell you, no!'" (13:2–3a)

The worst thing believers can do when they're going through painful times is think that God has abandoned them or is punishing them. It's no longer necessary to chastise us, because Christ has already taken God's punishment in our place. God brings suffering into our lives to bring us to spiritual maturity and to give us hope. He doesn't like inflicting pain. Few parents enjoy disciplining their children or watching them struggle through hard things in life, but wise parents know this is how their children grow up properly.

Also, our God is never aloof, content to watch tears stream down people's faces while he watches casually from his heavenly throne. On the contrary, as Isaiah 53 says, he became a man of suffering, familiar with pain. He was despised and took up our pain and bore our suffering. He was punished for our transgressions and was crushed for our iniquities. He did all of this because he knew that his suffering would lead to our joy and hope. This is why the Christian life can be not only weathered but also enjoyed, because we already know the ending. And, unlike someone spoiling the ending of *Star Wars,* this is wonderful to know! It's this truth that can keep us going when we don't think we can endure another minute of sorrow. The cross is our redemption. It's where Jesus stepped into the lightning for us.

The Light Chain

This chapter has been based on a sequence of emotional choices that Yoda warns will lead to the dark side. Let's end this discussion with a positive chain straight from the pages of God's Word.

Not only so, but we also glory in our sufferings, because we know that suffering produces perseverance; perseverance, character; and character, hope. And hope does not put us to shame, because

God's love has been poured out into our hearts through the Holy Spirit, who has been given to us. (Romans 5:3-5)

Isn't this astounding? Suffering is no longer the miserable end of all the bad stuff you've withstood. Quite the reverse. It's the beginning of all the marvelous blessings. At times, Yoda and Obi-Wan understand the value in suffering to accomplish the greater good. They both urge Luke to allow Han and Leia to suffer. Through their suffering, Luke would have time to finish his training, become a Jedi Knight, and have the abilities to defeat Vader and his Emperor.

Like Luke, we have a hard time realizing that every second we suffer is a second perfectly designed by God so that our character ends up resembling that of Christ. Just like Luke should have finished his training (even if that meant sacrificing Han and Leia), we must finish our difficult training on Earth so that we become the godly men and women God wants us to be.

Satan's schemes and living in this fallen world cause misery, but let's not forget the pain we bring upon ourselves when we sin. Some suffering is due to God's discipline, which is yet another manifestation of his deep love for us.

Because the Lord disciplines the one he loves, and he chastens everyone he accepts as his son. Endure hardship as discipline; God is treating you as his children. For what children are not disciplined by their father... but God disciplines us for our good, in order that we may share in his holiness. No discipline seems pleasant at the time, but painful. Later on, however, it produces a harvest of righteousness and peace for those who have been trained by it. (Hebrews 12:6,7,10b-11)

Again, God orchestrates everything (the good and the bad) for our spiritual profit. The above passage teaches that sometimes we must endure suffering in order to share in God's holiness. Not only does suffering lead to joy and hope for the believer, it also leads to righteousness and peace. Paul makes a similar connection in Romans 8:17 when he says, "we share in his [Christ's] sufferings in order that we may also share in his glory." He goes on to say in verse 18 that "our present sufferings are not worth comparing with the glory that will be revealed in us."

When you go through life, you will experience fear, anger, hatred, and suffering. Like Anakin and Luke, you will have the choice to sin or to not sin. Believers should take encouragement that every one of these situations can be redeemed for Christ. Fear God. Be angry, and yet do not sin. Hate what is evil. Suffer for the name of Christ. When you do these things, fear will lead to anger, anger will lead to hate, and hate will lead to suffering, all for the glory of God.

7

SPIRITUAL STAR WARFARE

○○○○○○●○○○○○○○○○○○○

The Spiritual Forces of Evil

As soon as you become a Christian, God declares you righteous and adopts you into his family. Like Chief Chirpa's grand pronouncement about Luke, Leia, and the others on Endor, God declares you a member of his eternal tribe. And, like the Rebels combining forces with the Ewoks to fight against the Empire, you also become a warrior, a defender of God's name—and a target for Satan.

Every Christian experiences spiritual warfare regularly. Even though it's not as mystical as it sounds, that doesn't make it any less real. Part of God's plan for our lives is that we battle with the "spiritual forces of evil" spoken of in Ephesians 6. Fortunately, he does not send us into war unarmed.

At the beginning of Luke's journey, Obi-Wan gives Luke a lightsaber, the weapon of a Jedi Knight. The first thing a new Christian often receives is a Bible, because the Word of God is, as Paul says in Ephesians 6:17, the sword of the Spirit. The author of Hebrews uses the same metaphor when he says God's Word is "sharper than any double-edged sword, it penetrates even to dividing soul and spirit, joints and marrow; it judges the thoughts and attitudes of the heart" (Hebrews 4:12). God also sends the Holy Spirit to strengthen us so that we can combine the knowledge and truth of Christ with the power of his Spirit. This gives us the ability to fight Satan with the ultimate weapon—Scripture—the same way Jesus did when Satan tempted him in the wilderness.

Even armed with God's Word and the Holy Spirit, your behavior (unlike your standing before God) is not perfected the moment you accept Jesus. The devil used to be our father and, as Aunt Beru says of Luke, we still have too much of our dark father in us. We are new creations, but we are still riddled with sinful thoughts and habits. The sanctifying process, including our war with Satan, will take the rest of our lives, and we'll only be without sin when we are finally in heaven with our Lord.

🔭 The word "Vader" means "father" in Dutch. Lucas says the name was a variation of "Dark Father." This may be only a coincidence, seeing as Anakin and Darth Vader were two separate characters in early scripts.

The fight against sin takes place in the spiritual realm. It's a conflict between living for God and living for ourselves. The Jedi deal with a similar conflict, only theirs is between living for the light side of the Force or choosing the dark. Indeed, Anakin battles as much spiritually as he does physically. Before he turns to the dark side, he's torn between following the Jedi way and turning his back on it to save Padmé. We have already explored his journey toward becoming a Sith. Now, let's consider the internal turmoil that occurs when the goodness that remains in Anakin fights against his growing wickedness. Analyzing Anakin's spiritual battles will help us even though, for believers, the roles are reversed. We battle the remaining evil that is in our hearts as we press forward to please God.

"I Feel the Conflict Within You"

For starters, where do we go in the Bible to learn about the clash between our side, which wants to live for Christ, and the side that wants to sin? The typical go-to passage for this topic is Romans 7, which describes Paul's fight against sin. But, a closer examination of the text reveals that Paul is actually describing his life as an unbeliever and the enormous power sin had in his life before he knew Christ. When Paul put his trust in Jesus, sin ceased to be his master.

For the first time in his life, he had the power to conquer sin. There is a dramatic shift in Paul's state of mind between Romans 7, where he is defeated and without hope, and Romans 8, where he declares that all believers are "more than conquerors," (Romans 8:37) specifically over demons and any other power in Creation. Consider the following two verses to see the stark difference between the control of sin in an unbeliever's heart and freedom from sin's control in the believer's heart.

> But I see another law at work in me, waging war against the law of my mind and making me a prisoner of the law of sin at work within me. (Romans 7:23)

> Because through Christ Jesus the law of the Spirit who gives life has set you free from the law of sin and death. (Romans 8:2)

To understand the unbeliever's conflict better, think of Darth Vader as a picture of Romans 7. Part of him doesn't want to do evil, as evidenced by him shedding a tear during his slaughter of the Jedi. His statement to Luke, "It is too late for me, son," shows that he knows he has chosen the wrong path but doesn't have the power to change. Hence, Vader either denies that the conflict exists, as he does to Luke in *Episode VI,* or he reasons that if he can persuade Luke to choose the dark side, it will "end this destructive conflict." The conflict to which he refers here is his conflict with Luke, who represents goodness and light. And yet, this is symbolic of the discord within Vader's own heart.

Unbelievers act similarly. If they don't have the power to overcome their sin, they may encourage others to join them in order to drown out any guilt they feel. They may also simply give up, saying, "It's natural" or "It's just the way God made me" or "God will forgive me." Few people enjoy confrontation, especially an internal conflict. To do what they really want, unbelievers will try to push down every conflict that gets in their way. This takes us back to Romans 1:18, which says people "suppress the truth by their wickedness."

When Luke and Vader talk on Endor in *Episode VI,* Luke urges Vader to, "Search your feelings… You can't do this. I feel the conflict within you." For the first time in years, Vader is conflicted with the lingering goodness in his heart. The task of turning his son over to the Emperor doesn't come easily. To combat this, Vader tries to entice Luke, saying, "If you only knew the power of the dark side," as if Vader is doing him a favor. In reality, the dark side has made Vader a slave. If Vader can satisfy himself that the dark side is stronger, maybe he will feel he has made the right decision, and his inner turmoil will subside.

Since Luke follows the light side, his spiritual warfare is a picture of Galatians 5:17, which is the appropriate passage to learn about the believer's battle with sin. Galatians 5:17 talks specifically about how the flesh (our remaining sin) desires what is contrary to the Spirit so that they are in conflict with each other. Therefore, we don't always obey God as we should. Luke doesn't make the right decision every time, but overall, he values goodness and strives to fight against the dark side.

Luke is so in tune with this clash between light and dark that he senses his father's conflict. In response to Luke's discovery that good still remains in him, Vader retorts, "There is no conflict." Luke presses Vader on this, confident that if his father fights it, he can turn back to the good. Unfortunately, Vader doesn't have Luke's faith. Hence, he has no real power to choose good over evil. This is the classic dilemma Paul describes in Romans 7. Vader doesn't want this evil life; but sadly, he can do nothing to free himself from it.

Luke's conflict is different from his father's in the sense that Luke has not succumbed to the dark side. Usually, choosing the dark side is like journeying into an inescapable black hole. As Yoda says, "If once you start down the dark path, forever will it dominate your destiny." While Luke must battle the seduction of the dark side, his faith in the light side gives him the power his father doesn't have. This is analogous to believers who fight against sin, buoyed by the Holy Spirit's strength, as described in Romans 8, a power unbelievers don't have.

Why is it so important to interpret Romans 7 as describing sin in the life of an unbeliever? If we subscribe to the defeated outlook Paul poses in Romans 7, Satan will have a good shot at making us ineffective for the Lord. The contrast between chapters 7 and 8 is as different as Vader is from Luke, Judas is from John, and the dark side is from the light. If we're going to be victorious in spiritual warfare, we must know the true promises of God, specifically that we have the power to defeat sin. If we don't have an accurate understanding of these principles, Satan will make sure we always feel wretched, irredeemable, and of no value to God's kingdom.

Know Your Enemy

Unlike Luke, Anakin doesn't know his true enemy at all. He doesn't know that befriending and trusting Palpatine will lead to harm. Even though his Masters try to warn him, Anakin ignores their reservations and insists that, "He is a good man. My instincts are very positive." Anakin couldn't be more wrong about his opponent, and the consequences for him and the galaxy are monumental.

Satan and his demons put little effort into tripping up unbelievers. Why waste time on people who are seeking only their own little kingdoms without any regard for God's kingdom? Satan has his targeting computer set on those who love God. He hates Christians and would like nothing better than to cause our spiritual destruction.

The Emperor, likewise, knows Anakin could be a great asset to the Jedi and the Republic. Therefore, he needs to either kill Anakin or turn him to the dark side. Palpatine senses Anakin's fear, anger, impatience, arrogance, and aggression and uses these against him. Anakin should realize that he could be a target for the dark side, and yet he keeps his guard down. Even though Anakin thinks he's in control, he is simply a tool of the Emperor. The deceitfulness of sin always makes us think we are in charge, but it's all a ruse. When we sin, we are just pawns in the hand of Satan, doing his bidding to accomplish his goals.

Palpatine's Sith name, Sidious, is derived from the word "insidious." Webster's Dictionary defines insidious as "awaiting a chance to entrap, harmful but enticing, having a gradual and cumulative effect, and developing so gradually as to be well established before becoming apparent."[16] This describes not only Palpatine but also Satan and sin itself.

> ✸ Ian McDiarmid, the actor who played Palpatine, compared his character to Iago in Shakespeare's Othello. Both characters looked like good guys on the surface but were actually highly manipulative and evil.

Palpatine's rise to power and Satan's deception in the Garden of Eden are also strikingly similar. From the beginning, Palpatine pretends to be Amidala's friend, but only for the chance to whisper lies about Chancellor Valorum's ability to rule and resolve the trade dispute. Soon after Palpatine's double-cross, a shocked Valorum laments, "Palpatine, I thought you were my ally, my friend. You have betrayed me! How could you do this?" I imagine that a comparable sentiment crossed Eve's mind after the Fall. The serpent seemed so nice and helpful. How could he have betrayed her trust so badly?

Satan didn't tell Eve that he hated God and wanted her and Adam as his slaves. His strategy was to find something Eve wanted, in this case, the nice-looking fruit, plant a lie in her heart, and wait until she succumbed to her desires. Likewise, Palpatine doesn't walk up to Anakin at the beginning and tell him he's a Sith Lord and that he wants to take over the galaxy. Instead, he uses clandestine moves over a period of years to take over Anakin's soul.

Now that we understand Palpatine's methods, let's examine how Luke defends against his tactics. The Emperor finds two vulnerabilities in Luke. One is Luke's compassion for his father and his desire for Vader to return to the light side of the Force. The second is Luke's love for his friends, especially Leia, which causes him to become angry when they suffer. Like young Anakin, Luke is a good kid, but he has a tendency toward anger, impatience, fear, and arrogance. During almost all of the Emperor's interactions with Luke, the Emperor tries to take advantage of Luke's weaknesses to cause him to turn to the dark side. Fortunately for Luke, before he ever sees Darth Vader or the Emperor, he knows they are bad news. Obi-Wan and Yoda told him all about them. Having this knowledge protects Luke from Vader's ploys. When Vader tells Luke that he is his father, Luke assumes it's a lie. His default assumption is that Vader would not tell the truth. Even though Luke was wrong in this case, his knowledge of his enemy is the number one reason

Luke is victorious. Through studying the Bible, we can also learn how our enemy operates and, more importantly, how to defeat him.

Before we come to Christ, Satan might say we don't need Jesus, that we are doing just fine on our own. After we come to Christ, Satan ramps up his sinister ways and tries to use our newfound faith against us. For instance, after preaching God's unconditional acceptance to ourselves so much, we might become a little too comfortable, thinking we can kick back and relax. In time, this attitude may cause us to neglect prayer and the study of the Bible. When this happens, we let down our guard. We may think we can coast for a while, that we have enough of God's Word in us and that we are not vulnerable to any spiritual dangers. This is exactly the type of situation the devil waits to exploit.

⚔ Just as "Sidious" is a form of the word "insidious," many believe "Vader" is derived from the word "invader."

Rarely does Luke let down his guard. One of the few times he does, Vader says, "You are unwise to lower your defenses!" God warns us to "Be alert and of sober mind. Your enemy the devil prowls around like a roaring lion looking for someone to devour" (1 Peter 5:8). Satan and his demons wait for us to lower our shields. By the time we do, it's too late. Our shields must always be up so that we can, as Ephesians 6:16 says, "extinguish all the flaming arrows of the evil one." Luke has a strong faith in his friends and his Master, but his faith in the light side is what protects him from the Emperor's evil advances.

The problem occurs when Luke doubts the Force. He fails during his "Trial of the Spirit" on Dagobah, because he rejects Yoda's advice to leave his weapons at the cave entrance. While the lightsaber is the Jedi's signature weapon, it is not the source of their power. Luke learns that he needs to have faith in the Force, not in his abilities and weapons. As Proverbs 28:26 tells us, "Those who trust in themselves are fools, but those who walk in wisdom are kept safe."

Satan uses our misplaced trust to make us fail. Maybe you have gone through something extremely difficult in your life that led you to place your trust and hope in something or someone, but whatever it was did not work out. Now you are tempted to become bitter and maybe even hate God. You know it's wrong, but Satan comes along and says that God has forgotten about you, doesn't love you, or is punishing you.

The Emperor tells Luke to "Strike me down with all your hatred and your journey towards the dark side will be complete." This is the same strategy Satan uses in these situations. The more we allow our anger, bitterness, and hatred to take hold of us, the more Satan wins. Vader lies to Luke when he says, "Give yourself to the dark side. It is the only way you can save your friends." We need to go back to the Word of God and read the truth so that Satan's lies will not work on us. God has not forgotten about you. If you are in Christ, he loves you with a love that is truly out of this world.

The Entangling Sin

The training lightsabers that younglings use are set on low. While they still hurt if touched, they cannot sever body parts or cause any other serious damage. Thus, the blades can deflect laser bolts without exposing the children to danger. But what if the younglings grew up thinking all lightsabers were like the sabers they used in training? Without meaning to, they would inevitably wound and possibly kill their friends or even themselves.

Sin is a lot like younglings training with lightsabers. We start off with just a little sin, some slight deviation from God's Word, because everybody else seems to be doing it, and it's enjoyable—at first. Since nothing bad appears to happen, we add a little more, taking things slightly further. The same sequence happens with every sin: lust, worry, greed, gossip, anger, impatience, laziness, envy, drunkenness, or deceit. At the onset, we see no major spiritual damage, so we take things further, and the path gets darker. If we don't repent, lust leads to sexual perversion, greed leads to stealing, gossip leads to broken relationships, and so on.

That's the way Satan and sin work. At the beginning, it seems like we are wielding lightsabers that merely leave a little bruise or burn on the skin, a small sacrifice considering how much pleasure the experience offers. As we go on, the power on the lightsaber increases while we swing it through the air with reckless abandon, enamored with the cool sounds and pretty light trails it leaves. Before we know it, the blade strikes hard against our body or against someone close to us, leaving a lot more than a singe. Even though Satan will continue to say that sin is safe and fun and that we should just give it a try, we need to know that there is no safe way to partake in sin.

The writer of Hebrews begins chapter 12 by commanding us to "throw off everything that hinders and the sin that so easily entangles." After Lando betrays Han, he comes to regret it, but by then it is almost impossible for him to get his friends and himself out of the mess he has created. Sin is similar. What starts out as a good idea backfires, because we are dealing with the father of lies. Lando makes a deal with Darth Vader and trusts that he will keep up his side of the bargain. Princess Leia trusts Grand Moff Tarkin when he says he will not destroy her home planet of Alderaan if she gives him the location of the Rebel secret base. These examples teach us that you can't trust those who are evil. Even if your back is up against the wall with no sign of an escape route, God promises to provide a way out so that you don't have to make a deal with the devil and fall into sin.

"So Certain Are You?"

The last time they talk, Luke says to Yoda, "Then I am a Jedi," somewhat unsure of his possible new status. For Luke, nothing is more important than answering this question. Regrettably, Yoda can't give Luke the answer he wants to hear and instead tells him he must face Vader again. This state of limbo is a frightening time for Luke. The dark side will test his faith like never before, and we are not sure he will prevail.

For the believer, nothing is worse than having the assurance of your salvation shaken. In terms of this confidence, Satan assaults professing believers in two ways. He will either convince you that you are saved when you are not or convince you that you are not saved when you are. This deals with the topics of both false and true assurance and can be a terribly destructive weapon in the devil's arsenal.

"I Assure You We Are Quite Safe"

Let's start with a look at the first one. At the end of *Episode III*, Anakin is convinced that he is good and the Jedi are evil. He considers his choice to become a Sith to be correct, the decision that will lead him to the future he desires. The Emperor does not need to deceive Anakin any longer, because at this point, Anakin deceives himself, having a false assurance that he stands in the better place. Only those looking on can see how twisted and evil he has become.

🔭 Lucas tossed around the idea of having Luke put on Vader's helmet and mask at the end of *Episode VI*, declare, "Now I am Vader," and try to take over the galaxy.

The book of James tells us that there are those who affectionately "consider themselves religious." They listen to the Word of God but still pollute themselves with the world. Vader's example and James' epistle teach how easy it is to deceive yourself. Satan loves people to think they are righteous when they are not. Like Vader comparing himself to the Jedi, we can be tempted to compare ourselves to others to boost our spiritual ego. However, God does not judge on a curve. His standard is perfection, and Jesus is the only person who meets it.

Anakin always judges his identity by how much power he has. He considers his strength in the Force as his righteousness, and it doesn't matter if he uses the power for good or evil. In the prequel trilogy, he commits himself to the Jedi faith only as far as he feels it is beneficial for him to do so. Deep down, his devotion is to himself, not to the Jedi or the light side. This is why he is so susceptible to Palpatine's subterfuge. He resists any sort of criticism from the Jedi, hating it when they point out his flaws. Yet, that is what he needs in order to repent and improve.

He carries this same insecurity and pride into his years as Vader. Satan loves to twist God's commands in our minds and make us think we are not doing enough. He also loves it when we think we are doing well. When people listen to the devil's lies and the deceitfulness of their hearts, they will develop a faulty view of themselves. God's Word says that no one is righteous. If Satan can prompt people to build up their righteousness by going to church, helping their community, and being good people, why would they need to seek out a savior to pay for their sins?

Amidst all his failings, eventually, Darth Vader accepts where he stands in terms of the dark side. When he tells Luke, "It's too late for me, son," he conveys his true heart assessment. Vader is wise enough to see his predicament but so entangled in the dark side that he cannot see how to escape. Vader is evil, and he knows it. He has no assurance of his Jedi heritage. But this awareness paves the way for his salvation, for it is far better for someone to recognize his or her spiritual condition as evil than to be oblivious to it. In episodes I-III, Anakin may have the Force, but it's questionable if he is a Jedi. He frequently fools himself and everyone around him. It's not until he picks up the Emperor and symbolically throws him back into the pit from which he came that Anakin shows a persevering Jedi heart and is redeemed.

Maybe I'm Not So Safe

Some believers love their Lord and obey him in all areas of life but still struggle with assurance from time to time. Demons attack us, hoping to get a few flaming arrows (or laser blasts) through the chinks in our spiritual armor. It is hard for believers to have joy if they do not defend themselves properly against these attacks. They become much like C-3PO, walking around with an "I'm doomed" attitude. So, let's look at how Satan can still agitate the assurance of those who are truly saved.

The devil's lie that we are not really believers is especially crafty, because he knows many of us are apt to rely on our emotions as a barometer to gauge how we are doing with God and how he feels about us. In our efforts to "be perfect as our heavenly Father is perfect," we can go too far in our expectations and condemn ourselves whenever we drop the ball spiritually.

The first thing we need to do is rule out the possibility that we are in the group described in the section above, those who assume they are Christians but really are not. Jesus teaches that people cannot simply say, "Lord, Lord," go through the religious motions, and expect to be saved. Therefore, we should examine our lives and invite other believers to judge us as well. This sort of introspection is something Anakin is never willing to do. Doing this is part of the "make every effort to confirm your calling and election" that 2 Peter 1:10 commands and will put us in a position to determine what our next step should be.

Going further with this concept, genuine faith produces good deeds that spring from a heart that loves God. The lack of this evidence will have a direct effect on how assured you are of your salvation. Vader can look at his track record and know that he is steeped in the dark side. This examination is why Vader's life ends well. He is redeemed only after examining his life and choosing to repent.

Up until this point, Anakin never does scrutinize his spiritual life. Not only does he have the dark qualities of fear, anger, and hatred, he also has the underlying problems of pride and self-deception, qualities that will always stand in the way of repentance. Satan doesn't want us to ponder our lives. He wants us busy with the temporary and superficial things of life so that when the end comes, we are unprepared to stand before God.

When we feel convicted, it is hard to determine the source. It could be from the devil, from our own hearts, or from the Holy Spirit. Regardless, when you feel any sort of condemnation causing you to question your salvation, ask yourself, "Do I *really* love Jesus or is my faith only words? Am I merely a resounding gong or a clanging cymbal?" If you really do love Jesus, stand firm in that truth, and resist the devil's accusations. We'll never think we are good enough by what we do. But if we allow Satan a foothold, he will intensify this feeling and convince us not only that we do not love God but also that God does not love us either.

Luke's anger burns in *Episode VI* when he releases a lightsaber onslaught on Vader. The Emperor watches with delight as Luke becomes darker. On the precipice of turning to the dark side, Luke has but one final task: kill his father and take his place at the Emperor's side. This is when Luke's faith breaks through. Like us, Luke drifts from the light path at times. He makes some bad decisions along the way, but when the Emperor directs him to kill his father, Luke exclaims, "Never! I'll never turn to the dark side. You've failed, your Highness. I am a Jedi, like my father before me."

Once the Emperor hears this, he knows he has failed to turn Luke. Luke has employed a strategy similar to the one James advocates in James 4:7, "Resist the devil, and he will flee from you." Luke's assurance wavers occasionally, but his commitment to the light side prevails in the end.

✴ Luke's lightsaber was blue in early *Episode VI* posters and trailers. It was changed to green to show up better against Tatooine's blue sky. Also, the color change prevented fans from thinking it was his original lightsaber and wondering, "How did he get it back?"

"And This is How We Know"

Wavering assurance can be a lonely and debilitating trial to endure. You might have tons of head knowledge about God, but if your heart and mind are not connecting the dots, the "rock" of salvation on which you stand is no more stable than the "ground" of a space slug's belly. It is during these times that Satan would love to swoop in and finish you off (Darth Maul style), if you let him. But praise Jesus that if our hearts condemn us, God is greater than our hearts (1 John 3:20). In 1 John 3, we find two ways that we can know for certain that we are saved. One of these we are responsible to do. The other is a work of the Holy Spirit.

Let's start with the second: "And this is how we know that he lives in us: We know it by the Spirit he gave us" (1 John 3:24b). This reiterates what Paul says in Romans 8:16, "The Spirit himself testifies with our spirit that we are God's children." One of the Holy Spirit's roles is to give us confidence that we belong to Christ. There is nothing you can do to give yourself or others assurance that comes only from God. If Satan is going after you in this area, ask God to fill your heart with the confidence that you are reconciled to him. Remember, we have confidence before God, because we believe in the name of his Son, Jesus Christ (1 John 3:22–23).

The second principle John provides that helps us to know our salvation is genuine is simple: Do we love others? If you do not love others, your heart will condemn you. Consequently, you will wrestle with assurance, because you are not behaving like a Christian.

Anakin tells Padmé in *Episode III* that he feels lost. "Something's happening. I'm not the Jedi I should be." Padmé tries to convince him that he is wrong, but she is unable. No one can. When we fail to think and act like we ought, when we obey the devil and strive to build our own kingdom, we will feel conviction deep in our souls, and no one can persuade us otherwise. If your assurance has been shaken, remember your first love, and do not forsake Christ. Salvation is not by works, but failing to obey God by not loving his Son or others will rob your heart of assurance and your life of joy.

"No Disintegrations"

Similar to Darth Vader rounding up a group of the galaxy's most feared bounty hunters to capture the crew and passengers of the *Millennium Falcon,* Satan summons his demons to hunt down Christians. In *Episode V,* Vader gives the bounty hunters free reign but with one nonnegotiable restriction: "No disintegrations." This is similar to God's command in Job 1:12. "The Lord said to Satan, 'Very well, then, everything he has is in your power, but on the man himself do not lay a finger.'" Like the restriction placed on Boba Fett and the other bounty hunters, Satan can only go so far in our lives.

Without God doing anything immoral or against his perfect character, God uses Satan's involvement to mature us as believers. Even though you might feel like Satan can cause you to sin so badly that you lose your salvation, the truth is, he can't. God has not given him that power. If Christ has died for you, he has also purchased your preservation. Not even the spiritual forces of darkness can take that away.

🔭 The head of the droid bounty hunter IG-88 was made from a Rolls Royce jet engine. This same part is seen as scrap metal behind Owen and Beru's smoldering corpses and as a drink dispenser in the cantina bar.

"Bury Your Feelings Deep Down"

When Luke discovers Leia is his sister, Obi-Wan says, "Bury your feelings deep down, Luke. They do you credit. But they could be made to serve the Emperor." We have already discussed that believers should not rely on their emotions to navigate the Christian life. This applies to spiritual warfare as well. Like the Emperor, Satan will use our emotions to lure us into sin. This includes lust, anger, greed, or any host of emotions that the Jedi also deem as dangerous.

Not keeping his passions in check, Anakin lets his desire for Padmé cause him to disobey Jedi law and marry her. He allows his anger to turn into hatred, to the point of trying to kill his Master, Obi-Wan, not once but twice. He lets his greed for power control him so that he becomes "more machine than man." The Emperor doesn't just flip a switch to control Anakin. Rather, he preys on what Anakin fears to lose and counts on his emotions to keep him on the dark path forever.

The same thing can happen to us when Satan uses our emotions against us. To illustrate, a marital affair doesn't just happen out of nowhere. It usually comes after a long time of disobeying God in other areas. Refusing to be thankful for your spouse, thinking you deserve better, and fantasizing about a different life are when demons hit us with ion cannons. We are not destroyed, but such attacks cause our internal spiritual circuitry to go haywire. At that point, all it takes is flirting with a coworker, sharing our emotional struggles, and maybe an occasional drink after work. Eventually, we are put into a compromising situation where we are all alone with only our lust to guide us. The potential for sin should have been detected far upstream before many spiritual battles were lost and several bad choices were made.

Joseph didn't spend time politely excusing himself from the sexual advances made by Potiphar's wife. Instead, he ran out of the house as fast as he could. During our spiritual battles, we need to follow Joseph's example. He understood that if he sinned against Potiphar, he would also be sinning against God (Genesis 39:9). Our choices affect more than our own little worlds. They are rebellious acts directed right at God. They steal God's glory as King.

The temptation to sin takes place in our minds. This is where we choose whether or not to obey God. Therefore, one of the best ways to defend against Satan's attacks is to stop an initial thought from developing into sin. Thoughts pop into everyone's mind. The question is, what are we going to do with those thoughts? We need to replace them with the promises of God and not let them develop into a mindset that no longer focuses on godly things.

If Anakin would have stopped his evil thoughts from flourishing, if he had recognized the spiritual battles occurring within, he might have avoided his tragic downfall. However, not only does he fail to submit to his Masters, he fails to submit to the Jedi tenets on which his faith is supposedly built. Anakin assumes his lightsaber and starship are the only weapons he needs to defend himself. Unfortunately, those weapons have no power against his inner demons.

While Luke lets his anger and impatience get the best of him at times, he always stops himself before going over to the dark side completely. Unlike his father, he understands the most important weapons of his warfare are spiritual not physical. This is why he throws his lightsaber away during his final confrontation with the Emperor. Knowing what will deliver the deciding blow, Luke declares that the Emperor has failed and that he is a Jedi like his father before him. This statement does more to defeat the Emperor than any damage Luke could ever inflict with a lightsaber or blaster.

The Emperor may be able to move objects around with his mind and influence the minds of the weak, but he cannot control Luke's heart, mind, or soul. He cannot govern Luke's decision to bow to him, and that is why the Emperor fails. In the same way, as powerful as Satan is, he is no match for Jesus Christ. Since we are united with Christ, we also have his power, the power to thwart all of Satan's plans to defeat us. Luke has the Force, because it runs strong in his family. He has it, because his father has it. Similarly, we have power at our disposal through the Holy Spirit because of our union with Jesus. We are already victors in this, because Jesus was the ultimate victor when he defeated Satan on the cross. We just need to buckle this belt of truth around our waist. Then we can escape Satan's influence like Luke using the grappling hook of his utility belt to whisk himself and Leia away from the Death Star stormtroopers.

🔭 Lucas originally envisioned Obi-Wan and Yoda returning to their bodies to help Luke in his final confrontation against the Emperor. This would better explain Obi-Wan's "I shall become more powerful than you can possibly imagine" line in *Episode IV*.

The Armor of Light

"The night is nearly over; the day is almost here. So let us put aside the deeds of darkness and put on the armor of light" (Romans 13:12). Both the Rebel Alliance and the Galactic Empire rely heavily on their armor to protect themselves in battle. The Empire feels safe behind the thick hull of the Death Star as the Rebel ships' firepower beat against it. Jango Fett's armor protects him when Obi-Wan deflects Kamino Kyber darts back at him. During the campaign on Hoth, Luke and his comrades try to shoot down Imperial walkers, which are approaching the power generator of their Rebel base, only to realize, "That armor's too strong for blasters!"

As mentioned earlier, Paul admonishes us in Ephesians 6 to put on the full armor of God so we can stand against Satan's attacks. The worst thing we can do is to go into a tempting situation without this protection. We see a few cases of this in the life of Peter, the Apostle. He was always charging into situations ill prepared, not realizing his weaknesses and Satan's power. In Luke 22, Peter says he is ready to follow Jesus into prison and death, but Jesus warns him that he will deny he even knows Jesus. Jesus prays explicitly that Satan would not cause Peter to turn away permanently.

Luke Skywalker is similar to Peter. Before he enters the cantina at Mos Eisley, he brushes off Obi-Wan's warning about how dangerous the place is and says he is "ready for anything." Of course, it's not long before Luke's life would have been taken if not for Obi-Wan's protection.

ⱺ The colored markings of the Phase I clone trooper armor are as follows: yellow = commander, red = captain, blue = lieutenant, green = sergeant, white = private. Later on in the war, color designates unit affiliation rather than rank.

Paul warns us that, "our struggle is not against flesh and blood, but against the rulers, against the authorities, against the powers of this dark world and against the spiritual forces of evil in the heavenly realms" (Ephesians 6:12). Sadly, both Anakin and Luke often forget that their battles are really on spiritual rather than physical fronts. Luke did not heed Yoda's advice that he would not need his weapons before entering in the cave on Dagobah. Anakin focuses more on the fact he did not receive the rank of Jedi Master than he does on protecting himself from Palpatine's influence. Instead of letting our arrogance get in the way, as it did at times for Anakin, Luke, and Peter, we should put on humility as we depend on the Holy Spirit and the full armor of God to protect us.

The battles that matter for us are not physical. And yet, how much of our time, effort, and money do we spend trying to make our lives on Earth long, safe, and pleasurable? Often we do this at the expense of protecting our souls from sin's deceitfulness. We need to understand that the battles that matter the most do not happen in the Middle East or in the rough neighborhoods of our cities but within our own heart. This is where we need to spend our time and effort raising defenses.

When the Rebels analyze the stolen plans of the Death Star, they discover the vulnerable exhaust port. Dodonna explains to Gold Leader that, "The Empire doesn't consider a small one-man fighter to be any threat, or they'd have a tighter defense." In this case, the Empire lacks two critical pieces of information: 1) its vulnerability and 2) its enemy, and they pay the price with their lives. In the same way, we need to know how susceptible we are to temptation and then tighten our defenses in weak areas. Sometimes, this requires drastic measures. If you're tempted to view pornography online, this might mean disconnecting your home's Internet service. If you're tempted to gossip, this may require you not to talk with certain friends who contend in the same way. Jesus thought sin was so bad that he said, "If your right eye causes you to stumble, gouge it out" (Matthew 5:29). Jesus is using hyperbole here, but his point is clear. We should take whatever measures are required to prevent ourselves from falling into sin.

God promises that he will always provide a way out of the temptation so that we can avoid sin. Martin Luther penned the words to the remarkable hymn about spiritual warfare, "A Mighty Fortress is Our God." He uses the imagery that God is a bulwark or a castle that protects us from the devil's attacks. We should remind ourselves continually of the good standing we have with God because of

Christ. When we pray to God and meditate regularly on biblical truth, we put on the armor of God, an armor that Satan's firepower cannot penetrate.

🔭 All of the clone troopers' armor in *Episode III* was done with CGI.

Satan and his demons will always target believers, because we are their enemies now instead of their allies. However, even with all of their spiritual power, demonic forces can never cause us to lose our salvation. The most they can do is entice us so that we are ineffective for our King. Think of them like the mynocks that chew on the power cables of the *Millennium Falcon*. Demons try to drain the spiritual strength we need to live for Christ. Like Han Solo with his blaster, we must shoot them down immediately before they cause too much damage.

Shooting demons with a blaster gun and utilizing a utility belt are not too far from the battle imagery Paul uses in Ephesians 6 to describe how we should engage Satan during his attacks. Throughout this passage, Paul speaks of putting on the full armor of God so that we can take our stand against the devil's schemes. Paul uses the analogy of a Roman soldier's armor, something to which his audience would have been able to relate.

Continuing with Paul's theme via the grid of *Star Wars,* clone troopers and stormtroopers wear body armor that includes a breastplate. This piece protects the heart, lungs, and other vital organs. When we stand with the breastplate of righteousness in place, we remember our standing with God is based on Christ's death, not on the good we achieve. Like Luke remembering who he is as a Jedi, we fight Satan by remembering who we are in Christ.

When we become lethargic in our Christian walk, the devil can shoot us as easily as Luke bullseyes womp rats in his T-16. When we fit our feet with the readiness that comes from the gospel of peace, we are nimble and can dodge the enemy's attacks. Yoda trains Luke to use the Force while on the run. It would be great if all Luke had to do is stand there and use the Force, but that's not usually how battles play out. Life comes at you quickly, and you need to be able to do spiritual somersaults to prevent Satan from landing a strike.

Most of the time, not only must you fight back in defense, you have to do so while moving out of the way of deadly offensives. We receive peace with God through his gospel, a gospel of peace that Satan will try to pervert into a false gospel. Our job is to be aware of these dark tactics and find cover in the true good news of Jesus.

Shields protect the good guys and the bad guys in *Star Wars.* A shield protects the Death Star during its construction. Shields protect the *Millennium Falcon* during its dogfights against the TIE fighters. The Jedi and Sith also use Force push to deflect attacks. As an illustration, Yoda deflects Dooku's lightening back at him rather than generating his own. In spiritual warfare, Satan uses all sorts of tactics to shake our faith. He tries to cause us to doubt God, whether that means questioning his goodness, his promises, or his control over situations. Any of these assaults to our faith can leave us lying on the battlefield, spiritually debilitated. When we experience these attacks, we must put up our shield of faith to deflect the evil one's "blaster shots."

🔭 While writing *Episode IV*, Lucas watched several classic war films. The space combat in the first *Star Wars* film was based on actual World War II dogfight footage.

Leia, Luke, starfighter pilots, stormtroopers, Death Star gunners, Imperial guards, and, of course, Darth Vader all know the importance of wearing helmets. If your head takes a hard hit, you're done for. Your mind is the number one target of Satan. If you let him sway you to think in a way that runs counter to the Bible, there is no area in your life he can't damage. This is why Paul tells us to strap on the helmet of salvation. When we remember the fullness of our salvation—who died for us, why he died, and the spiritual riches we receive because of it—we can defend against the devil when he strikes against the sound doctrine that supports our faith.

The lightsaber is the offensive weapon of the Jedi and the Sith. Unlike the breastplate, helmet, and shield, it can deliver a counterstrike to the opponent. The Jedi respect their civilized weapon and use it not to conquer but to protect. Paul says the Sword of the Spirit is the Word of God. It is the weapon that Jesus used against

Satan when he was tempted in the wilderness. We must know the Bible so well that we can use it not only to defend against the dark forces trying to take us down but also to know when the Word is being misused.

All sorts of false teachers and even well-intentioned Christians use verses out of context. Satan attempted to use Scripture as a sword to hurt Jesus, but Jesus knew when Scripture was being misapplied and was able to strike back with the true Word that was planted in his heart.

Paul ends his "armor of God" teaching with a command to be alert and to pray: "And pray in the Spirit on all occasions with all kinds of prayers and requests. With this in mind, be alert and always keep on praying for all the Lord's people" (Ephesians 6:18). We need to be alert at all times, because the spiritual forces of evil never cease to do battle with our souls.

Anakin does not understand the real war that goes on with himself and with Palpatine. When he becomes Darth Vader, he recognizes his internal struggle but chooses not to fight for his remaining goodness. In contrast, Luke knows how to protect himself with his utility belt, helmet, and lightsaber, but more than guarding his physical body, he knows how to protect his spirit. When we look at his example, we realize that we cannot rest on the battlefield for a moment. We can never lower our defenses. We must not become arrogant in our own strength. Hordes of demonic forces wait patiently for us to lower our shields for just a moment. It is our job to put on the full armor of God, never take it off, be alert, and ask God to give us the strength to win the battles. If we do this, he is faithful to make us victorious to the very end.

GOD'S
TRACTOR BEAM

*We've spent a lot of time thinking about Satan, Palpatine, and the dark side.
We needed to do this to make sure we get off on the right foot spiritually, learn
how to handle our emotions, and avoid falling for the devil's deception. In this
part of the book, we will turn our attention more to God's rescue plan for us.*

*In Chapter 8, we'll consider how God from the beginning devised a plan to
save his people. In Chapter 9, we'll study God's New Covenant and how that
differs from what God did before. In Chapter 10, we'll begin our exploration
into the doctrines of grace and see how God chose to love us despite us being
unlovable. In Chapter 11, we'll learn how not only Jesus died to rescue us, but
that his death purchased our eternal preservation. Finally, in Chapter 12, we'll
see how even though God accomplished everything for us in Christ; we are still
responsible to live a godly life.*

8

PURSUED ACROSS THE GALAXY

○○○○○○○●○○○○○○○○○

The Parable of the Lost Droid

Suppose one of you has a hundred droids and loses one of them. Doesn't he leave the ninety-nine and go after the lost droid until he finds it? And when he finds it, he joyfully puts it on his landspeeder and goes home. Then, he calls his friends and neighbors together and says, "Rejoice with me; I have found my lost droid!"

This is a very loose paraphrase of Luke 15, where Jesus tells the "Parable of the Lost Sheep," but you get the idea. It also harkens back to Luke going into the dangerous territory of the Tusken Raiders to bring back his runaway droid, R2-D2. Both of these stories remind us about how God did everything to pursue us and bring us into his fold.

God doesn't need humans to satisfy a longing or fill a void in his heart. God has always been content within the relationship of the Trinity. Father, Son, and Holy Spirit exist in a perfect union of love and holiness. However, as the parable above illustrates, God is love (1 John 4:8), and he sacrificed in order to rescue his enemies, namely you and me.

God's pursuit of his people is a thread that is woven through-out Scripture. God already had a rescue plan when Adam and Eve disobeyed him in the Garden of Eden. "And I will put enmity between you and the woman, and between your offspring and hers; he will crush your head, and you will strike his heel" (Genesis 3:15). God had given Adam and Eve paradise, showering them with love, provision, and protection. They responded to his faithfulness with disloyalty, to his rule with insurrection, and to his protection by putting their lives at risk. God, in turn, punished them as his just and holy character requires, but he also committed immediately to a plan of deliverance.

Similarly, some of the most satisfying elements in *Star Wars* are the friendships that are forged, but these relationships almost always get off to a rocky start. Think of the first time Han meets Leia or Leia meets Lando. But, when our heroes commit to the good of others, deep love and respect develops, and beautiful acts of sacrifice occur.

When Luke is in trouble, dangling from a weather vane beneath Cloud City, he calls out to Leia. Without a moment of hesitation, she puts herself in danger to rescue him. When Luke doesn't come back from his patrol on Hoth, Han goes out to look for him despite the warning that he might not survive. Thirty men put their lives in jeopardy to rescue Shmi from the Tusken Raiders. Only four return, and yet her husband still plans to go back as soon as he heals enough to make the journey. *Star Wars* is filled with stories like these. Sacrificial love will always appeal to people, especially believers, because these serve as pictures of our ultimate rescue.

The Need to be Pursued

While God cares for all of his creatures, he reserves his friendship for believers only. Before trusting in Jesus, we were God's enemies and in desperate need of rescue. Since none of us were good enough to stand before God, he could have just blasted us into a million pieces at the moment we came into existence, a reasonable punishment for rebellion according to C-3PO. Even though God would have been justified in doing this, he didn't. Rather, he chose to be patient, to endure all of our law-breaking, fist-shaking, and cosmic blow-offs until the appointed time when his rescue plan could be carried out. "The Lord is not slow in keeping his promise, as some understand slowness. Instead he is patient with you, not wanting anyone to perish, but everyone to come to repentance" (2 Peter 3:9).

To appreciate God's pursuit of us, it is important to remind ourselves routinely of what he has rescued us from. Unlike movies, the Bible can only describe hell with words, but that's often more than enough to make the point. John, through a vision that includes God's final judgment, describes hell as a fiery lake of burning sulfur into which God tosses his enemies. Keep in mind that the Bible's hyperbole and apocalyptic language convey truths that are usually not as harsh or intense as the realities themselves. So, actually, compared to hell, a lake of burning sulfur would be a nice respite.

The planet Mustafar helps us imagine hell by immersing us into a fire-and-brimstone environment. The volcanic planet embeds a truly terrifying picture into our minds with its obvious allusion to the biblical hell. Mustafar is where Anakin kills the Separatist leaders, taking Nute Gunray and the others completely by surprise. It's also where Obi-Wan judges Anakin for his wickedness and strikes him down. For almost everyone, Mustafar is a place of final judgment and retribution. Incidentally, Mustafar is the appropriately hellish place for Anakin to travel to in bodily form since his spirit has already metaphorically made the journey.

🎬 Much of the exploding lava of Mustafar was taken from real footage of Mount Etna, the largest volcano in Italy. It erupted during the filming of *Episode III*.

Before God saved us, we were his enemies, locked in a spiritual lightsaber duel with him. Ignorant of sin's dangers and God's wrath, we plodded down narrow bridges with lava spewing up everywhere, swinging in futility at God with every sinful act. God could have delivered the strike that launched us into the lake of fire at any moment, our hope incinerated in an instant as eternal torment begins.

Shifting metaphors, before trusting in Christ, you were on the plank above the Sarlacc's mouth, peering down and waiting to plummet into the abyss. Perhaps your pride was waiting for God to play the role of R2-D2, who provides Luke with his lightsaber and thus a way to save himself. But God opened your eyes to the uselessness of trying to save yourself. Then he grabbed you from the precarious plank, did a headfirst dive into the Sarlacc's mouth, and satisfied the monster's appetite so that you were no longer in jeopardy.

You and I were the ones spiritually frozen in carbonite, dead to God's goodness. But like Han's friends entering Jabba's palace (another hive of scum and villainy), God condescended to come to a sinful world and sacrifice himself, to melt away our cold hard exterior and our frozen heart as well.

We were the ones in the garbage compactor, wallowing in the filth of this world, with all of its sin and perversions, unaware that the walls were closing in on us. Just as our heroes need C-3PO's help from above, we needed God. God showed his great love for us despite the fact we reeked of rotten garbage. During the rescue, God did more than just stop the walls from closing in. He allowed the walls to crush him, but he broke them in the process, so those walls can never close in on us again. As if saving us was not enough, God also promised to wash off the stench of our old life so that we can smell good to the world.

The main principle to understand is that we needed to be saved not only from sin but also from God himself. "It is a dreadful thing to fall into the hands of the living God" (Hebrews 10:31). Yet, in our pride, we denied our need to be rescued. God had to do it all. Jesus embraced the rescue mission knowing of his imminent death. Han Solo's line, "Attacking that battle station ain't my idea of courage. It's more like suicide," is selfish, but it's also accurate. In Han's mind, taking on that mission was a guarantee of death. But this is exactly what Jesus did for all those who trust in him. God had to pursue us with the certainty of the ultimate sacrifice, specifically, the death of his only Son.

After thinking about how badly we needed rescuing, let's dig deeper into God's promises and see how he carried out his wonderful plan of salvation.

Biblical Covenants

"This deal's getting worse all the time." With this line, Lando Calrissian reminds us that deals don't always go the way we hope. Lando enters into an agreement with Darth Vader expecting one thing but receiving something very different. Deals in the Bible are given a fancier word, "covenants." The Bible tells us that God made five covenants: the Noahic, Abrahamic, Mosaic (or "Old"), Davidic, and the New.

A covenant can be thought of like a contract or an agreement between two or more parties. When Luke sells his land speeder, he agrees to transfer ownership in exchange for money. When Luke bargains with Jabba the Hutt for Han Solo's life, he proposes an arrangement that would be mutually beneficial. Qui-Gon tries to work out various deals with Watto for both a T-14 hyperdrive and Anakin's freedom. Similarly, we can think of all sorts of covenants into which we enter on a daily basis. Students agree to do academic work in exchange for a degree. Employees pledge to labor for a company in exchange for wages. Children might do extra jobs around the house to earn a special treat from their parents.

⚞ Lucas made a bet with Steven Spielberg that *Close Encounters of the Third Kind* would be more successful than *Star Wars*. Lucas lost the bet and has paid Spielberg over $40 million so far.

God pursues his people through covenants. In the remaining sections of this chapter, we will explore the first four of these covenants and see that if anyone has the right to say Lando's line, it's God, not us. God's covenants have different purposes, and he makes them with different people. But one thing is certain: God is always faithful to keep his promises.

The Noahic Covenant

Talk is cheap, and many of the promises throughout *Star Wars* reflect this. While some of these are kept (Obi-Wan training Anakin, Luke returning to Dagobah, and Lando finding Han Solo), many of them are not (Anakin doesn't free his mom from slavery, he doesn't save Padmé from dying, and Palpatine doesn't bring democracy back to the Republic).

We've all been guilty of breaking our word at some point. For example, many times, I'll tell someone I'll pray for him or her. Most of the time I do, but there are occasions when I fail to deliver. You can probably think of a few cases when you said you would do something but didn't. Thank God that he is not like us. God doesn't lie, and never breaks a promise.

After God flooded the earth, he promised Noah and every living creature that would come after, "I establish my covenant with you: Never again will all life be destroyed by the waters of a flood; never again will there be a flood to destroy the earth" (Genesis 9:11). Noah didn't need to do anything in return for this gracious promise, which we call the Noahic Covenant. It doesn't hinge on anything we do either. God has kept his word all these years, and the rainbow reminds us of his mercy upon man and his keeping of this covenant.

God keeping his promise to Noah is crucial to his plan of salvation for us. If he had wiped out the earth again before Jesus atoned for our sin, we would have had to spend eternity paying off that debt. But God kept his promise! The earth has survived, and everything God decreed has occurred right on schedule.

Darth Vader suggests to the Emperor that they attempt to turn Luke to the dark side. Vader says if Luke does not join them, he will die. The implications of this statement are huge. If Luke had died, he would not have been able to save his father, and the Emperor would have gone on to commit even more evil. The Force would have remained out of balance, and the galaxy would still be under the totalitarian rule of the Empire. Just as Luke had to survive for the story to continue, so did Earth.

The Abrahamic Covenant

When it comes to promises, few people in the Bible receive more from God than Abram (or Abraham, as he is called later). Let's review these promises in order and determine how they parallel the promises made in *Star Wars*.

First, God promised to make Abram into a great nation. The Lord had said to Abram, "'Go from your country, your people and your father's household to the land I will show you. I will make you into a great nation, and I will bless you; I will make your name great, and you will be a blessing'" (Genesis 12:1–2).

God's second promise was to give Abram's descendants a land of their own. Referring to the land of the Canaanites, "The Lord appeared to Abram and said, 'To your offspring I will give this land'"

(Genesis 12:7a). God also promised that, "all peoples on earth will be blessed through you" (Genesis 12:3b).

Qui-Gon, in *Episode I*, doesn't promise Anakin descendants, freedom, or a new land, but he does make a deal with Watto with some of these goals in mind. This agreement allows for all these pivotal events to happen eventually in Anakin's life. Ultimately, Anakin gains his freedom, moves to a new land (Coruscant), and fathers Luke and Leia. Moreover, because Anakin eventually destroys the Emperor, he blesses all people (and creatures) in the galaxy.

The Abrahamic Covenant was an arrangement between God and Abraham that was fulfilled both physically and spiritually. For now, we'll focus on the physical aspect of the covenant and address the spiritual one later.

In an attempt to create his own descendants, Abraham had a child (Ishmael) with Hagar. But Paul explains in Galatians 4 that God rejected Ishmael, because he was born according to the flesh rather than the result of a divine promise. God proved his faithfulness to Abraham and kept his promise when he miraculously caused Abraham's wife Sarah to become pregnant with Isaac. "And by faith even Sarah, who was past childbearing age, was enabled to bear children because she considered him faithful who had made the promise" (Hebrews 11:12). As a side note, while this is a foreshadowing of Mary becoming pregnant with Jesus, it also parallels how the midi-chlorians inexplicably make Shmi pregnant with Anakin.

Isaac, Abraham's child of the promise, fathered Jacob. Jacob, in turn, fathered Judah and his brothers, and so on. Through God keeping his promise to Abraham, things were in place for the next phase of the Abrahamic Covenant to be realized, which was making Abraham's physical descendants into a nation.

Unlike Abraham, who died before he could enter the promised physical land, Anakin goes to Coruscant right away. However, God did fulfill his promise by giving the land to Abraham's descendants. "So the Lord gave Israel all the land he had sworn to give their ancestors, and they took possession of it and settled there" (Joshua 21:43). Likewise, once Vader kills the Emperor and the Empire is defeated, Anakin's descendants (Luke and Leia), now have the freedom to live in a land of their own without the tyranny of the Empire looming over them. As stated before, when Anakin (as Darth Vader) repents of his evil ways and hurls the Emperor down the shaft, he saves not only Luke, but also everyone else in the galaxy. It's here that we see the final fruits of what Qui-Gon did for Anakin so many years before. In the same way, when we study the New Covenant, we'll see how believers all over the earth are spiritually blessed through Abraham's belief and his true seed, Jesus Christ.

The Mosaic (Old) Covenant

After God led Abraham's physical descendants, the Israelites, out of slavery in Egypt, God made a covenant with them, and with this covenant came laws. Since Moses was Israel's representative to God, he received the new body of decrees, collectively called the Mosaic Law. There are 613 commandments altogether, but they are often summarized as the Ten Commandments. We refer to this covenant as the Mosaic Covenant or the Old Covenant.

Like the agreements we see in *Star Wars,* the Mosaic Covenant was basically a deal between God and his chosen people, the nation of Israel. In short, the covenant said that if Israel performed certain religious duties *perfectly* and offered sacrifices in the correct manner, God would bless them. "The Lord commanded us to obey all these decrees and to fear the Lord our God, so that we might always prosper and be kept alive, as is the case today" (Deuteronomy 6:24). The inverse was also true. "'Cursed is anyone who does not uphold the words of this law by carrying them out.' Then all the people shall say, 'Amen!'" (Deuteronomy 27:26).

To understand this covenant fully, we need to figure out what the Bible says about the Israelites. As we read how the Israelites responded participating in this covenant, we notice that most of them never loved God. They simply preferred receiving his benefits rather than his punishments. After years of Israel's heinous behavior, God gave this evaluation: "The Lord says: 'These people come near to me with their mouth and honor me with their lips, but their hearts are far from me. Their worship of me is based on merely human rules they have been taught'" (Isaiah 29:13).

Jesus himself said this about the Israelites, "but I know you. I know that you do not have the love of God in your hearts" (John 5:42).

A great illustration of the Old Covenant is Han Solo and his deal with Ben and Luke. Han agrees to his side of the contract, which is to deliver his passengers to Alderaan. If he does this, Ben will give him money. Of course, much more is required of Han after he's captured by the Empire and agrees to try to rescue Princess Leia. During all of this though, he lets no one forget why he's doing this. "Look, I ain't in this for your revolution, and I'm not in it for you, Princess. I expect to be well paid. I'm in it for the money!"

If you saw only a snippet from *Episode IV,* when Han is helping in Princess Leia's escape, you might think that he's a chivalrous, sacrificial hero. But if you were able to peer inside his heart and read his mind, you would discover discreditable motives. He's actually selfish and has no genuine love for others.

Princess Leia's detention cell on the Death Star is #2187. This is a nod to the Arthur Lipsett short film 21-87, which deeply influenced Lucas as a director.

The same could be said of those under the Old Covenant. Since that covenant was based on observing the Mosaic Law, the Israelites focused merely on obeying rules. They ended up just going through the religious motions and had little genuine affection for God. Like watching only certain scenes of Han Solo, if you read nothing but certain passages of the Bible, you'd think the Israelites really loved God. But in reality, virtually all did not (Romans 11).

So, why is it important to learn about Israel and their covenant with God? First, the Old Testament comprises the bulk of our Bible. If we misunderstand Israel and the Old Covenant, we misunderstand most of God's Word. Not only will we misread the Old Testament, we'll misread a lot of the New Testament, too, because so much of it requires a proper understanding of God's relationship with Israel.

In the year *Episode V* came out, George Lucas and Harrison Ford teamed up to film *Raiders of the Lost Ark* (as in "Ark of the Mosaic Covenant").

Second, we need to know if the laws given to Israel are still binding on us today. For instance, is it a sin to work on Sunday? Should we vote for only politicians who are pro-Israel? What about getting tattoos? Does it please God to baptize our children (or circumcise our baby boys)? The list of questions is lengthy, and many Christians have differing opinions. If you love God, you want to obey every command he gives. But that's the key question. Which laws does he give Christians (who are mostly Gentiles) in this new era that started at the cross? It's hard enough battling sin without adding a bunch of obsolete rules to the mix. You want to make sure you heed only the ones he intends for you and ignore the others. In the next chapter, you'll learn more about how God wants believers to live in the New Covenant era. For now, let's press on and tackle another one of God's covenants.

The Davidic Covenant

God continued to be the one dedicated to pursuing his people, through covenants, with his ultimate goals being to save them from ceaseless punishment, give them eternal rest, and rule them as their King in heaven. The next covenant God made is also named after the person with whom he made it—David.

> Now I will make your name great, like the names of the greatest men on earth. And I will provide a place for my people Israel and will plant them so that they can have a home of their own and no longer be disturbed (2 Samuel 7:9b-10a). The Lord declares to you that the Lord himself will establish a house for you: When your days are over and you rest with your ancestors, I will raise up your offspring to succeed you, your own flesh and blood, and I will establish his kingdom. He is the one who will build a house for my Name, and I will establish the throne of his kingdom forever. (2 Samuel 7:11b-13)

Lineage is very important in God's redemptive plan, just as the Skywalker family plays a significant role in saving the galaxy in *Star Wars*. Consider the life of Princess Leia, one of the offspring of Anakin, the "Chosen One," and Padmé Amidala, former Queen of Naboo. From the opening crawl of *Episode IV,* we learn of Princess Leia's strength and determination for good. She's the princess of an oppressed world who is "racing home aboard her starship, custodian of the stolen plans that can save her people and restore freedom to the galaxy." Unfortunately, she, like King David, doesn't have any lasting political power past her term in the Senate. Even with her remarkable heritage, her power and influence is limited, and she doesn't have enough of either to deliver the deathblow to the Empire.

🔭 Princess Leia's ship in *Episode IV* is a Rebel blockade-runner named *Tantive IV*. Also referred to as a Corellian corvette, the ship's design was created from early concept sketches of the *Millennium Falcon*.

Leia is similar to David and Solomon in the sense that while she has the desire to live honorably, fighting for peace, justice, and goodness, she doesn't qualify to fill the role of saving the galaxy. That role is destined for another of Anakin and Padmé's offspring. Likewise, God didn't question David's heart, but God knew that if a *spiritual* temple was to be built for him (1 Peter 2:5), the builder would have to fulfill certain righteous criteria that no human being could meet.

The impetus for the Davidic Covenant started with King David wanting to build God a permanent house, a lasting temple to replace the transportable tabernacle. But God flipped the proposition and told him that *God* would build a temple for David—and he would use one of David's descendants to do it. It would be more than just a temple though; God promised David a kingdom, a dynasty that would last forever!

The covenant God made with David continued God's plan of redemption. It highlights again that no man or woman can do anything to make something (including him or herself) acceptable before God. This is why God had to take the initiative and provide, in essence, his own flesh and blood to establish his kingdom. This covenant had physical implications, but it also stretched far beyond the physical. God promised David that he would provide the righteous seed, and his kingdom would not end at Israel's borders or with any earthly king's death. This everlasting kingdom would be the Church comprised of a spiritual people from every tribe, nation, and tongue!

"But God said to me, 'You are not to build a house for my Name, because you are a warrior and have shed blood'" (1 Chronicles 28:3). God didn't want his kingdom to be ruled by a "man of war." This must have surprised David, because he seemed the most likely candidate for the job. Again, analogous to Princess Leia, David's spirit was willing, but he was simply not qualified because of his sin.

By the end of *Episode III*, it looks as though Anakin has failed to bring balance to the Force. Obi-Wan puts it so well as he expresses his extreme disappointment in Anakin. "You were the Chosen One! It was said that you would destroy the Sith, not join them. It was you who would bring balance to the Force, not leave it in darkness." At this point, because of Anakin's turn to the dark side, Obi-Wan must look to another person to fulfill the prophecy.

King David thought he would be the one to build God's house, but God had other plans. He corrected David, telling him that Solomon would build the temple. Again, all of this is symbolic of what was to come. Eventually, neither David nor Solomon or most of their descendants were righteous enough to usher in the everlasting kingdom that God had in mind. The only person destined to do this would not be a warrior like David or Anakin, quick to shed others' blood. He would be a prince of peace.

Jesus would fulfill the Davidic Covenant by, in fact, shedding his own blood. The temple wouldn't be a structure of stones; it would be Jesus Christ himself. Because Jesus imputed his righteousness to David and Solomon through his death on the cross, they are saved and fully accepted by God, not having any stain or blemish counted against them. In a way, the Son redeems the father(s). The resemblance of stories continues as we have Luke (the son) redeeming Vader (the father) not through violence but through a single act of self-sacrifice. In the same way, although David and Solomon were not counted worthy to redeem God's people, their descendant, Jesus, was.

Now that we have surveyed the Noahic Covenant, the Abrahamic Covenant, the Mosaic Covenant, and the Davidic Covenant, focus on the fact that God, from beginning to end, does it all. He is the one who steps in repeatedly to make sure his people are saved. He is the one who continues to show grace when sinners deserve condemnation. Indeed, at any point in history, God could have wiped out the human race and gone back to his perfect relationship within the Trinity. But he didn't. He kept pursuing us. He continued to press forward and endure our sin, generation after generation, because of his great love for us.

If you are in Christ, he did that for you, by name. Keep God's love, sovereignty, and promises in mind as we jump into the New Covenant. In the words of Han Solo, "Go strap yourselves in!" This is when God's plan really takes off!

9

THE NEW COVENANT

○○○○○○○○●○○○○○○○○

Better Than the Movie Poster

"This R2 unit of yours seems a bit beat up. Want a new one?" Considering the insufficiency of the Mosaic Covenant, a.k.a., the Old Covenant, to save its adherents from sin, God's people needed a new covenant. Not only that, God needed a new people with spiritually regenerated hearts who would have the ability to love him. Therefore, God chose a new people who comprised more than just the Israelites. This new chosen group included people from every tribe and nation. This new opening up of God's plan of salvation is also why the New Testament changes its language to describe God loving the "world" rather than just a single nation. We call this new arrangement the "New Covenant."

God never designed the Old Covenant to actually pay for the sins of those under it. God only used the Israelites under the Old Covenant to show everyone the impossibility of trying to earn his approval by obeying rules. Paul has this to say about the Old Covenant,

> Now if the ministry that brought death, which was engraved in letters on stone, came with glory, so that the Israelites could not look steadily at the face of Moses because of its glory, transitory though it was, will not the ministry of the Spirit be even more glorious?" (2 Corinthians 3:7-8)

The Old Covenant was glorious, because it was part of God's plan of salvation, but it was also a "ministry of death," because it left people stuck in their sin. It wasn't the way God was going to save people. It only served as a picture, a shadow of what was to come.

Consider the relationship between the Old Covenant and the New Covenant like this: Imagine going with your friends to see the new *Star Wars* movie. For months, everyone has been talking about how awesome it will be. You go to the first midnight showing.

As you stand in line outside the theater, a spotlight draws your attention to the movie poster for the new episode. It's a beautiful work, framed perfectly in an anti-glare glass case, showing both old and new characters. Your inner geek salivates as you analyze every pixel. After gazing at the poster for a long time, you finally turn to your friends and say, "This has been awesome! I'm going to go home, now." In complete shock, your friends watch you get into your car and drive away.

✴ Jeff Tweiten and John Guth, two members of the Seattle *Star Wars* Society, camped out for 136 days to buy the first two tickets to *Episode II*.

The next day, your friends describe spectacular action scenes, thought-provoking character development, and fascinating plot twists from the movie, all of which the poster failed to deliver. They also seem to have enjoyed the night far more than you did. Depression hits as you realize what you missed. All you saw was a movie poster. While it was an awesome poster, it was just a poster, something that might end up in a trash can—or sold on eBay. In all the excitement, you missed the point of going to the theater in the first place—to see the movie!

I bet you're thinking the above analogy is a little silly. Who would ever trade looking at a poster for watching the actual movie? But when it comes to God's covenants, that's exactly what the Israelites did. It's also what the church in Galatia did, what the believers in the book of Hebrews considered, and what you and I do if we add any part of the Old Covenant to our faith.

Think of the Old Covenant as a *Star Wars* promotional poster, not the full, glorious movie itself. Meaning, the Old Covenant Jews were trying to get their sins forgiven using methods (the Mosaic Law) that God would later say had no lasting effect. The Old Covenant didn't encompass the wonderful reality of salvation that God put into effect in the New Covenant through Jesus' death on the cross. The Old Covenant was only meant to point to what would happen in the New Covenant, just as a movie poster only gives you a glimpse at what will happen in the movie. We're supposed to leave the Old Covenant behind just as we leave the poster behind and take our seats in the theater to experience the actual movie with all the wonderful elements that bring us such lasting satisfaction.

A Hologram of Good Things to Come

When I first became a Christian, I didn't know much about the Bible nor how to study it correctly. The fact that I was a Padawan without a Master didn't help matters either. I didn't understand how the Old Covenant related to the New Covenant, and I was confused about which laws applied to me. No, I was not sacrificing bulls and goats; I knew that much. I also understood that salvation was not by works, but many Christians told me I should give ten percent of my income to my church, refrain from working on Sunday, and look to the Ten Commandments as God's golden standard of law. As I look back on this, it was similar to looking at the movie poster rather than watching the movie itself. Eventually, I learned that with this New Covenant came a new "law of Christ" that replaced the Mosaic Law and that the New Testament—not the Old Testament—gave me my marching orders as a Christian.

> Therefore do not let anyone judge you by what you eat or drink, or with regard to a religious festival, a New Moon celebration or a Sabbath day. These are a *shadow* of the things that were to come; the reality, however, is found in Christ (Colossians 2:16-17, emphasis mine). The law is only a *shadow* of the good things that are coming—not the realities themselves. For this reason it can never, by the same sacrifices repeated endlessly year after year, make perfect those who draw near to worship. (Hebrews 10:1, emphasis mine)

So, what did the biblical authors, who wrote under the inspiration of the Holy Spirit, mean by "shadow of the good things"? To help clarify, substitute another word for *shadow* like *foreshadow, illustration, picture,* or *symbol.* Basically, God used the Mosaic Law as well as the entire Old Covenant era (roughly 1,500 years) to teach us to set our hearts on Jesus and not try to earn our righteousness. "Nevertheless, God was not pleased with most of them; their bodies were scattered in the wilderness. Now these things occurred as examples to keep us from setting our hearts on evil things as they did" (1 Corinthians 10:5–6). That time period, including the people and the laws, was not intended to be part of the everlasting kingdom God promised to David, only to point to it.

God meant for the Old Covenant to serve a purpose similar to a hologram. In *Episode II,* Dooku has a hologram of the ultimate weapon, the Death Star, which the Imperials would eventually build. The hologram acts as a sort of blueprint for the real battle station. It's not the battle station itself, but it's needed to give the Empire and its engineers an idea on which to base their efforts. No one is foolish enough to point the hologram toward a planet and expect the image to blow it up. Likewise, the Old Covenant serves as a type of hologram for the New Covenant. The New Covenant is the spiritual fulfillment of the Old Covenant hologram.

> "Dejarik" is the name of the game R2-D2 and Chewie play on the way to Alderaan. The holographic game pieces resemble actual creatures in the galaxy. In this match, Artoo's Mantellian Savrip defeats Chewie's Kintan strider.

A perfect example of this is the Old Covenant's sacrificial system. Under this covenant, the Jews thought their sins were being forgiven when they performed sacrifices. But, the New Testament gives us the extra information needed to understand God's bigger picture of salvation.

It is impossible for the blood of bulls and goats to take away sins." (Hebrews 10:4)

Day after day every priest stands and performs his religious duties; again and again he offers the same sacrifices, which can never take away sins. But when this priest [Jesus Christ] had offered for all time one sacrifice for sins, he sat down at the right hand of God, and since that time he waits for his enemies to be made his footstool. For by one sacrifice [Jesus' death on the cross] he has made perfect forever those who are being made holy. (Hebrews 10:11–14)

Through reading Hebrews, we learn the Israelites' sins were forgiven only in the ceremonial sense, meaning they were accepted back by the physical nation of Israel but not by God. All of their religious work, their effort to earn God's acceptance, never ultimately saved them. In God's kindness, though, their faithlessness serves as an example to us so we don't fall into the trap of thinking God accepts us more when we do activities like go to church, read the Bible, or volunteer to help the needy. We do, of course, honor God by doing these things with the right attitude, but his unconditional love is based on Christ's death, not our works.

The Last Remnants of the Old Covenant

Hebrews 8:13 says, "By calling this covenant 'new,' he has made the first one obsolete; and what is obsolete and outdated will soon disappear." When Jesus died on the cross, rose from the dead, and sent his Holy Spirit to Earth, the New Covenant era began and the Old Covenant era came to an end. The verse above says that the Old Covenant was obsolete and would disappear soon. This alludes to the Romans destroying the Temple in AD 70.

Think of this like when the Senate (a holdover from the Old Republic) still exists at the end of *Episode III*. There were still remnants of the Old Republic even after the formation of the Empire, just as there were still traces of the Old Covenant after the cross. Tarkin announces its official end when he says the Emperor dissolved the Imperial Senate permanently and that "the last remnants of the Old Republic have been swept away." Even though the Republic, for all intents and purposes, is done for back in *Episode III* when the Empire is formed, it's not until this point in *Episode IV* that the last traces of the Republic are snuffed out.

When Jesus died on the cross, he did everything needed to close the door on the Old Covenant and usher in the New Covenant. When he did this, the Old Covenant was done with just as the Republic is when the Empire is formed. Similar to it taking many years for the Senate to be eradicated, it wasn't until AD 70 when the Romans destroyed the Temple in Jerusalem that the Old Covenant's sacrificial system was officially over. In other words, the Old Covenant just took some time for the last remnants to be swept away completely. This is why it's so important for us to not go back under any part of the Mosaic Law. Those laws are over and done with.

You might be saying, "Now wait a minute, the Old Testament says to obey the Ten Commandments. Why shouldn't I want to do that?" These commandments are all good moral statutes, and versions of most of them (except for keeping the Sabbath) are restated in the New Testament. But if we look to the original Ten Commandments, we look to a law that was never given to us. If God made a covenant with a particular people (Israel), and that covenant has drawn to a close, it makes sense that neither it nor its corresponding laws apply to us.

Sometimes, reality seems one way until we receive new information (like the teachings found in the New Testament) that sheds a whole new light on things. Consider when our heroes try to escape from the Death Star in *Episode IV.* At every turn, it seems that incredible odds are stacked against them, and they barely escape each time. Whether it's freeing Leia from the detention area, escaping the trash compactor, swinging across the chasm, squeezing through the closing blast doors, or destroying the pursuing TIE fighters, it looks like they could be recaptured at any moment. The last thing we think is that this rescue operation is easy. That being said, Leia says to Han afterwards, "They let us go; it's the only explanation for the ease of our escape." "Easy?" Han retorts. "You call that easy?"

It's not until we get to eavesdrop on Tarkin's conversation with Vader that we discover they were allowed to escape so that the Empire could track the *Millennium Falcon* to the Rebel secret base. All along, we thought one thing, but after receiving new information, everything gets turned on its head. Looking back, it makes a lot more sense that the Empire lets our heroes escape. Obi-Wan comments earlier how precise the blaster fire of Imperial troops is. Now it's believable that the stormtroopers (whose entire existence is serving as soldiers) are purposely missing if a farm boy, a princess, and a smuggler can outshoot them at every encounter.

🔭 Mark Hamill improvised his phone number (326-3827) as the garbage compactor's hatch number. For several takes, Harrison Ford said the line substituting his phone number instead, leading the two actors to bicker about whose number to use.

Another example happens when Yoda says, in *Episode V,* "No. There is another," in response to Obi-Wan's statement, "That boy is our last hope." If you watch *Episode V* before ever watching *Episode VI,* you'll scratch your head wondering who this other hope is. But after you receive new information in *Episode VI,* you can look back and understand that Yoda is referring to Leia. Both of these analogies remind us to filter our reading of the Old Testament through the lens of the New Testament's teaching passages.

We've been getting pretty scholarly in this chapter. You may be thinking, "What's the point of going down this road?" We're going deeper into theology, because we need to know the Bible as much as possible. Doing so helps us to learn how to show our love for God and others.

Think about the relationships in *Star Wars.* One way for Han to show his love to Leia is to serve the Rebel cause, because that's what's dear to her heart. Obi-Wan shows his love for Luke by guiding and instructing him as not only a Jedi Master but also as a father figure. All of us have particular ways we like to be loved. It could be through encouraging words, an act of service, or a big hug. Scripture teaches that we demonstrate our love for God by obeying him, "In fact, this is love for God: to keep his commands" (1 John 5:3a).

So, if we love God by keeping his commands, we need to make sure we obey the commands he gives to believers in the New Covenant era. If we don't know the appropriate commands to follow, it's like giving someone a big hug when what he or she really needs is to borrow your car for a job interview.

Understanding how God has divided up history and how certain commands were intended only for a distinct people helps us avoid spinning our wheels spiritually. As Christians, hopefully we spend most of our lives thinking about God and how to serve him best.

We're wasting time and not honoring God if we spend our energy on things that he, in his Word, has deemed unimportant.

The Old People of God

After centuries of God being faithful to Israel, he made a final evaluation of them. He determined that they were wicked, did not keep their end of the bargain (obey perfectly), and needed to be punished for their sin. "But God found fault with the people… they did not remain faithful to my covenant and I turned away from them, declares the Lord" (Hebrews 8:8a, 8:9b). "God will remember their wickedness and punish them for their sins" (Hosea 9:9b).

When we read the Old Testament, it's natural to view the Israelites as the good guys. It certainly seems like they are God's chosen people, set apart in a world of pagans. Still, eventually we find out most were actually evil in God's sight. This is like watching Han Solo collect his reward after helping save Princess Leia. As he packs up his money and plans to run out on the Alliance, it's obvious that he was always only looking out for himself, because a real "good guy" would never act like that.

The Israelites were only "God's people" in a movie poster/hologram sort of way. Scripture's language (disobedient, wicked, evil, complaining, stiff-necked) makes it clear that the Israelites could not possibly be the true holy people of God.

> You stiff-necked people! Your hearts and ears are still uncircumcised. You are just like your ancestors: You always resist the Holy Spirit! (Acts 7:51)

> But concerning Israel he [Isaiah] says, "All day long I [God] have held out my hands to a disobedient and obstinate people." (Romans 10:21)

> How long will this wicked community grumble against me? I have heard the complaints of these grumbling Israelites. (Numbers 14:27)

> Then the Israelites did evil in the eyes of the Lord and served the Baals. (Judges 2:11)

Now, let's contrast these terms with the words the Bible uses to describe Christians under the New Covenant: *new creation, saints, loved by God, accepted,* and *forgiven.* The distinction could not be starker.

Granted, there were men and women in the Old Testament who loved God sincerely and will be saved. People like Abraham, Noah, Moses, and David are part of the "remnant," Paul talks about in Romans 11. God chose to save a small percentage of Israel based on Christ's future work on the cross. But, we make a big mistake when we think the Israelites, as a whole, are believers just like us. It's important to know that if we're in Christ, God will never describe us as evil. He is always for us and never against us. This is a critical principle to get right. The quality of our life and walk with God hinges on trusting that we are accepted unconditionally.

Let's use another analogy from *Star Wars* to understand Israel better. The clone troopers mirror the Israelites in many ways. They take orders from the Jedi and fight against the Jedi's enemies, as Israel did for God. The clone troopers are an easily defined group of people with their own look and feel, just like the nation of Israel. And if someone watches only *Episode II,* he or she walks away thinking that the clone troopers are the good guys.

In actuality, the clone troopers are bad guys with bad hearts whose true master is the Emperor. This is reminiscent of the Israelites, who were bad people (just like most everyone else on Earth) with evil hearts whose true ruler was Satan. After watching the last act in *Episode III,* when the clones show their true colors during Order 66, no one would dare argue that the clones are the good guys. In the same way, the Israelites were not God-lovers even though they looked like it for so many years. Like the clones, they were just going through the motions of obedience but with hearts that would later betray.

The last thing I want to do is slander another group of people, and I'm not trying to encourage anti-Semitism in the least. If it's any consolation, if God would have made the Old Covenant with the people of Estonia, Australia, or Tupelo, Mississippi, then I would be talking about them. Without Christ, we are all slaves to sin, and no group of people would have done any better at obeying God than the Israelites. Furthermore, of course we should love Jewish people just the same as anyone else. Being descended from Israel shouldn't dissuade us from sharing the gospel either.

I hope I'm not beating a dead Bantha with this section. My purpose in belaboring these points is that we need to understand the role Israel plays in God's plan of salvation, because it affects us. It's only when we know accurately what the Bible says about this or any given subject that we can live for God in ways that honor him. If we look to the wrong pattern, we fail to bring glory to God and get terribly misdirected and hurt in the process.

✶ Darth Vader's suit control panel (in *Episode V* and *VI*) contains three lines of Hebrew text. Many speculate the words translate as, "His deeds will not be forgiven until he merits."

The New People of God

Realizing that most of the Israelites were not part of the true spiritual people of God, we ask, "Then, who is?" Paul gives a partial answer when he says, "For not all who are descended from Israel are Israel. Nor because they are his descendants are they all Abraham's children" (Romans 9:6–7). He goes on to say, "In other words, it is not the children by physical descent who are God's children, but it is the children of the promise who are regarded as Abraham's offspring (Romans 9:8). Paul connects the dots that God's plan of salvation depends on God's promise, the one he made to Abraham so long ago. Simply put, the Church (with a capital "C"), that is, all believers from every tribe, nation, and tongue, are the legitimate people of God, because they are under a New Covenant, a covenant built on the promises of God and sealed in Christ's blood. "Spiritual" Israel is made up of all who are chosen by God.

Unlike the Israelites under the Old Covenant, Christians are characterized in the New Testament as loving God and growing in holiness. Sure, we continue to have days when we don't feel like doing the right thing, but those days no longer describe our personalities and motivations as a whole. Due to the Holy Spirit's work in our hearts, we don't want to remain in sin any longer. We desire to repent. This is the mark of a Christian and the evidence of a new spiritual life that a typical Israelite never showed.

🔭 The word Yoda (or specifically *Yodea*) means "one who knows" in Hebrew. However, it may also come from the Sanskrit word *Yoddha*, which means "warrior."

All of us, before we gave our lives to Jesus and trusted in him for salvation, were much like the Israelites. We were characterized by self-centered behavior without any love for God. Previously, I used Han Solo as an illustration of someone under the Old Covenant. But really, Han Solo acts like two different people. The Solo of *Episode IV*, as his name implies, looks out only for himself. He's arrogant, selfish, and only brave and sacrificial if there's enough money to merit the risk. When the Rebels need his piloting skills to destroy the Death Star, he's too self-centered to join them.

But then, a remarkable transformation happens in Solo's heart in the third act of *Episode IV*. We don't see this on screen, but I imagine this change begins by him thinking about Luke, Leia, and the others. As he flies the *Falcon* into the cold, dark loneliness of space, he probably feels guilty for treating them badly and regrets the things he said. Most of all, he thinks about how Obi-Wan sacrificed himself so that they could escape.

As Han contemplates this, it hits him how his life is all about him and his insignificant, little kingdom, and he doesn't like it. In fact, he detests it. For the first time in his scoundrel life, he wants his life to matter for something more. He doesn't want the phrase, "Take care of yourself, Han, I guess that's what you're best at," to characterize him. It's at this point that Han has a true change of heart. In an instant, he turns his ship around and flies full speed back to the battle. Now he's willing to risk his ship, his future, and his life like a real "good guy." He goes on to play a pivotal role in defeating the Empire at the Battle of Yavin, but the "new" Han is just getting started.

By *Episode V*, Han has learned all about love and sacrifice from his new friends, evidenced by the fact that he ignores the warning of the deck officer on Hoth and rides out into the icy deathtrap to rescue Luke. Soon after saving Luke, Han has the option to leave the Rebel base on Hoth before the Empire arrives, but he chooses to put himself in jeopardy to ensure Leia makes it to her transport.

Watching Han transform so much from *Episode IV* to *V* should inspire us, because it's much like the change we see over time in a believer's life. Unfortunately, like Han, we continue to have our occasional rude and selfish moments, especially when dealing with real world versions of a certain protocol droid. But when a person puts his or her faith in Christ, the Holy Spirit produces a real heart change, like we see in Solo. The selfish ways of the "former life" no longer appeal the way they once did. We desire to repent of sin and strive to live for Jesus, our new King.

We never see changed hearts and transformed lives in nearly all of Israel. When you read your Old Testament, pick up on all the times God was gracious, all the times he pursued the Israelites, giving them a second chance even though they didn't deserve it. Notice also, most of the Israelites would always return to their old sinful ways, showing no lasting love or devotion to the God who showered so many blessings upon them. When you read the Bible, refrain from the trap of thinking you are like the Hebrew people under the Old Covenant. You are not. If you're a Christian, you're a new creation, a post-*Episode-IV* Han Solo. You could not be more different from the typical Israelite. The days of looking out for only yourself are long gone.

10

MAN'S SIN & GOD'S GRACE

○○○○○○○○○●○○○○○○○

Total Depravity

A Wretched Hive of Scum and Villainy

Before experiencing the Trial of the Spirit in *Episode V,* Luke asks Yoda what's inside Dagobah's ominous cave. Yoda answers, "Only what you take with you." To Luke's surprise, he finds Darth Vader, lightsaber in hand! After Luke decapitates the Sith Lord, Vader's helmet explodes, revealing Luke's face. For the first time, Luke comes face to face (literally) with the notion that he's not the Force's squeaky-clean gift to the Jedi. On the contrary, Luke learns that he has a dark side, and if he chooses the wrong path, he'll end up just like his evil nemesis.

This scene embodies an important biblical truth referred to as "total depravity." Total depravity, sometimes called "radical corruption" or "pervasive depravity," teaches that sin affects every aspect of an unbeliever's heart. In the context of salvation, this principle teaches that sin dominates a person's heart, mind, and soul so much that he would never pursue a holy god of his own volition. Paul recognized how his utter sinfulness leads to a desperate need to be rescued. "What a wretched man I am! Who will rescue me from this body of death?" (Romans 7:24).

As we will see, the total depravity of man is conveyed clearly in the pages of Scripture. The tenet, as we know it, derives from the study and teachings of John Calvin, a 16th century French theologian. Calvin had a very high view of God's Word and a conviction that God is sovereign in rescuing his chosen people. His ideas on salvation would later be referred to as "the doctrines of grace, "the five points of Calvinism," or by the acrostic, "TULIP." The "T" in TULIP stands for this first point.

Total depravity is not "total" in the sense that the person is as bad as he could possibly be. Through his common grace upon all mankind, God restrains evil. To illustrate this, Luke is not cruel like Grand Moff Tarkin or greedy like Greedo. Luke actually has more good qualities than bad. Instead, total depravity means that there's no area in a person's character that is off-limits to sin. Even though Luke is not deceitful like Palpatine or gluttonous like Jabba the Hutt, he could be if the dark side took over. In fact, Luke does lose his temper, patience, and humility on several occasions, revealing his "inner Vader."

Smoldering Spiritual Skeletons

The Bible teaches that Adam represented humankind when he sinned in the Garden. Therefore, every man and woman receives the curse of Adam's bad record and bad heart (Romans 5). The depravity inherited from Adam affects our ability to respond positively to God's holiness. From our first moment of existence, we are morally dead, a spiritual corpse, incapable of choosing Christ without God first making us spiritually alive.

> As for you, you were dead in your transgressions and sins, in which you used to live when you followed the ways of this world and of the ruler of the kingdom of the air, the spirit who is now at work in those who are disobedient. All of us also lived among them at one time, gratifying the cravings of our flesh and following its desires and thoughts. Like the rest, we were by nature deserving of wrath. But because of his great love for us, God, who is rich in mercy, made us alive with Christ even when we were dead in transgressions—it is by grace you have been saved. (Ephesians 2:1–5)

In *Episode IV,* Luke finds the smoldering skeletal remains of his uncle and aunt. We know they're gone and not coming back.

So, with basic anatomy in mind, try to imagine Uncle Owen and Aunt Beru changing themselves into living people again. After they grow new bones, a heart, a brain, lungs, and skin, they jump up, ready to tackle the morning's chores. Ridiculous, isn't it? But no more unreasonable than a person coming to Christ without God breathing new spiritual life into him first. This is why Paul uses the word *dead* to describe those who are not in Christ. He could have used the words *injured, sick, confused,* or *needy* to describe us in relation to sin, but he didn't. He used the word that applied. Likewise, in talking with Nicodemus in John 3, Jesus taught that we must be reborn spiritually to see the kingdom of God.

🔭 Many fans speculate that Boba Fett murdered Owen and Beru. Evidence supports this theory, especially since *Episode IV* "Special Edition" establishes Fett being on Tatooine during this time.

Before the gift of faith (Ephesians 2:8), I was spiritually unable to come to God. Since I was born with a self-centered disposition, it was impossible for me to submit to a holy God who demands complete self-denial. This is similar to why Han Solo mocks the Force and wants nothing to do with it. He doesn't want to be humble and rely on something outside himself.

Granted, there are plenty of nice people around us who seem morally upright enough to deserve God's acceptance. But despite how innocent they appear to us, are they living to honor Jesus? Are they obeying Colossians 3:17: "And whatever you do, whether in word or deed, do it all in the name of the Lord Jesus, giving thanks to God the Father through him"? Before God changed my heart, I sure didn't have Jesus' glory in mind. And if honoring Jesus was not the reason for my behavior, then all I was doing by trying to be a "good" person was storing up God's wrath for me (Romans 2). Like the first R2 unit Luke and his uncle almost buy from the Jawas, as an unbeliever, I had a "bad motivator," that is, a bad heart, and on my own, I could do nothing to change it.

He [Jesus] went on: What comes out of a person is what defiles them. It is from within, out of a person's heart, that evil thoughts come—sexual immorality, theft, murder, adultery, greed, malice, deceit, lewdness, envy, slander, arrogance and folly. All these evils come from inside and defile a person. (Mark 7:20-23)

Unfortunately, we like to grade our sin on a curve. Using our own moral compass, we might say, "I'm not that bad. At least I'm not like *that* person." Without a doubt, Luke looks as pure as Hoth's snow if you put him next to a hideous alien who has the death sentence in twelve systems. But God's standard of righteousness is not at all like ours. Sometimes, we have such a low view of God's holiness that we don't realize how bad we were before Christ.

Luke's Disbelieving Heart

When Luke arrives on Dagobah, his heart is already in a hardened state. He looks around at the slimy mudhole, considers his search for Yoda, and wonders if the Jedi Master even exists. Luke needs a heart change. It's the reason Yoda says at the beginning, "I cannot teach him. The boy has no patience." He goes on to list several other reasons, including anger and recklessness.

Yoda knows that the heart must be right before training can begin. Luke struggles constantly to believe. It's hard for him to believe a Jedi Master could be in such a small package. It's hard for him to believe Yoda's council of not needing weapons in the cave, and it's virtually impossible for him to believe that Yoda lifted the X-wing out of its swampy incarceration.

Nobody seeks the God of Scripture due to an unbelieving heart. "As it is written: There is no one righteous, not even one; there is no one who understands, no one who seeks God" (Romans 3:10–11). Luke needs faith. To become a Jedi, he needs an internal change. Similarly, for you to become a Christian, God needs to regenerate your heart supernaturally. With a new heart, the depravity that once characterized and enslaved you no longer prevents you from believing in Jesus.

For believers, acknowledging our former depravity is essential for understanding a host of other crucial principles in our Christian walk. For example, appreciating this doctrine allows us to grow in holiness, because it promotes humility. In addition, it paves the way for assurance, knowing that God will finish the good work in us because he's the one who began it. It also takes the pressure off evangelizing, because we recognize that God is in the business of changing hearts. While it's still necessary to pray for unbelievers and share the gospel, it's up to the Holy Spirit, not us, to convince their hearts.

Lastly, I'm certain that this doctrine will be hard for some to accept. Pride never likes to acknowledge sin. But a person's love for God and others will always be proportional to how much he views the holiness of God and the depravity of his former self. The more you and I recognize how bad we were, the more we'll appreciate how God pursued and rescued us. In turn, this will increase our love for Christ. Think of John the Baptist's words: "He must become greater; I must become less" (John 3:30). If you think your sin required little forgiveness, then the love you have for God will reflect that. The sinful woman in the Gospel of Luke knew she was a sinner and loved her Savior fervently because of his mercy.

Notice I said "former self" earlier. If we are in Christ, our hearts and our behavior are not sinful in the way they once were. Paul lists wrongdoers in 1 Corinthians 6 (sexually immoral, idolaters, adulterers, thieves, drunkards, slanderers, and swindlers) but then punctuates it with, "And that is what some of you were. But you were washed, you were sanctified, you were justified in the name of the Lord Jesus Christ and by the Spirit of our God" (1 Corinthians 6:11). These sections on total depravity are intended to open your eyes to what was really going on in your heart before God saved you. Like Luke, you and I were not as bad as we could have been. In fact, Luke acts very admirable at times. He cares for his friends and family, rescues Princess Leia, and is generally a nice guy. This demonstrates God's common grace and his general love for all humanity at work. After all, "He causes his sun to rise on the evil and the good, and sends rain on the righteous and the unrighteous" (Matthew 5:45b).

Because of God's common grace, most people are reasonably pleasant, like Luke. They do many good things even if saving the galaxy is not one of them. They care for their friends and family. They work hard. And for the most part, they treat others well. Still, there was a time when you and I wanted to run our own lives without God, and that is the essence of depravity. These next sections are not intended to make you feel bad. Their purpose is to turn your gaze inward for a while to understand your sin better so that you can direct your eyes back to Jesus, back to the cross, and delight in his forgiveness.

Unconditional Election

"No Such Thing as Luck"

In *Episode IV*, when Luke manages to deflect the training remote's laser blasts, Han calls it "luck." Ben is quick to point out that there's no such thing as luck. Christians who have a firm grasp of God's sovereignty will agree wholeheartedly with Obi-Wan. God didn't just create the universe; he is in complete control over everything in existence, right down to the last molecule billions of light years away. Be that as it may, many say that his control stops when it infringes on a person's free will, especially the choice to accept or deny Christ. This brings us to the second point of Calvin's five points (the "U" in TULIP), "unconditional election." This doctrine, also known as "sovereign election" or "unmerited favor," states that God elects or chooses who will come to faith and thus, by elimination, who will not.

The word *unconditional* means salvation is not based on the person ever showing any interest or favor toward God or earning God's affection by living well. This is one of the hardest doctrines for people, even believers, to swallow. Nevertheless, it is a crucial truth that we need to embrace in order to have a more complete view of God.

The book of Revelation describes the Book of Life written at the creation of the world, which contains the names of who will be spared God's wrath. The question is, how did God choose those names? Before anyone was born physically, God decided who would trust in Christ. Scripture does not give us much information about why he chooses some and not others. The Bible only teaches that he does it this way for his own pleasure and purposes. "For he chose us in him before the creation of the world to be holy and blameless in his sight. In love he predestined us to be adopted as his sons through Jesus Christ, in accordance with his pleasure and will" (Ephesians 1:4–5).

God's choice isn't like Luke and his uncle picking out an R2 unit. On that occasion, the Jawas line up their best droids, and Uncle Owen decides based on which he thinks will do the best job. When the first R2 unit malfunctions, Owen rejects it. Bad performance equates to dismissal. God, on the other hand, knew that no human being would ever meet his standard of perfection. Yet, he chose to show mercy on some.

🔭 When Luke returns to discover his dead uncle and aunt, the wind blows from left to right during both the shot of the homestead and the reverse shot of Luke.

Paul argues for election in Romans 9. The editor's section heading in the NIV translation labels it "God's Sovereign Choice." In this chapter, Paul describes how God used Isaac and Rebekah's twins Jacob and Esau to illustrate the point that God would choose whom he would love. God's choice was not dependent on either of the twin's merit.

> Yet, before the twins were born or had done anything good or bad—in order that God's purpose in election might stand: not by works but by him who calls—she was told, "The older will serve the younger. Just as it is written: "Jacob I loved, but Esau I hated." (Romans 9:11–13)

"It Just Isn't Fair!"

After Uncle Owen, the authority in Luke's life, tells Luke he has to wait to go to the Academy, Luke cries foul. People always think they deserve better, because they have a biased and unbiblical idea about what is fair. For instance, many disagree that God will actually send someone who was "bad" most of his life to eternal paradise, while another who devoted his life to the study of religion and helping mankind might be sent to everlasting punishment. To our human minds, this does not compute.

This is not a new complaint. People addressed this with Paul. "What then shall we say? Is God unjust? Not at all!" (Romans 9:14). Paul goes on to quote Exodus. "For he says to Moses, 'I will have mercy on whom I have mercy, and I will have compassion on whom I have compassion'" (Romans 9:15). This sounds harsh and arbitrary, but the reality is that God is not indebted to save any of us. In other words, he does not owe us grace. Our guilt is twofold: 1) we are guilty because Adam represented us, and 2) we sin every day. Either one of these is enough to warrant God's just punishment. It is man's pride to think he is good enough or can act morally enough to win the acceptance of a holy God.

> One of you will say to me: "Then why does God still blame us? For who is able to resist his will?" But who are you, a human being, to talk back to God? "Shall what is formed say to the one who formed it, 'Why did you make me like this?'" Does not the potter have the right to make out of the same lump of clay some pottery for special purposes and some for common use? (Romans 9:19-21)

George Lucas has been tinkering with the original trilogy for years, to the chagrin of fans. I, like most, do not like the majority of changes he's made. In my opinion, Greedo shooting first, CGI Jabba at Mos Eisley, and Vader yelling "Noooooooooo!" as he grabs the Emperor diminish rather than add to the story. I was fortunate to see the original *Star Wars* in theaters in 1977 (my older brother said we saw it at least twenty-five times). The original trilogy as the public first saw it has more than just a place in my heart. It influenced me as a person. So, I understand why fans are so angry about the changes. But they're not just angry. They're angry at George Lucas, the creator who gave the fans the movies in the first place.

As unhappy as I am with Lucas' alterations, I understand that he has every right to make these choices. These movies are his babies, not mine. The fans' reactions exemplify how a lot of believers handle God's Word. Throughout their Christian life, they have thought about God in a certain way, but then they learn what the Bible really says about a subject, and their faith is turned upside down. The doctrines of grace incite this sometimes, and, like Luke, believers want to cry out, "It's just not fair! It shouldn't be that way. I want it to be my way!" But what matters are not our opinions or preferences but what God's Word says.

"We Seem to be Made to Suffer"

Using the metaphor of the potter from the earlier passage, the Bible teaches that God, as Creator, has the right to make and predestine some people to be his children and some not to be. Not only does he predetermine this, he controls situations to bring his plans about.

In *Episode V,* Luke says, "Now all I have to do is find this Yoda . . . if he even exists." At first, Yoda disguises who he really is. This seems a little unfair and deceitful, but Yoda has good reason. Luke starts off with a bad attitude and is bent on disbelieving. Knowing this, Yoda acts in a manner that brings Luke's arrogance to the surface.

In a way, God used a similar approach with Israel. Instead of doing everything in his power to help the Israelites, he did the opposite. He hardened their already wicked hearts so that they had no chance of turning to him to be healed.

> He [the Lord] said, "Go and tell this people: "'Be ever hearing, but never understanding; be ever seeing, but never perceiving.' Make the heart of this people calloused; make their ears dull and close their eyes. Otherwise they might see with their eyes, hear with their ears, understand with their hearts, and turn and be healed." (Isaiah 6:9–10)

If it is not God's plan for a particular person to believe in him, that person never will. It is people's nature to reject God. So, when God hardens their hearts, he only makes the downward slope they are already on steeper. That being said, people go to hell because they are sinners, first and foremost, not because God doesn't choose to save them. Luke becoming angry and impatient and the consequences of his emotions are not Yoda's fault. Yoda's actions only serve to bring out what is already in Luke's heart. Before his change of heart, Luke does not want to believe in a wrinkly, pint-sized, creature with funny ears. He wants his Master to be in his image, not the other way around. Yoda has every right not to train Luke. It's Yoda's choice, not Luke's and in a "Romans 9:15-like" fashion, Yoda lets Luke know this. "Ready, are you? What know you of ready? For eight hundred years have I trained Jedi. My own counsel will I keep on who is to be trained!"

Because of our depravity, left to ourselves, we would never choose Christ. As a mark of further judgment, sometimes God withholds his grace even more so that people spiral deeper into unbelief and sin (Romans 1).

They [unbelievers] perish because they refused to love the truth and so be saved. For this reason God sends them a powerful delusion so that they will believe the lie and so that all will be condemned who have not believed the truth but have delighted in wickedness. But we ought always to thank God for you, brothers and sisters loved by the Lord, because God chose you as firstfruits to be saved through the sanctifying work of the Spirit and through belief in the truth. He called you to this through our gospel, that you might share in the glory of our Lord Jesus Christ. (2 Thessalonians 2:10b-14)

While wandering in the wilderness of the Jundland Wastes, C-3PO bemoans, "How did I get into this mess? I really don't know how. We seem to be made to suffer. It's our lot in life." I am not saying that God makes most humans just to suffer. But it does seem that way. Let's think this through biblically so we can have a correct understanding.

🔭 Harrison Ford broke his leg during the filming of *Episode VII* in 2014 when the hydraulic door of the *Millennium Falcon* fell on him. Less than a year later, the plane he was piloting crashed due to engine failure.

First, God is sovereign over our birth as well as our life. Psalm 139:13 speaks of God knitting each of us together in our mother's womb. Second, for the most part, we suffer during the years we have on Earth. People experience natural disasters, illnesses, hunger, loneliness, poverty, betrayal, murders, car accidents, burglaries, wars, terrorist attacks, aging bodies, estranged relationships, divorces, loss of jobs, sleepless nights, shipwrecks, plane crashes, and death of loved ones—and this list only scratches the surface. There's so much suffering that God's Word says it's better for someone to never have been born than to experience the evil of this world (Ecclesiastes 4:3). We live in a cursed world. But let's remember who cursed it: God. Why did he curse it? Man's wickedness. "The wrath of God is being revealed from heaven against all the godlessness and wickedness of people, who suppress the truth by their wickedness" (Romans 1:18).

After years of suffering judgment on Earth, unbelievers will suffer punishment forever.

> He [God] will punish those who do not know God and do not obey the gospel of our Lord Jesus. They will be punished with everlasting destruction and shut out from the presence of the Lord and from the glory of his might. (2 Thessalonians 1:8-9)

I know it may be tough to think of the God you love in this way, but be comforted by the following verses:

> What if God, although choosing to show his wrath and make his power known, bore with great patience the objects of his wrath—prepared for destruction? What if he did this to make the riches of his glory known to the objects of his mercy, whom he prepared in advance for glory. (Romans 9:22-23)

Every one of us deserves only punishment, not mercy. And yet, we in Christ are the objects of his mercy, chosen before we were able to show an ounce of faith. We don't know why he chose to save some of us and not others. We could just as easily have been the objects of his wrath. But the doctrine of unconditional election should cause us to love God, more not less, because he directed his fierce judgment at his Son on the cross rather than us.

God Chose the Lowly

Luke and Leia are twins who are separated at birth, raised differently, and go on to very different destinies. Luke, from man's point of view, brings little to the table, a farmer from the most desolate planet in the galaxy. Sound familiar? Not only was Jesus from a humble background, so are most of those God calls to follow him.

> Brothers, think of what you were when you were called. Not many of you were wise by human standards; not many were influential; not many were of noble birth. But God chose the foolish things of the world to shame the wise; God chose the weak things of the world to shame the strong. He chose the lowly things of this world and the despised things—and the things that are not—to nullify the things that are, so that no one may boast before him. It is because of him that you are in Christ Jesus, who has become for us wisdom from God—that is, our righteousness, holiness and redemption. Therefore, as it is written: "Let him who boasts boast in the Lord." (1 Corinthians 1:26-31)

God chose people so that he can be glorified, not the other way around. Most Christians are not billionaires, professional athletes, beauty queens, or Nobel Prize winners. Most are people whom the world regards as nothing special. God chose these persons, because this brings more glory to him. When God draws them to faith, they realize they contribute nothing to their salvation. This is exactly what God requires from us: humility and belief.

🔭 The actors playing Jedi and Sith were allowed to choose their lightsaber design. Despite this fact, Hayden Christensen was not allowed, because he needed to use the same hilt that Obi-Wan gives Luke in *Episode IV*.

Both the Jedi and the Sith know all about destinies. Obi-Wan tells Luke, "Your destiny lies along a different path than mine." While Vader tells Luke, "Your destiny lies with me, Skywalker!" The truth is, no one knows someone's eternal destiny except God. Just because God chose who will be saved and who will not should not stop us from praying for others' salvation or sharing the gospel. On the contrary, knowing how incredibly sovereign God is during his pursuit of his people, this should cause us to pray and share all the more. Fortunately, we don't have to convince people they need Christ. If they are part of God's elect, nothing will stop them from coming to saving faith.

More than Clairvoyance

God's sovereignty in election is a disputed topic among Christians, and the perspective I'm putting forth is not the most widely accepted view. Many believers take the Arminian stance, which is based off the teachings of Jacobus Arminius (1560–1609), a Dutch theologian who emphasized man's free will as the dominating factor in salvation.

A believer's view of predestination is not crucial to having saving faith. I consider Christians who hold to Arminianism just as much my brothers and sisters in Christ as those who embrace Calvinism. Since I am convinced the doctrines of grace are biblical, my goal is to have these principles shape our view of God.

Nevertheless, I would be remiss in not dealing with at least one counterargument during this study. One or two chapters are not enough to tackle every verse that seems to refute God's sovereignty in election. Indeed, an entire book is needed to properly handle the arguments. That being said, let's look at a popular passage that our Arminian brothers and sisters often bring up to defend their view.

> For those God foreknew he also predestined to be conformed to the image of his Son, that he might be the firstborn among many brothers and sisters. And those he predestined, he also called; those he called, he also justified; those he justified, he also glorified. (Romans 8:29-30)

Typically, an Arminian will interpret the word "foreknew" in verse 29 to mean God used clairvoyant powers to look into the future, saw who would respond positively to the offer of salvation, and chose those individuals on the basis of their first choosing him. This argument hinges on the meaning of the word "foreknew." Webster's defines it as "to have previous knowledge of and know beforehand, especially by paranormal means or by revelation."[17]

If this is how it happens, we're left with a situation where God is not really in control of events. If God does not orchestrate everything beforehand, then the future, as Yoda puts it, would truly be "always in motion." Yoda can't see Han and Leia's fate, because their future might change. *Star Wars* is inconsistent here. The Jedi and the Sith speak of people having destinies. If this is true, then Yoda should be able to look down the corridors of time to see the fate of Luke's companions. But whenever you add man's free will to the mix, inevitably, you end up with a future that can change due to a practically infinite number of factors and whims.

Admiral Motti's complaint of Vader in *Episode IV* is that the Force has not given Vader clairvoyance enough to find the Rebel hidden fortress. Obi-Wan alludes to this deficiency when he says that even Yoda cannot see Han and Leia's fate. This reminds us that a clairvoyant God who is not omnipotent leaves us with a God who cannot know a future event for certain. Therefore, for his sovereign will to come to pass, he must be able to control all the variables that could alter the outcomes.

Of course, God is all-knowing, but the word *foreknew* in the above verse does not refer to knowledge. "Knew" is the past tense of "know." So, this text says that long ago, God knew those he predestined. Let's take a closer look at how else the Bible uses the word *knew* so that we can figure out what Paul means in this verse.

The ESV translation of Genesis 4:1a is "Now Adam knew Eve his wife, and she conceived and bore Cain." However, the NIV translates the verse as, "Adam made love to his wife Eve, and she became pregnant and gave birth to Cain." Wow! It's one thing to know a woman; it's quite a different story to make love to her. Here, the word "knew" implies a deep intimacy between a husband and wife. Likewise, Romans 8:29 means that God set his affection on a particular group of people (referred to as "those") before the foundation of the world. This is completely consistent with the other verses we looked at, such as Ephesians 1:4–5.

When cloud cars fire on the *Millennium Falcon* in *Episode V,* Leia says to Han, "I thought you knew this person." What does she mean by that? As movie watchers, we must interpret her statement logically in the context of what is going on. She doesn't mean simply knowing what Lando was all about, that he once owned the *Millennium Falcon,* used to be a professional gambler, and is now the administrator of Cloud City. Her statement implies friendship. A friend doesn't allow his friend to be shot at. That's the reason for her comment.

Let's look at one more example. When Jesus explains that not everyone who says to him, "Lord, Lord," will enter the kingdom of heaven, he goes on to say, "Then I will tell them plainly, 'I never knew you. Away from me, you evildoers!'" (Matthew 7:23) Again, the use of the word "knew" connotes a relationship rather than mere knowledge. Of course, Jesus knew all *about* them, but that's not what he was getting at. He meant that he didn't know them personally, i.e., intimately. Quite the reverse, God knew by name those whom he would glorify one day.

We can go on all day with word studies. I'm not a big fan of them, because the context should trump a word's potential meaning. We shouldn't allow reading a word or verse in a vacuum to override what the rest of Scripture says. We must take the entire Bible into account when determining a verse's meaning. In this case, think of what you've already learned about the depravity of man. Meditate on Romans 3:10–11. Ask God to help you understand this better. "Foreknew" couldn't possibly mean that God looked into the future to determine who would respond to the gospel. No one would choose God unless God *first* chose to replace the person's bad heart with a good one.

Irresistible Grace

"It's Pulling Us In!"

The *Millennium Falcon* made the Kessel Run in less than twelve parsecs. Solo's ship may not look like much, but she's got it where it counts. But when it gets caught in the Death Star's tractor beam, there's little she or her captain can do to stop being drug, kicking and screaming and (in Chewie's case) howling, into the moon-sized space station. The force field reaches out, grabs, and pulls our heroes in. Han, Luke, and Obi-Wan would have never set foot on the Death Star if the Empire had not used their own invisible force to pluck them from outer space.

In the case of God and people, the reverse is true. Corrupt people would never want to approach a holy God. So, God had to use his power to make sure it happened. The tractor beam illustrates the Holy Spirit's role in our salvation and, thus, God's sovereignty in election.

"No one can come to me unless the Father who sent me draws them, and I will raise them up at the last day" (John 6:44). Jesus taught that God must draw or literally drag people to himself. Given what we have learned about man's complete inability to seek anything spiritually good, it makes sense that God would need to do the heavy lifting.

🔭 The Kessel Run was 18 parsecs long. Smugglers traveled it to circumvent Imperial blockades. A parsec is a measurement of distance equaling 3.26 light years.

This brings us to the doctrine called "irresistible grace." You probably notice I'm skipping the "L" for now and jumping to the "I" in our TULIP acrostic. We'll study that one in the next chapter. The order we learn these doctrines isn't essential, and there's actually some benefit in studying irresistible grace now.

Irresistible grace (sometimes called efficacious grace) is the work of God whereby the Holy Spirit gives a person the spiritual ability and desire to respond to the gospel. Here's how John Calvin described it: "As to the kind of drawing, it is not violent, so as to compel men by external force; but still it is a powerful impulse of the Holy Spirit which makes men willing who formerly were unwilling and reluctant."[18]

This Is the God You're Looking For

God doesn't just perform some sort of Jedi mind (and heart) trick on everyone who believes even though, from a certain perspective, it may seem that way. Rather, he gives the person a new spiritual heart that wants to believe. Doing so keeps the promise God made in Ezekiel 36:26: "I will give you a new heart and put a new spirit in you; I will remove from you your heart of stone and give you a heart of flesh." Without this new heart, the gospel rolls off the backs of unbelievers the way a Jedi mind trick rolls off the backs of Hutts and Toydarians. As I said earlier in this chapter, an unbeliever has a "bad motivator," meaning his heart motivates him to do wrong. Since darkness wants nothing to do with the light, God must change a person's desire supernaturally so that he will choose Jesus.

Unlike the stormtroopers who are duped into believing Obi-Wan's suggestion about the droids, we're completely aware of the decision we make to follow Christ. It's not as though we wish we could resist God's powerful influence somehow, but he's just too strong. On the contrary, in a way that we can't understand completely, we make the decision voluntarily even if we don't realize the supernatural work that undergirds it. I imagine the effect of a Jedi mind trick wears off later on, leaving the victim wondering why he did such a stupid thing. But a true belief in and love for God only deepens over time, so that we look back with even more joy at having made the decision to follow him.

"I Can't Shake Him!"

There are cases when people put up more of a fight when coming to Christ. Once God's tractor beam (which always includes conviction over sin) kicks in, some try to put their spirit in full reverse, locking in the auxiliary power in an effort to deny the truth of their own ugliness. This is futile though, because if you're one of God's elect, his chosen people, then his grace will be efficacious even if you resist (hence, irresistible grace). Christ gave up his life to pay for the sins of every single one who will believe. As a result, there's no chance that God will let Christ's death go to waste, not even concerning one of his children. His death guarantees the salvation for all those whom the Father has chosen. "All those the Father gives me will come to me, and whoever comes to me I will never drive away" (John 6:37).

If you're a believer, God locked on the coordinates of your soul before the foundation of the earth. But, before the appointed time came for you to believe the gospel, you had to be convicted of your sin, and this is never a fun time. In fact, some people resist by distracting themselves with all sorts of worldly things. Yet, no matter how much we try to fight the Holy Spirit's pursuit of us, eventually, we, like Biggs Darklighter, figure out that we can't shake this sort of determination.

Often, the Holy Spirit's conviction causes reactions like those from our heroes when they realize they're caught in the tractor beam. Han Solo is particularly hostile about being captured and vows to fight! Obi-Wan reminds him that he can't win, but there are alternatives to fighting. We can't thwart any part of God's plan for our salvation. At last, Solo must admit that the tractor beam is more powerful than his ship's engines. He shuts down and accepts his fate.

When God targets a sinner in need of his grace, it's not always obvious to onlookers or to the sinner himself. Occasionally, we witness night-and-day testimony. But in other situations, like in my life, it takes years of wrestling with the gospel before finally believing. There's no way to know for sure if God is drawing someone until the person becomes a believer, looks back on his spiritual journey, and sees God's hand at work.

When God attracts people to himself, some may be bold and fearless like Han, others reserved and collected like Obi-Wan or panicky like Luke. But almost all fear what it will mean to give up their lives to this God. Will they lose their identity? Will this new identity be good? Will their family and friends accept them? Like our heroes being caught in the tractor beam, it can be an unnerving experience.

Once you are through with this tractor-beam experience, whether it was incredibly joyful or terribly painful, you realize that becoming a Christian was the best thing that could possibly happen. To have your sins washed away, to be able to stand in the presence of God and enjoy him forever is beyond words. For our heroes in the *Falcon,* they should've been scared. The Death Star is not exactly the Hilton. However, for the person caught in God's tractor beam, there is no better or safer place to be.

11

JESUS DIES FOR & PRESERVES GOD'S PEOPLE

○○○○○○○○○○●○○○○○○

Limited Atonement

Obi-Wan's Congregation

"You can't win, Darth. If you strike me down, I shall become more powerful than you can possibly imagine."

When I first heard Obi-Wan say these words, I didn't know what he meant, but man, did I think he was cool! It's not too different from when Jesus predicted his own resurrection, saying, "Destroy this temple, and I will raise it again in three days" (John 2:19). When Vader slashes Obi-Wan down, we, along with Luke, can't believe our eyes. That's not what was supposed to happen! Even if the odds are stacked against them, the good guys should always win. I'm sure Jesus' disciples wrestled with this as they stared up at Jesus on the cross. But similar to Jesus knowing more about the purpose of his crucifixion than his onlookers, Obi-Wan has a much larger plan than just winning a lightsaber duel. It's a plan of salvation not for himself but for his friends.

As we continue our study of God's pursuit of his people, this scene with Obi-Wan will help us understand the next doctrine of grace, "limited atonement," (the "L" in TULIP). Also called "particular redemption," limited atonement means that Jesus died only for a particular group of people, the ones described in the last chapter as being chosen unconditionally by God.

So, who does Obi-Wan have in mind when he lifts his civilized blue-bladed weapon for the last time, and who will receive the benefits from his sacrifice? Obi-Wan knows that if his friends wait for him, they may not escape. Not only that, they must escape with the plans to the Death Star or else the entire galaxy will be doomed. From a certain perspective, since the Rebels defeat the Empire in *Episode VI,* you could say Obi-Wan dies for the whole galaxy. But let's take a closer look. In *Star Wars,* what are the two things from which people need to be saved? One is from physical death. The other is from the tyrannical clutch of the Empire, which closes in like a Sith stranglehold, squeezing away people's freedom, dignity, and joy. Under the rule of the Empire, people have their life, but is it really theirs?

Obi-Wan has one particular group in mind when he raises his lightsaber. That group comprises Luke, Leia, Han, Chewie, Artoo, and Threepio. Not only does Obi-Wan save their lives, by doing so, he helps them to live free from the oppression of the Empire. Did Obi-Wan die for everyone? Yes and no. He does not die only for humans. He also dies for a Wookiee and for two droids. This is similar to Jesus dying for people from every tribe, nation, and tongue. Obi-Wan also dies for those who aren't Jedi. You could say that Obi-Wan, because of his lack of discrimination and the benefits his sacrifice has on the entire galaxy, gives himself up for all.

Obi-Wan's sacrifice, as wonderful as it is, does not help Jek Porkins, Biggs Darklighter, or the others from Red, Gold, Blue, and Green Squadrons who die just hours later at the Battle of Yavin. Obi-Wan's death does not help Dak Ralter, who was crushed by an AT-AT in *Episode V,* or Nanta the Ewok who was shot by an AT-ST in *Episode VI.* Through his sacrifice, Obi-Wan saves only his five immediate companions, the ones in the forefront of his mind when he surrenders his life.

🔭 Biggs Darklighter is Luke's best friend from Tatooine. Numerous scenes were filmed with him but were cut later. One scene includes Biggs telling Luke that he has joined the Rebellion.

Let's peel this back even further and ponder the second benefit that Luke and his friends receive because of Obi-Wan's death. While our heroes must continue to struggle and fight, ultimately, they regain their full freedom, truly a new life, free from the Empire. By doing so, they reap everything for which Obi-Wan died.

This is like the magnificent benefits we inherit because of Christ's death. When we trust Jesus to save us, we receive the work of the Holy Spirit, who sanctifies us during our life on Earth. He gives us a new life free from the slavery of sin. But we get so much more. The Holy Spirit is only our "down payment." Eventually, after we struggle and fight through our life in this fallen world, we get a permanent new life in heaven.

All the nations will be gathered before him, and he will separate the people one from another as a shepherd separates the sheep from the goats. He will put the sheep on his right and the goats on his left. (Matthew 25:32-33)

Statements like the above are scattered throughout the Bible, many times uttered by Jesus himself, where a division is made, a distinction is declared, separating people into two groups. Sometimes, these statements use metaphors. Other times, they are literal. But the basic idea is that one road leads to everlasting life with him, and the other road, the wider road, leads to destruction.

Jesus says, "I am the good shepherd. The good shepherd lays down his life for the sheep" (John 10:11). When Obi-Wan notices Luke and the others near the *Millennium Falcon*, he contemplates his dilemma. He knows that if he continues to fight Vader, he will jeopardize his friends' escape. He looks over to Luke, back to Vader and chooses to sacrifice himself for the good of his companions. His passive stance emphasizes the willingness of his death. In "Isaiah 53:7-like" manner, Obi-Wan lays down his life for a specific group of people, even a group that includes a scoundrel—a lost sheep.

Jesus Died for the Whole World, Right?

Christian brothers and sisters who fall into the Arminian camp disagree with limited atonement. They feel it diminishes the love of God if he died only for some. While most would say that not everyone will be saved, they will say the decision to be forgiven rests solely on the person to accept or deny Jesus. To their credit, those who emphasize man's free will use several Bible verses to prove their point. The most popular verses for their argument are the ones which mention the word "world" or "all." Let's examine one of the most quoted verses and see if it contradicts a limited atonement.

1 John 2:2 says, "He is the atoning sacrifice for our sins, and not only for ours but also for the sins of the whole world." So, the key is to find out how the word *world* is used. Does it mean everyone on Earth or does it mean something different? This is where a proper understanding of what God was doing in the Old Covenant era plays an important role in our analysis.

During the Old Covenant era, God focused his love on one people, one nation, the Israelites. That changed when Jesus ushered in the New Covenant. "And they sang a new song, saying: 'You are worthy to take the scroll and to open its seals, because you were slain, and with your blood you purchased for God persons from every tribe and language and people and nation'" (Revelation 5:9).

This verse illustrates how God expanded his love to include Gentiles. God did not purchase every tribe and nation but rather *persons* from every tribe and nation. Therefore, "world" in the context of 1 John 2:2 does not mean every single man and woman on Earth. Rather, it means people from places other than just Israel. In the context of God's love, he is no longer focused solely on Israel. He has changed the shadow (or hologram) of the priest, the sacrifices, and the forgiven group of people spoken of in Hebrews into their true fulfillment.

When Obi-Wan tells Luke, "You have taken your first step into a larger world," this statement could be interpreted (out of context) as Luke leaving his old physical world of Tatooine and stepping into the larger unknown galaxy. But that is not what Obi-Wan means. Luke has just felt the Force for the first time. Given the larger framework, Obi-Wan means Luke has stepped into the larger world of controlling the Force.

When Padmé tells Anakin, "We live in a real *world*. Come back to it." What does Padmé mean? Does she mean that Anakin is trapped in the Matrix like Neo and needs to escape his artificial reality? Or does she mean that Anakin is living under the delusion that a romantic life with each other is possible?

Just like you and I talk, people (unless they are writing something obviously meant for interpretation like poetry) try to convey a specific idea when they use language. The men that God used to write the Bible are no different. John did not write his letter to be interpreted however the hearer wanted. Instead, when he used the word *world,* it was meant to be understood in the context of the rest of Scripture.

Representation

In Romans 5, Paul describes how God used a system of representation to both condemn man and save his elect. Adam represented every human being in the Garden when he sinned. On the other hand, Jesus represented on the cross only those who trust in him. In Genesis 3, Adam rebelled against God. From that point on, everyone inherits his bad standing before God. "Consequently, just as the result of one trespass was condemnation for all men, so also the result of one act of righteousness was justification that brings life for all men" (Romans 5:18).

When God judges any unbeliever, there is a two-fold condemnation. He accounts for Adam's sin as well as the unbeliever's own unscrupulous behavior. On the flip side, Christ represents all believers. Meaning, God views the believer (even though he sins) and sees only the righteousness of Jesus, who paid the ransom.

The Ewoks do not like outsiders. They prove this when they take Luke, Han, Chewie, and Artoo prisoner. In *Episode VI,* the Ewoks light a fire under them, and it is only a matter of time until they will be cooked. Fortunately, the Ewoks think Threepio is a god. Because of his "divine influence," and Luke causing him to levitate, the Ewoks let our heroes go.

Luke and the others need a representative, someone who will go to bat for them and save them from the Ewoks. Threepio does this for a select group of individuals. Even though the group is made up of humans, a Wookiee, and a droid, Threepio does not represent *all* humans, Wookiees, and droids. This is proven when the Empire attacks. The Ewoks fight and kill many stormtroopers in the battle. Threepio provides salvation for his friends only.

When "All" is Not All

Note that the previous verse from Romans uses the word *all*. This trips people up sometimes, because Paul says that Jesus represented all men in Romans 5:18. Still, we must not assume anything but let Scripture interpret itself. Paul figures his audience understands what it means to be accepted by God, and we can go to another of his letters to find out to whom this "all" refers. "For as in Adam all die, so in Christ all will be made alive. But each in his own turn: Christ the firstfruits, then when he comes *those who belong to him*" (1 Corinthians 15:22–23, emphasis mine).

It's helpful to remember how we use the word *all*. We don't usually use it to refer to everybody on the planet. In *Episode V,* Leia says, "Vader wants us all dead!" No one would argue that the Princess means he wants everyone in the universe dead, including the Emperor, his stormtrooper legions, and the rest of the underlings who show the fear and respect he craves. Instead, it's obvious that she means all the Rebels. This is the way to understand communication in everyday life as well as in the Bible, not by scrutinizing every possible meaning of a word but by knowing and applying the context. The verses in 1 Corinthians 15 make clear that punishment applies to everyone whom Adam represented, and forgiveness applies to everyone whom Jesus represented.

There are times when "all" in Scripture means all types of people. "For the grace of God has appeared that *offers* salvation to all people" (Titus 2:11, emphasis mine). Everybody needs the gospel preached to them, and so God makes no distinction in who hears the good news of Christ. A king needs the gospel just as much as a homeless person. The rich need Christ just as much as the poor. Americans need to have their sins forgiven just as much as those living in Borneo. These examples could go on to comprise everyone. But what is being given to all of these people? Not salvation itself but only the *offer* of salvation.

Other words that need to be qualified include *everyone, everybody, nobody,* and *no one.* Consider Matthew 24:36: "But about that day or hour no one knows, not even the angels in heaven, nor the Son." After a cursory glance, it seems that *no one,* not even Jesus knows. But if we include more of the context, the verse goes on to qualify itself, "but only the Father."

In *Episode I,* Anakin says, "Mom, you said the biggest problem in this universe is *nobody* helps each other." Does Shmi actually mean nobody without exception, that no one (not even Anakin) has ever helped her with anything during her entire life? While that statement could be taken literally, *no one* (and I really mean no one) ever does.

As you come across Bible verses that seem to support an unlimited atonement, ask yourself, "Is the use of the word *world* simply referring to all the nations?" Given the context of the verse, does the "all" refer to all of the elect? Is the "all" referring to just all kinds of people? We haven't enough time in this book to address every single verse that supports limited atonement and the ones that appear not to. Your homework is to dig into Scripture and figure out more of this on your own. Learning what you have about total depravity and unconditional election, did Jesus make it merely possible for everyone to trust in him, or did he guarantee the salvation of all those whom his Father chose to save?

Summary

To summarize the doctrines of grace up to this point, our salvation is the powerful and unstoppable work of God. "Total depravity" means that sin so affects the unbeliever's heart that he is incapable of desiring the holy God of the Bible. "Unconditional election" means that God chose by name the people to whom he would show mercy, and his choice is not based on anything good or bad that people do. "Irresistible grace" is the all-encompassing work of the Holy Spirit that God uses to bring sinners to himself. "Limited atonement" means that Jesus' death on the cross does not give the possibility of salvation to everyone but rather the guarantee of salvation to everyone God chooses to save. Since our hard, rebellious hearts had to be changed supernaturally to be receptive to the gospel, we cannot take credit for our salvation; it is the work of God.

Perseverance of the Saints

The Holy Spirit Will Be With You Always

Why is it so important that Obi-Wan tack on the little word "always" to the already powerful statement, "The Force will be with you"? For the first two movies of the original trilogy, Luke is only a Padawan learner. At the beginning, he does not even know what the Force is, much less all the ins and outs of how it functions or how it benefits its devotees. As he learns that it can be a powerful ally, he begins to trust it and eventually depend on it. If the Force were not with him in the ice cave (when his lightsaber is out of reach), he would have been dinner for the wampa. If the Force had not been with Luke when Jabba tried to execute him, he would have been lunch for the Sarlacc. Again and again, Luke proves that Obi-Wan's statement is true. By the last act of *Episode V,* Luke goes into every duel, battle, or other challenge trusting that the Force will be with him.

This brings us to the last doctrine of grace called "perseverance of the saints," also referred to as "preservation of the saints," or "eternal security." This is the "P" in the acrostic "TULIP." This doctrine teaches that God guarantees our salvation and causes us to love Jesus forever. We can think of it as, "the Holy Spirit will be with us always." This principle serves as a bookend to our faith and a testimony to God's faithful and successful pursuit and rescue of his chosen people.

Many Bible passages describe this encouraging truth of God. Let's start off with Philippians 1:6, where Paul states that, "being confident of this, that he who began a good work in you will carry it on to completion until the day of Christ Jesus." This means that when God begins the work of our salvation by choosing us, dying for us, drawing us, and justifying us, he will complete our salvation by glorifying us, which is, giving us eternal life in heaven. The "golden chain of salvation" found in Romans 8:29–30 states this truth in similar words:

> For those God foreknew he also predestined to be conformed to the image of his Son, that he might be the firstborn among many brothers and sisters. And those he predestined, he also called; those he called, he also justified; those he justified, he also glorified.

Luke's Tight Grip

A lightsaber is so valuable to a Jedi that Obi-Wan tells Anakin in *Episode II*, "This weapon is your life." This certainly holds true when Luke uses his lightsaber to defend against the wampa. In fact, in most scenes when Luke uses the Force to attract his lightsaber, he does not lose it or let go of it again but rather keeps an extra tight grip on it. That's how it is once God has a spiritual grip on us. He knows how valuable we are, not because of anything intrinsically good in us but because we were bought with the blood of his Son.

🎥 Some of the real world components of Obi-Wan's *Episode IV* lightsaber include an Armitage Shanks Starlite handwheel, a Browning ANM2 machine-gun booster, and a Rolls Royce Derwent Mk8/Mk9 jet-engine balance pipe.

When Vader severs Luke's hand, Luke loses his lightsaber lifeline. This, of course, is not Luke's doing and something he does everything in his power to prevent. Unlike the case with Luke and his lightsaber, nothing and no one can ever loosen the embrace God has on us. "I give them eternal life, and they shall never perish; no one will snatch them out of my hand" (John 10:28).

As believers, we are criticized often for our faith. This may lead to family members or friends cutting ties with us. Around the world, some governments stop at nothing to try to force believers to renounce their Christian faith. The thing all these opponents of Christ do not understand is that God will not let his children be plucked from his hand.

> For I am convinced that neither death nor life, neither angels nor demons, neither the present nor the future, nor any powers, neither height nor depth, nor anything else in all creation, will be

able to separate us from the love of God that is in Christ Jesus our Lord. (Romans 8:38-39)

Not even Satan can cause us to lose our salvation. Once we have trusted in Jesus Christ alone through faith alone, once we have repented of sin in our lives, God declares us righteous forever. We are sealed with the Holy Spirit! The devil and his demons will try their hardest to peel back God's fingers, but they will never succeed. Remember Princess Leia's cool retort to Governor Tarkin? "The more you tighten your grip Tarkin, the more star systems will slip through your fingers." There's no danger of that with God. No matter how hard your situation in life, how bleak your future seems, or how much your love for God wavers, God will hold on to you. If you are in Christ, God's unconditional love grips you so tightly that nothing can cause you to slip through his fingers.

As a side note, the previous metaphor is another use of anthropomorphism. This literary technique is used to ascribe human characteristics to God. The purpose is to convey an idea that we can understand. God does not literally have his hand around us, but he does in the sense that we are his. He cares for us, and because of the powerful work he does in the life of every believer, he will not allow any of his children to fall away. Referring to Luke, Yoda asks, "Will he finish what he begins?" We might be tempted to ask the same question of God. But we can be confident that God will finish what he begins, which is nothing short of our complete and eternal salvation!

God's Restraining Bolt

R2-D2 is able to run away from Luke, because Luke removes Artoo's restraining bolt. Restraining bolts are not just to keep droids in a certain location. The small device actually overrides the droid's internal will so that they obey. Without the restraining bolt, Artoo does what he wants, which is to leave his master's presence.

The restraining bolt God attaches to us is on the *inside,* deep within our heart, free from the possibility of removal. God's restraining bolt doesn't override our will; it transforms our will to one that seeks to please him. This causes believers to be motivated internally (not externally) to persevere. The result is that we stay with our Master even when outside pressures are great.

Some religious folks only profess Jesus. They say they worship Christ, but they do not have a genuinely changed heart. They are motivated to persevere by things other than the Holy Spirit. In their case, the most they have to keep them on the right path is an external restraining bolt in the form of societal constraints, family pressure, or pride. This sort of external restraining bolt can be knocked off easily by life's worries, riches, and pleasures (the stuff Jesus warns about in the "Parable of the Sower" in Luke 8). When the Tusken Raider causes C-3PO to fall backward, not only does the droid lose his arm, he loses his restraining bolt. Presumably, it is broken off when he hits the ground. The Israelites had a restraining bolt in the form of the Mosaic Law, with all its rules and regulations, attached on the outside, away from their heart. God took off their restraining bolt because of their wickedness and rebellion. He will never do that to Christians under the New Covenant. Believers will persevere because of the work God does in our hearts.

In *Episode VI,* the Rebels must deactivate the Death Star II's shield generator. If they can neutralize the shield around the giant space station, the Rebel fighters can fly into the super structure and destroy the main reactor, thus causing a reaction that will blow up the galactic superweapon. For the Empire, that shield generator protects their very existence, especially considering their leader is on board the space station.

🔭 Wedge Antilles is the only Rebel pilot to survive the Battle of Yavin, the Battle of Hoth, and the Battle of Endor.

If you are in Christ, God has destroyed your old heart and given you a new one that is capable of loving him and others in a biblical way. Since this world has all sorts of temptations and distractions that could try to lure you away, God, in his wisdom and mercy, has put an impenetrable shield around your heart. Like Luke says of Imperial walkers, "their armor is too strong for blasters," the Holy Spirit's shield is too steadfast for anything to extinguish your love for Jesus. Unlike the Rebels destroying the power source of the

Death Star II's shield, God will never let anything lower his shield. Sure. Your heart will come under attack, and from your perspective, the shield may weaken, but this happens only so that your faith can be strengthened. When you see what kind of pounding God's shield can take, yet you still come out on the other side serving God, your faith and love for him will grow even stronger.

Trials and Discipline

We have learned that our salvation, from the beginning, was not really our idea; it was God's. He pursued us and rescued us and continues to strengthen, protect, and preserve us so that we will continue to love Jesus forever.

From our point of view, serving God day in and day out, is not always an easy endeavor. All the diversions of life can make our perseverance seem downright impossible. Fortunately, God will never let us veer too far off course. Consider when Han and the others in the *Millennium Falcon* are approaching Cloud City. Two twin-pod cloud cars fire upon them and warn them not to deviate from their present course. Sometimes, God places trials in our lives or disciplines us to make sure we don't deviate from our present course of living for him.

Trials do not give us the luxury of relaxing spiritually. It's the painful times in life when we are at the end of our rope that we fall to our knees and rely on our Father. God designed trials and his discipline to be like blaster fire that singes us just enough so that we don't stay on a path that does not have God as our focus. This is why James says the following:

> Consider it pure joy, my brothers and sisters, whenever you face trials of many kinds, because you know that the testing of your faith produces perseverance. Let perseverance finish its work so that you may be mature and complete, not lacking anything. (James 1:2-4)

Hebrews 12 describes how God disciplines his children. An essential part of our walk with Christ is to understand that everything that happens to us (good or bad) is motivated by God's love. His discipline can be thought of as "tough love." Parents know all about this. When moms and dads discipline their kids this way, the process is miserable from the children's perspective. Be that as it may, not disciplining their kids shows a lack of love. Children need to be taught what is allowed and what is not. In the same way, God disciplines us through hardship so that we might mature and share in his holiness.

The Lord's discipline is essential for our spiritual growth and part of how God causes us to persevere in our faith. "No discipline seems pleasant at the time, but painful. Later on, however, it produces a harvest of righteousness and peace for those who have been trained by it" (Hebrews 12:11). On Dagobah, Yoda employs physical exercises to train Luke in the use of the Force. The training exhausts Luke and even causes some bumps and bruises, such as when Artoo distracts Luke, causing him to lose concentration and fall to the ground. Still, Luke must learn to use the Force in the midst of the distractions, trials, and temptations of life. God's loving discipline, while not pleasurable at times, helps shape our character to resemble that of Jesus.

When Luke cannot get the vision of Han and Leia in pain out of his mind, he leaves his new Master and flees into the unknown to help them. Yoda and Obi-Wan could have easily prevented Luke from leaving. Luke would have been no match for their power. Yoda could have ripped Luke's X-wing apart, removing his only way to leave. But, in their wisdom, neither of the Jedi did this. Instead, they let Luke go, even though they realize he could suffer greatly or possibly die. They know that if Luke is going to mature and learn patience, he must persevere through some difficult situations. This is partly why Obi-Wan refuses to help Luke confront Vader.

In the same way, it's part of God's plan for our lives to be rocky at times. Sometimes, God has you walk through the Jundland Wastes of life in order to get you where he wants you spiritually. This does not mean he has given up on you. The Lord disciplines you and brings trials your way to help you grow in Christ. Unlike Obi-Wan with Luke, God will never leave or refuse to help. He is committed to helping us increase in holiness, and he orchestrates the entire universe so that we will persevere. As believers, even though we will die (the ultimate ordeal), God will preserve our spirits and bring us home to be with him forever.

Final Thoughts

God has always been in the business of choosing people to receive his extraordinary grace, affection, and blessings. For instance, in the Old Testament, God saved only Noah and his family and destroyed the rest of mankind. God chose and blessed Abraham but did not do this for all of Abraham's physical descendants. God set his special love upon the nation of Israel, but he did not lavish it on the other 99.8% of the world. Redemption of only certain individuals in the New Covenant era shouldn't shock us as God doing something radically out of character. Focusing his grace on a separate group of people is what he has always done.

For those who live in the New Covenant era, salvation includes full forgiveness of sin, because Jesus died for us by name. The Holy Spirit regenerated our hard hearts and gave us the desire and faith to seek out the God who rescued us. The only shock here is that God shows everyone incredible kindness even though the majority are spiteful or indifferent toward Him. Every plate of food, every air conditioner in the summer, every tear-free day, and millions of other gifts are examples of God's remarkable common grace to the general population.

Arminianism posits that in some way Jesus died for everybody in the world, thereby making salvation possible for everyone. It leaves the ultimate decision completely in the hands of the individual person to accept Jesus as Savior. The problem is that it is impossible to reconcile this view with much of what the Bible says.

There are good reasons why the doctrines of grace are described as "gracious." We use the term *grace,* because we didn't deserve to be rescued. God gives us grace, not justice. If God ever gave us what we deserve, we would be punished. But he does not punish us. Instead, he punished his Son in our place. This is all part of God's rescue plan for his people, and it is guaranteed to succeed. Jesus' death on the cross pays for the sin of all those whom the Father gave Jesus to save. If we can approach what the Bible says about God's sovereignty in our salvation with humility, our relationship with him will improve as we become less in our own eyes and he becomes greater.

While learning about the doctrines of grace is important, God loves us because of Christ's work on the cross, not how much theology we know. Christians who believe Jesus died for everyone or that God's grace is resistible can still love God just as much as their Calvinist brothers and sisters do.

Believing or not believing in the doctrines of grace is, by no means, central to the gospel or your salvation, but it matters very much. How you view yourself and others in relation to God's holiness and sovereignty will affect a great number of areas including assurance, evangelism, and the fight against sin. The next part in your journey will be learning how your efforts fit into God's larger plan.

12

OUR RESPONSIBILITY

○○○○○○○○○○○○●○○○○○

Luke: "I Don't Believe It."
Yoda: "That is Why You Fail."

We've spent a lot of time discussing God's grace and how he controls everything, right down to our salvation. The next logical questions are: Why pray? Why share the gospel? Why obey or strive for righteousness when God already accepts us? These are good questions. So, to avoid concluding this book by giving you a laissez-faire attitude toward your walk with God or sending you off the other side of legalism, let's examine our responsibility in the midst of God's grace and sovereignty.

The first thing to realize is that certain biblical truths seem paradoxical. For instance, how can God be three separate persons of Father, Son, and Holy Spirit yet be one God? How can Jesus be fully God and also fully man? How can God control all things but not be blamed for evil? These are not contradictions but rather complex principles that our finite minds are simply unable to grasp. Just as Luke must reconcile the idea that the Force mysteriously controls his actions yet also obeys his commands, we must wrestle with how our duty fits into what Jesus has already done for us.

In terms of salvation, God chose who will be in Christ, but from our perspective, we must still choose him. For us to be saved, God requires us to believe.

If you declare with your mouth, 'Jesus is Lord,' and believe in your heart that God raised him from the dead, you will be saved. For it is with your heart that you believe and are justified, and it is with your mouth that you profess your faith and are saved. (Romans 10:9–10)

We should consider trusting in Jesus for salvation our utmost responsibility. Everything else hinges on it.

After all this talk about God's sovereignty, you might think that our responsibility is to just wait around until God zaps us into believing in Jesus. On the contrary, we should strive with all our might to believe! You may be on the fence with your own belief. Are you similar to Luke after Yoda raises the X-wing out of the swamp? Do you struggle to believe that Jesus is who he claims? If something is holding you back from believing, ask God for the gift of faith. Ask Christians to pray that God would give you the eyes to see. If you find it difficult buying in to a particular biblical concept, then read, study, and ask mature believers to explain it.

By all means, take the necessary steps to believe, and don't put off making the choice to live for Christ. As Joshua said to the tribes of Israel, "Choose for yourselves this day whom you will serve" (Joshua 24:15). Luke did not stop at his unbelief. He kept pursuing. He kept training. He kept learning about the Force until the time when he did believe. Nobody knows when or how God works, and that's okay. We only need to be faithful to do our part, which begins with believing the gospel.

When Obi-Wan suggests that Luke leave Tatooine, learn about the Force, and rescue Princess Leia, Luke wants nothing to do with it. Obi-Wan's reaction is to trust the Force and let Luke come to his own decision. He does not belabor all the good reasons through argument or demand that Luke do anything. He understands Luke's destiny will be realized. On the other side of the coin, Obi-Wan knows that, eventually, Luke must make the choice to leave his old life and learn the ways of the Force.

🪐 Travelers to Matmata, Tunisia can stay at the Hotel Sidi Driss. This is the actual location where they filmed the Lars' homestead on Tatooine.

Even though God predestined every believer long ago, we are still responsible to confess our guilt, trust in Jesus, repent of sin, and follow Christ as Lord for the rest of our lives. But before we start patting ourselves on the back, even if we wrestle and sweat for years to believe the gospel, God still gets all the credit for saving us. Knowing this helps us from becoming prideful. Paul knew God's sovereignty backwards and forwards. Nevertheless, he still called for all people to repent and believe.

"What is Thy Bidding, My Master?"

Once a sinner makes the sincere decision to follow Jesus as Lord, God declares that person forever innocent. But, the Christian life is not just praying a single prayer and living however we want for the rest of our lives. Quite the reverse. We say goodbye to our old master, the devil, and welcome Jesus as our new Master. Early in *Episode IV*, Threepio tells his counterpart, "Behave yourself, Artoo. You're going to get us in trouble. It's all right, you can trust him. He's our new master." We should behave ourselves in the sense that we need to obey God. Unlike Threepio's warning, we needn't fear getting into trouble with God. While God may discipline us (Hebrews 12), he does so as a loving Father with our good as his ultimate goal. Like the droids with Luke, it is all right for us, we can trust our Master.

New believers usually don't know how to live the Christian life at first. I sure didn't, and I spent years floundering spiritually. New believers know their sins are forgiven, but oftentimes they don't know what should happen next. We are going to look to an unlikely candidate to get a better handle on this topic.

When Darth Vader asks the Emperor the ominous question, "What is thy bidding, my Master?" he actually sets a great example for us. Creepy as this may sound coming from Vader, we should admire his humility, loyalty, and enthusiasm when it comes to serving his Emperor. Few creatures in the *Star Wars* universe are more power-hungry than Vader, and yet he knows his rightful place before his Master. He is willing to submit to the Emperor and ask how he may serve him. This is the attitude we should take before

Jesus. But this brings us back to the following question: How do we serve Jesus the right way?

We should obey God, because this is how we prove we love him. The New Testament is replete with God's commands for us. The Bible also tells us that we show our love for God through actions, not merely words. Our love for God is manifested in the good deeds we do even though these works do not save us. Earlier in this book, we studied the different covenants God made throughout history, noting that Christians have been under the New Covenant ever since Christ's death and resurrection. "For when the priesthood is changed" (which there was when Jesus became our high priest before God), "the law must be changed also" (Hebrews 7:12). Knowing how the law has changed will keep us from spinning our wheels spiritually by obeying or trying to obey laws that God did not intend for us to follow.

Which Laws to Keep?

The Jedi have tenets they are supposed to follow. They are to serve others, avoid emotional attachments, and not seek revenge. A faithful Jedi thinks about these laws and corrects himself when he falls short. Anakin fails to live up to the Jedi's high standard when he forgoes the Jedi tenets for his own reasoning. If we don't know the Bible very well, we can fall into the same trap.

Sometimes, we make it a lot harder to follow God's laws, because we fail to learn which ones still apply to us. In short, as we touched on in Chapter 9, Christians should follow what Paul calls Christ's law. This phrase "Christ's law" or "law of Christ" is mentioned only a couple of times in the Bible, but Paul distinguishes it from the Mosaic Law. The law of Christ is comprised of the commands found in the teaching passages of the New Testament, excluding much from the Gospels and Acts. Why not include those? The Gospels chronicle a special time when Jesus ushered in the New Covenant era while still living under the Old. In addition, Jesus directed specific individuals with commands intended only for them. Consider Luke 18:22, when Jesus tells the rich ruler to sell all his possessions and give his money to the poor. That doesn't mean a Christian who doesn't give all his money to the poor is sinning.

In the fuller revelation of the letters to the churches, we are commanded simply to "give generously" (Romans 12:8). Our primary marching order for giving is not donating all our possessions but rather, as 2 Corinthians 9:7 says, "Each of you should give what you have decided in your heart to give, not reluctantly or under compulsion, for God loves a cheerful giver."

Other times, Jesus spoke in parables only to make a point to his specific audience. Jesus said the following when having a meal at a Pharisee's house:

> Then Jesus said to his host, "When you give a luncheon or dinner, do not invite your friends, your brothers or sisters, your relatives, or your rich neighbors; if you do, they may invite you back and so you will be repaid. But when you give a banquet, invite the poor, the crippled, the lame, the blind." (Luke 14:12-13)

Jesus needed to say this, because his host only intended to be hospitable in order to gain something for himself. This was not intended to be a blanket rule for everyone. Someone who invites his relatives over for dinner does not sin. We know this, because when we go to the teaching passages of the New Testament, we read these words of Paul, "Anyone who does not provide for their relatives, and especially for their own household, has denied the faith and is worse than an unbeliever (1 Timothy 5:8). See how quickly we can confuse our lives by adding rules or misunderstanding laws that God not intend for us to follow?

When Luke offers to take Obi-Wan to Anchorhead, Obi-Wan responds, "You must do what you feel is right, of course." Too many of us use our feelings as a guide to our behavior. If we feel we should do something, we do it. If we feel we shouldn't, we don't. This is not a good strategy for the Christian life. God commands all sorts of things that I might not *feel* like doing. I rarely feel like taking care of a sick child at 3:30 a.m. I might not feel like doing yard work under the hot sun to help someone at church, and I seldom enjoy apologizing to my wife for sinning against her. All of that doesn't matter. What matters is that God's Word commands me to love. There is also a host of things that I might feel like doing, but the Bible tells me to refrain from them. For the believer, we need to rephrase Obi-Wan's statement to, "You must do what God's Word says, of course. Feelings are inconsequential."

🔭 Anchorhead is an old settlement about fifty miles from Mos Eisley. It is close to both Beggar's Canyon and Tosche Station.

Apostolic example is not legally binding for the believer either. For instance, just because the apostles cast lots to help determine who should take Judas' place does not mean we should take a similar action when making decisions. The book of Acts is a historical book. It's like watching *The Making of Star Wars.* If you watch this *Star Wars* documentary, you'll see snippets of the movie and the behind-the-scenes work, but you will not get the full account of either. To try to fill in the gaps would be an exercise in guesswork and lead inevitably to a host of wrong beliefs. The same applies to Acts. God gave all sorts of unusual experiences to specific believers. Unless we are commanded in the rest of the New Testament to do a similar action, we should assume we are not supposed to reproduce the experiences. In the case of casting lots, we are never commanded to do this.

During the Sermon on the Mount, Jesus raises the Old Covenant laws to a heart level like never before. There are laws in the New Covenant that were also laws under the Old Covenant, such as the law against adultery. But under the New Covenant, Jesus teaches that even a lustful thought is adultery. It was nothing new to be told not to murder. But now Jesus says even having a feeling of ill will toward another is sin. Jesus prepares us to view law in a completely different way. It's also why Paul says: "For the entire law is fulfilled in keeping this one command: 'Love your neighbor as yourself'" (Galatians 5:14).

As believers, we actually have a lot of freedom with respect to law. Unlike if we were under the Mosaic Law, we are allowed to get a tattoo of Yoda. We are allowed to wear a cotton-polyester blended shirt of Boba Fett. And we're allowed to eat barbeque pork during *Star Wars* marathons. We can gather together with other believers to worship God on any day; we are not necessarily bound to any sort of special day like the Sabbath. We are told to "give generously" instead of an exact ten percent tithe. The list goes on to touch many areas of the Christian life. Unfortunately, too much freedom can get us into trouble.

Both Paul and Peter warn us to not take advantage of our liberties in order to sin. Even though we are not under the Mosaic Law and are free to do things that the Jews were not, we are not living in anarchy. We are under Christ's law. Remember, 1 John 5:3 tells us we love God by keeping his commandments. Since we are not under the Old Covenant, then we show our love for God by obeying the commands given for the New Covenant era. And these commands are not burdensome, because following those flows out of a love for God. Believers will not take advantage of God's grace so as to sin without intention of repentance (Romans 6:1–2).

During these times, we fall back under the assumption that God will just forgive us. If it gets too hard to try to figure out what to do, we stop trying. Oftentimes, this problem stems from the fact that many of us want the Christian life to be a formula that allows us to just plug in what we are told to do. We think if we read the Bible, pray to God, and go to church, then that should equal a successful walk with God. But it's so much more than that. When Yoda explains the dark side to Luke on Dagobah, Luke asks, "But tell me why I can't—" Yoda interrupts him and refuses to give him any more answers. Luke is looking for a formula. He wants a neat little compartment into which to fit his new faith. Yoda realizes it's not that simple. Likewise, we must still figure out how best to serve, obey, and honor God in each and every situation, even when life gets complicated and even though the Bible might not address our circumstances exactly.

"Don't Look Back"

God's command to Abram, "Go from your country" is something Anakin and Luke are also called to do. Both are called to leave Tatooine, leave family, leave friends, and leave familiar surroundings. In essence, they are called to leave home in order to go to a different place that is unfamiliar, possibly unsafe, and potentially overall worse than their home. Anakin and Luke must step out in faith to follow Qui-Gon's and Obi-Wan's appeal to leave their old lives behind.

When we commit our lives to serving Jesus as King, God calls us to leave our "country" behind—not a physical land but a place where we had set up ourselves as king. God's Word teaches that Christians have no business dabbling in the sin of their old life. There are warnings for the person who wants to straddle the fence saying that he serves Christ but is unwilling to repent of sin. Anakin's mother knows the danger of trying to forge a new life while trying to keep a tight hold on the old. She tells Anakin, "Now be brave, and don't look back." This warning is practically verbatim from Genesis 19:17, when the angels commanded Lot and his family to flee from Sodom and Gomorrah and to not look back. But Lot's wife did look back and suffered for her disobedience (Genesis 19:26).

Jesus speaks in no uncertain terms about what he demands of us. We are to be completely devoted to him. He knows the risks of trying to serve both God and the world. In Luke 9, people give reasons why they need to delay following Jesus. Everyone wants to do something related to their old life. Jesus gives a caution similar to Shmi's when he said, "No one who puts a hand to the plow and looks back is fit for service in the kingdom of God" (Luke 9:62).

Slaves to Righteousness

The word "slave" has a bad connotation for most people. We think of the atrocities that have been committed by evil men against the oppressed throughout history. So, when the Bible calls us "slaves," we may bristle. Our pride may take a hit the way Anakin's does when Padmé says, "You're a slave?"

"I am a person!" he responds angrily. As naïve as Anakin is supposed to be in *Episode I,* he already knows what it means to be a slave. To be a slave means you are not your own. Someone else owns you, controls you, and dictates much of your life. Anakin's defiant statement tells Padmé that even though Watto technically owns him, Anakin will call the shots in his life.

Paul reminds the church in Corinth that, "You are not your own; you were bought at a price" (1 Corinthians 6:19b–20a). He uses this same master/slave language in Romans 6 when he describes sin's control.

> For sin shall no longer be your master, because you are not under the law, but under grace. What then? Shall we sin because we are not under the law but under grace? By no means! Don't you know that when you offer yourselves to someone as obedient slaves, you are slaves of the one you obey—whether you are slaves to sin, which leads to death, or to obedience, which leads to righteousness? But thanks be to God that, though you used to be slaves to sin, you have come to obey from your heart the pattern of teaching that has now claimed your allegiance. You have been set free from sin and have become slaves to righteousness. (Romans 6:14-18)

Jesus doesn't just free you from the oppression of Satan and then let you live however you want. Instead, Jesus becomes your new Master. Unlike the heavy yoke that was on you before Christ, the yoke God gives you is easy and the burden is light. Paul never implies that the Christian life is stress-free. But if you are in Christ, your new heart causes a desire to live for your new Master. Living morally is not the crushing weight that it once was when sin was your master.

In the passage above, Paul also addresses those who, like Anakin, still want to call the shots. Anakin grows up as a renegade even within the Jedi Order. When Padmé asks Anakin to talk with the Chancellor, he lashes out, "I'm not your errand boy. I'm not anyone's errand boy!" Anakin hates to be told what to do. Sometimes, we don't like to be told what to do either. But we forget that when God redeemed us, he bought us. Not only does he own us, because he created us, he also owns us, because Christ purchased our lives through his death. Romans 6 addresses the fact that we will be slaves to someone. We will either be slaves to the devil or slaves to God. Yes, God is gracious, but Paul states emphatically that *by no means* should we ever sin with the mindset that God will forgive us.

✦ The "Great Schisms" were times when Jedi broke away from the Jedi Order. The "Fallen Jedi," a.k.a. "Dark Jedi," devoted themselves to the dark side of the Force.

For years, I thought I became a Christian when I was nineteen years old. I say "thought," because looking back on it now, I'm not so sure. I remember getting down on my knees in my room and praying the "sinner's prayer." I didn't want to go to hell and was convinced that Jesus was the only way. I prayed the prayer, thought I was saved, and started reading a devotional every night before going to bed. Except, nothing major in my life changed. I was in college and continued to party. I was doing all sorts of things that God's Word says not to do. I was also neglecting the things that he commands us to do. I was still my own master.

Fast-forward about two years. I was dating an unbeliever and still living a sinful lifestyle, but something different started to happen inside me. For the first time, I felt convicted over my sin and began repenting. I stopped getting drunk, ended things with my girlfriend, and sought out believers with whom I could meet. In retrospect, I didn't become a Christian when I was nineteen, because, like Anakin, I still wanted to call the shots. Perhaps God was beginning to draw me around that time. Nevertheless, the Bible is clear that lordship is required for salvation. If you have not submitted to God as Master, then he is not your Savior.

A slave gaining his freedom is a motif found throughout *Star Wars*. Anakin is enslaved to Watto. Shmi is held prisoner to the Tusken Raiders. Vader is subjugated to the Emperor. Leia and Han are in bondage to Jabba. And most are shackled to the Empire.

This theme is also found throughout the Bible. One of the promises found in God's covenant with Abram was that God would rescue Abram's descendants (the Israelites) from their bondage in Egypt. God fulfilled this promise and freed his people through the supernatural parting of the Red Sea.

> Then the Lord said to him, "Know for certain that for four hundred years your descendants will be strangers in a country not their own and that they will be enslaved and mistreated there. But I will punish the nation they serve as slaves, and afterward they will come out with great possessions." (Genesis 15:13-14)

It's important for us to understand the themes of slavery in *Star Wars* and in Scripture, because without Christ, every man and woman is a slave to sin. Jesus said, "Very truly I tell you, everyone who sins is a slave to sin (John 8:34). God's pursuit of Abram and his descendants resulted in God freeing them from physical bondage, symbolic of Jesus freeing people spiritually. Paul's argument in Romans 6 is that either you are slave to your sin or you are a slave to righteousness. There is no way around the fact that we are creatures. As such, we are not our own. We must serve somebody. Paul says serving your sin leads to death, meaning hell. Serving Christ leads to eternal life.

It takes cooperation with and trust in the Force for Anakin to win the pod race that gains his freedom. Qui-Gon is able to help set Anakin free from his physical slavery but not from his spiritual bondage. Anakin is still a slave to his ambition, his pride, his jealousy, his anger, his fear, and a host of other sins. He also becomes a slave to the Emperor. He becomes his errand boy. Anakin wants so badly to be in control, to have power, but, as Princess Leia warns Governor Tarkin, the more Anakin tightens his grip, the more what he desires slips through his fingers.

Abram also tried to take matters into his own hands regarding the promise that God made to him about giving him children. Abram and his wife Sarai were getting too old to have kids. So, Abram slept with a slave woman, Hagar, in order to build a family. This action did not fulfill the plan that God ordained and only caused problems. In Galatians 4, Paul uses these events to set up a compelling illustration about how trying to earn God's favor by obeying rules (in this context, the Mosaic Law) locks a person out of his inheritance. We must be slaves to Christ, not to religion.

🕊 Jango Fett was sold into slavery after the Jedi turned him over to the Governor of Galidraan. Some fans speculate that this is why Jango's (and later Boba's) ship is named Slave I.

We are slaves to righteousness, but we are so much more. We are coheirs with Christ, children of God, and friends of Jesus. Jesus says, "No longer do I call you slaves, for the slave does not know what his master is doing; but I have called you friends, for all things that I have heard from my Father I have made known to you"

(John 15:15, NASB). Moreover, our Master is kind and gentle with us, not cruel and harsh like so many human slave masters.

C-3PO has many character flaws, but his submission to Luke is not one of them. He works hard for his master. He obeys Luke and submits to him in every way. Likewise, as a master, Luke is very kind to Threepio. He even risks his life, sticking around Sand People territory, so that he can find Threepio and carry him to safety. Luke and C-3PO remind us how important our attitude is when living out some of the other roles mentioned in Ephesians 5 and 6, such as parent and child or husband and wife. Threepio provides a great model to us, showing how we submit to our Master when we submit to those in authority over us. Paul includes another example when he states that if we don't submit to the civil authorities that God has placed over us, then we are not submitting to God (Romans 13:2).

The Evidence

"What good is it, my brothers and sisters, if someone claims to have faith but has no deeds? Can such faith save them?" (James 2:14). Why is bearing fruit so important? Why is it crucial that professing believers show evidence of a transformed life? Because the evidence, as James notes in his letter, is the proof that our sins are forgiven. If Jesus represented you on the cross, he did not just pay for your sin, he also purchased a changed life for you.

> Likewise, every good tree bears good fruit, but a bad tree bears bad fruit. A good tree cannot bear bad fruit, and a bad tree cannot bear good fruit. Every tree that does not bear good fruit is cut down and thrown into the fire. Thus, by their fruit you will recognize them. (Matthew 7:17-20)

In the "Parable of the Talents", the master says to his servant, "Well done, good and faithful servant!" This praise is not just an extra pat on the back that some Christians will receive and others will not. Every believer has his sins forgiven. Every believer has good deeds predestined by God. Every believer loves God. And every believer will have his or her life characterized by obeying God.

In fact, this is love for God: to keep his commands. And his commands are not burdensome, for everyone born of God overcomes the world. This is the victory that has overcome the world, even our faith. Who is it that overcomes the world? Only the one who believes that Jesus is the Son of God. (1 John 5:3-5)

Han and Leia's relationship, like a Christian marriage, serves as an allegory for Christ and the Church. During the middle of the original trilogy, Han is caring, patient, and committed to pursuing Leia despite the fact she gives back only coldness and insults ("stuck-up, half-witted, scruffy-looking nerfherder"). However, as *Episode V* progresses, Han wins Leia over with his devotion, and her hard heart softens.

🐾 A nerf is shaggy-haired, hoofed, four-horned animal indigenous to Alderaan. They were exported throughout the galaxy for their delicious meat (nerf steak, nerf sausage, and nerfburgers).

Moments before Han is frozen in carbonite, Leia says, "I love you," and Han's reply, "I know," became an instant classic. Han's "I know" helps us see the importance of our Bridegroom's confirmation of our love for him. Let's examine this exchange more closely.

Han already knows Leia loves him due to her new behavior. This is the same way that we want our Lord to respond to us. The first time I see Jesus in heaven, I hope it's not necessary for me to say, "I love you." Instead, I want him to say, "Because of your life, I know that you love me." As the author of 1 John 3:18 says, "Dear children, let us not love with words or tongue but with actions and in truth." This verse reminds me to not simply say I love God or my wife or friends or even my enemies but to show them love to the point where they have no doubt.

It is vital that Leia's love is genuine. "Not everyone who says to me, 'Lord, Lord' will enter the kingdom of heaven, but only he who does the will of my Father who is in heaven" (Matthew 7:21). Emotions were running high that day in Cloud City. Could it be that Leia was simply moved with pity for the "scruffy-looking nerfherder"? Absolutely not, and it demonstrates that this is not a princess' last-minute decision. In the same way, Jesus' words above are frightening but necessary to help us remember the importance of proving our sincere love rather than just saying we love him at the last moment.

Han confirms his own love for Leia by his past commitment. So, why doesn't Han tack on, "I love you, too"? In short, he doesn't have to. He has already shown Leia that he loves her by protecting and caring for her at every turn. I can ask the same sort of questions about God. Why do we love God? "We love because he first loved us" (1 John 4:19). I don't need God to do or say anything more. When he sent his only Son to die for my sin, he showed me a million times over that he loves me. That is all the assurance I need.

Han loves Leia even when she is not lovable. There is no love more beautiful than unconditional love. Just look at the opposite way the world loves. Worldly love is based completely on a what's-in-it-for-me attitude. So, when we see Han love Leia, putting his life in peril to save her time and time again, we should think of Christ and how he loved us, even though he knew we would never do anything to deserve it.

Even when Han is facing imminent death, he is still most concerned about Leia. He stops Chewie from trying to rescue him and tells him to take care of Leia. This is the stuff of which real heroes are made, and it's what Jesus demonstrated on the day he was crucified. "Jesus said 'Father, forgive them, for they do not know what they are doing'" (Luke 23:34). Jesus takes a gigantic step further than Han Solo and is actually concerned about the welfare of people who are mocking him and approving of his excruciating death. We are also called to be others-centered even if we're in the midst of a terrible trial.

Final Thoughts

This chapter addressed what we are obligated to do as Christians. In a universe where God is sovereign, this isn't always easy to sort through. Even though God controls all things, we are still held accountable to do certain things. God is gracious, but we are commanded to repent of sin. God plans all things in eternity past but says that our prayers can affect outcomes. He tells us to share the gospel with all unbelievers, even though only his elect will come to faith. God saved us not because of our merit, yet we are commanded to follow Jesus as Lord.

This seems contradictory, but our Father wants us to live in and trust him through this tension. As we go through our daily lives trying our best to live in a way that pleases God, we can rest in the fact that he is already and forever will be pleased with us. He loves us unconditionally because of Jesus' work on the cross. As you mature in Christ, you will actually see more of your sin, not less. This is normal and means that the Holy Spirit is sensitizing you to your sin. Don't be discouraged but know that God is refining you. As time goes on, your character will continue to resemble that of Jesus' even if you don't feel like it. Keep pressing on. Fight the good fight. You will make it. God has guaranteed it!

PART IV

THE HOLY SPIRIT

Similar to the Jedi having the Force to help them in their spiritual journey, God gives Christians the Holy Spirit. "But the Helper, the Holy Spirit, whom the Father will send in my name, he will teach you all things and bring to your remembrance all that I have said to you" (John 14: 26, ESV). The Holy Spirit gives us the awesome power to escape the control of sin so that we persevere in loving Jesus until we die. Problems occur, though, when we try to feel the Holy Spirit's guidance in life as a Jedi feels the Force. In addition, just as the Force might give the Jedi special powers, some Christians think the Holy Spirit infuses them with supernatural powers to heal, prophesy, and speak in tongues.

The next two chapters will discuss where Christians can veer off course when it comes to their understanding of the Holy Spirit. Once again, I'm not questioning any believer's love for God. I'm just trying to help us express our love in the most God-honoring way possible. Also, in my experience, misunderstanding the Holy Spirit's work may result in unnecessary stress and sadness. My hope is to help believers avoid the pain that an improper perspective might cause. In Chapter 13, we'll study the filling of the Holy Spirit, and the gifts of the Holy Spirit. In Chapter 14, we'll look at the role of the Holy Spirit in making choices in our daily lives.

FILLING & GIFTS

○○○○○○○○○○○○●○○○○

Filled with the Spirit

The Jedi increase in the knowledge of the Force by feeling the energy field around them. A common practice for the Jedi is to calm their hearts and minds so that nothing within obstructs the flow of the Force. For the most part, they try not to think in order to feel and manipulate the Force in a greater way. Even though the Force is everywhere, only certain individuals with a high enough midi-chlorian count can benefit from its power. Likewise, we may think that, as believers, we are only taking advantage of a small part of the blessings God wants to dispense upon us. We think, like Yoda instructs Luke, that we need to calm our minds and hearts so that the Holy Spirit can flow in and through us unobstructed and his power can pour into our lives.

Scripture commands believers to be filled with the Holy Spirit. "Do not get drunk on wine, which leads to debauchery. Instead, be filled with the Spirit" (Ephesians 5:18). Therefore, Christians around the world, in an endeavor to grow closer to their Lord, try desperately to have more of the Spirit in them. But should we assume with the above command that Paul thinks the Holy Spirit can become depleted over time? Occasionally, does more Spirit need to be poured into us like Aunt Beru fills a glass with blue milk?

🔭 A scene of Aunt Beru dispensing blue milk into a pitcher was deleted from *Episode IV*. Blue milk comes from female banthas and is nutritious and delicious.

Few regard the Holy Spirit in these spatial terms, but they might think of him as ebbing when they feel far from God. This, too, misunderstands what it means to be filled with the Spirit. Since Ephesians 5:18 is the only place in the teaching passages of the New Testament that mentions being filled with the Holy Spirit, we need to look to other verses to shed light on what Paul means. The best place to go is Colossians 3. Ephesians and Colossians are very much alike in both structure and content. If you put Ephesians 5 and Colossians 3 side by side, you will see those chapters, in particular, are strikingly similar. Let's focus on the parallel verse for Ephesians 5:18 which is Colossians 3:16.

> Do not get drunk on wine, which leads to debauchery. Instead, be filled with the Spirit, speaking to one another with psalms, hymns, and songs from the Spirit. Sing and make music from your heart to the Lord, always giving thanks to God the Father for everything, in the name of our Lord Jesus Christ. (Ephesians 5:18–20)

> Let the word of Christ dwell in you richly, teaching and admonishing one another in all wisdom, singing psalms and hymns and spiritual songs, with thankfulness in your hearts to God. And whatever you do, in word or deed, do everything in the name of the Lord Jesus, giving thanks to God the Father through him. (Colossians 3:16–17, ESV)

As we can see in the passage from Colossians, to "Let the word of Christ dwell in you" can be used in the same manner as Paul telling us to be filled with the Spirit. In the context of both Ephesians 5 and Colossians 3, this is all about being obedient. It's about putting off the sin of your old life (sexual immorality, greed, anger, and cursing) and putting on compassion, kindness, humility, gentleness, and patience. If you are being an obedient Christian, you are, by definition, filled with the Spirit. If you have let sin take over in a certain area of life, you need to repent. When we obey God's Word, the phrase "filled with the Spirit" can be used to describe us. Again, it's not the Spirit himself departing our body and then returning like a capricious friend who must go off and stew for a while. The Holy Spirit never leaves us. Being filled with the Holy Spirit simply means obeying the Lord.

Think of the statement: "The Force is strong with this one." What is Vader saying? To be strong in the Force is two-fold. Yes, it's a measure of midi-chlorians, but more importantly, it's how the person uses the Force. When Luke uses the Force to help blow up the Death Star, it could be said that he is strong in the Force. However, when he fails to lift his X-wing out of the marsh, you could accurately describe him as weak in the Force. Luke's midi-chlorian count does not change. What changes are Luke's faith, mindset, and self-control. On Dagobah, he believes it is more a matter of his physical strength than relying solely on the power of the Force. In the same way, the Christian life is not about trying to muster up more Holy Spirit like a Jedi trying to increase his midi-chlorians. On the contrary, God has given us his Holy Spirit, and we are told only to walk in obedience. When we do that, we can be described as Spirit-filled Christians.

The Gifts

Speaking in Tongues

Along with the filling of the Spirit are the gifts of the Spirit, another misinterpreted concept in some churches. Not to be confused with the fruit of the Spirit, which is love, joy, peace, patience, kindness, goodness, faithfulness, gentleness and self-control, the gifts of the Spirit are acts such as serving, teaching, encouraging, giving, leading, and showing mercy. There is also another category of gifts called sign gifts. From these, we will focus on tongues, healing, and prophecy. As we begin, think about how all Jedi can manipulate the Force to some extent, but only some can heal others or see into the future. This will help us as we move forward.

Let's start with the subject of speaking in tongues, because it's both the most commonly sought after and most misunderstood gift. What exactly is a "tongue"? No, we're not talking about what the opee sea killer uses to catch its prey. In the biblical sense, a tongue is a language, but it's important not to stop there. It's a real language, an actual dialect spoken in the world. More notably, it is an unusual way God reveals truth to his people.

"All of them were filled with the Holy Spirit and began to speak in other tongues as the Spirit enabled them" (Acts 2:4). This verse, an account from Pentecost, is one of the key verses folks give to defend speaking in tongues as a legitimate occurrence in modern times. The very next verses are the essential ones to get right, specifically verses 6–11, which describe how each one in the crowd heard his own language being spoken. This was shocking, because Galileans were speaking other people's native languages.

> Parthians, Medes and Elamites; residents of Mesopotamia, Judea and Cappadocia, Pontus and Asia, Phrygia and Pamphylia, Egypt and the parts of Libya near Cyrene; visitors from Rome (both Jews and converts to Judaism); Cretans and Arabs—we hear them declaring the wonders of God in our own tongues! (Acts 2:9-11)

When the Bible mentions tongues, we should understand that these are forms of communication that use nouns, verbs, and everything else you learned in elementary school. Tongues are not just random sounds. A tongue is not incoherent speech that only God can understand. Tongues are languages that you can actually learn.

The miracle at Pentecost was that these men did not take the time to learn these languages. The Spirit poured out the ability on them without them asking for the gift or striving for it in any way. Consider a Pentecost-like event happening to Luke, Leia, and Lando. I use Lando instead of Han, because Han seems to have invested the time to learn a few different languages like Shyriiwook (Chewbacca's language) and Huttese (what Greedo speaks in the cantina). It's no longer miraculous if Han already knows the language. So, at *Star Wars* Pentecost, Luke, Leia, and Lando start talking in other languages, such as Huttese, Jawaese, and Bocce. If someone recorded their utterances, he would be able to play them back later to creatures like Hutts and Jawas. The Hutts and Jawas would hear their language being spoken, no big deal. In the same way, in Acts 2, the languages themselves are not significant. What is important is how the Holy Spirit gifted people to speak them.

🦅 Greedo's home planet is Rodia, and his native tongue is Rodese. Huttese is the most popular language in the galaxy next to Galactic Basic.

If you find it hard to relate to Acts as well as our *Star Wars* example, imagine a group of English-speaking believers gathered and then one starts speaking new revelation from God in French, another Italian, and another Russian without ever knowing a single word of the language. In the biblical sense, we would classify this as speaking in tongues.

Private Prayer Language

Some say speaking in tongues is a private prayer language and point to Romans 8:26 as the proof text. Let's look at that verse (shown in italics) in the context of the passage.

> We know that the whole creation has been groaning as in the pains of childbirth right up to the present time. Not only so, but we ourselves, who have the firstfruits of the Spirit, groan inwardly as we wait eagerly for our adoption to sonship, the redemption of our bodies. For in this hope we were saved. But hope that is seen is no hope at all. Who hopes for what they already have? But if we hope for what we do not yet have, we wait for it patiently. *In the same way, the Spirit helps us in our weakness. We do not know what we ought to pray for, but the Spirit himself intercedes for us through wordless groans.* And he who searches our hearts knows the mind of the Spirit, because the Spirit intercedes for God's people in accordance with the will of God. (Romans 8:22–27, emphasis mine)

If "wordless groans" is some sort of spiritual tongue, we need to determine to what the phrase "in the same way" refers. The same "groans" in verse 26 point back to the verses 22 and 23. The whole creation groans as it waits for the children of God to be revealed, and we groan inwardly as we wait for the redemption of our bodies. The "wordless groans" of Romans 8:26 in the context of the rest of the chapter is not a private prayer language. We don't speak in a special prayer language any more than the whole creation does in verse 22. The meaning of verse 26 is that the Holy Spirit works in the life of every believer in a behind-the-scenes way, interceding for us and strengthening us in the midst of our sufferings.

The Jedi and Sith communicate through everyday words and never any sort of special Force dialect. Even when Luke communicates telepathically to Leia in *Episode V,* he uses his native language.

Couldn't he have communicated his need to be rescued to Leia in a deeper way so that she simply felt a strong urge to turn the ship around? No. That would have been a bad move. Luke only has minutes, maybe seconds, before his arms and legs give way. Why cloud the message so that even he would be unclear of its content? Luke speaks the phrase, "Hear me, Leia," not only for our benefit but also so that Leia would understand his message and respond immediately.

🔭 The sound of Luke dangling from a Cloud City weather vane was made by moving around a TV antenna.

Admittedly, sometimes we're too distraught to formulate thoughts, or we don't pray for the right things. That's when our helper, the Holy Spirit, talks to God the Father on our behalf. But often, we do know our requests and should engage our minds when we talk to God just like we would if Jesus were sitting in front of us. We don't need to create a special prayer language. When we look for instruction about prayer from other Scripture, we are told things like, "Do not be anxious about anything, but in every situation, by prayer and petition, with thanksgiving, present your requests to God" (Philippians 4:6). It's apparent from the rest of God's Word that we don't just unplug our minds and let our mouths make sounds. We formulate thoughts about what we need, and then we ask God. Our prayers don't need to be free of grammatical errors or overly formal. They just need to be sincere.

Praying to God for help is not for only God's ears. The Bible tells us to gather together and pray for one another (Matthew 18:19; James 5:16). When Luke uses words to call out to Leia, we, as movie watchers, share his struggle with him. Most of us have felt like we have dangled for dear life (metaphorically speaking) on more than one occasion. When we pray out loud in a way that others can understand, we allow them to help carry our burdens by praying for and with us. Similar to Paul advocating prophecy over speaking in tongues in 1 Corinthians 14:5 so that the whole church may be edified, we need to also consider others when we pray publicly.

Purpose

Now that we have a definition, we need to study why the Spirit gave the gift of tongues in the first place. "Tongues, then, are a sign, not for believers but for unbelievers" (1 Corinthians 14:22a). In the preceding verse, Paul quotes Isaiah 28:11–12, which prophesies that God will speak to people with foreign lips and strange tongues. The context of Isaiah 28, just like much of the entire book of Isaiah, is God's judgment on Israel for rejecting him. Tongues are not a good sign for unbelievers. They are fulfilled prophecy that God is angry at them and his wrath awaits.

In *Episode V*, Han, Leia, and General Rieekan discover a strange signal being transmitted across the airwaves on Hoth. They don't know what it is and do not understand its language. Threepio reminds them that he is fluent in six million forms of communication, and that this signal might be an Imperial code. The Rebels don't need a word-for-word translation. They just need to know to prepare to defend themselves from the wrath of the Empire.

The Israelites, though familiar with the prophecy of Isaiah, never put two and two together that speaking in tongues was a sign of God's judgment against them. The New Covenant era, which had already started by the time of Paul's letter to Corinth, is a radical new time in the unfolding plan of God. God is finished showing his love to Israel. They broke his covenant, causing God to curse almost all of Israel. Now, he shows a love that leads to not physical salvation but spiritual salvation and not just to a single nation but to people from every nation, tribe, and language.

Use

Since, first and foremost, tongues are not a sign for believers, the Corinthian church was making a mess when they gathered together. They didn't understand how tongues should be used. So, Paul had to instruct them. First, he says that there should be intelligibility in the words. "So it is with you. Unless you speak intelligible words with your tongue, how will anyone know what you are saying? You will just be speaking into the air" (1 Corinthians 14:9). As explained earlier, speaking in a tongue should be an actual language and not merely speech-like syllables. Second, there must be an interpreter.

If God has not gifted anyone to interpret the language, then the speaker must keep silent out of consideration for the persons who wouldn't know what he is saying (1 Corinthians 14:28).

No matter which *Star Wars* movie you watch, you quickly realize your need for an interpreter. You either need Han translating for Chewie, Threepio translating for Artoo, or good old-fashioned subtitles to know what in the world creatures like Greedo and Jabba are saying. Threepio is the master interpreter. As he's proud of saying, he is fluent in over six million forms of communication. I am thankful for Threepio's interpretation, and he serves as a good illustration of the importance of having a means to understand the language that you're hearing.

> ✠ *Episode III* and *Episode V* were the only two *Star Wars* movies that didn't use subtitles to interpret alien languages.

This pinpoints why focusing on tongues can be detrimental to a believer's walk. Too often, a believer, in his zealous quest for the gift of tongues, forgets to be both Christ-centered and others-center and instead becomes self-centered. An interpreter allows the speaker of a tongue to be understood. It's no accident that Paul's teaching on spiritual gifts spills over into 1 Corinthians 13, the chapter on love. The church in Corinth may have been a gifted church, but they were not doing a very good job at loving one another. Keeping silent unless there is an interpreter is a way to love others, because we want others instructed in the Lord and encouraged, not confused and feeling out of place.

Furthermore, any sort of giftedness will always be a huge temptation to turn inward and become boastful. *Star Wars* is full of people who, because of their giftedness with either the Force or a blaster, become arrogant and self-centered. Paul instructs the believers in Corinth that speaking in tongues is not a big deal compared to loving others. In fact, he says that he would rather speak five intelligible words to instruct others than ten thousand in a tongue.

Are Tongues Still Used?

"At that moment the curtain of the temple was torn in two from top to bottom. The earth shook, the rocks split and the tombs broke open. The bodies of many holy people who had died were raised to life" (Matthew 27:51–52). When Jesus died on the cross, several phenomenal events occurred. This period, including his resurrection and the giving of the Holy Spirit, marked a monumental transitional time in God's plan of salvation for humanity. This ended the Old Covenant era; an age characterized mostly by disbelief in God, and marked the beginning of the New Covenant era, an age when God would motivate people at the heart level to love him. This window of time, especially Pentecost, included events that no one had ever experienced. Pentecost was when God put a big spotlight on what he was doing for his people.

When a new *Star Wars* movie is about to be released, there's a tremendous amount of buzz. In the past, people would pay for a ticket to another movie just to watch the two-minute trailer of the new episode in the saga. Fast-food restaurants gave out *Star Wars* drinking glasses, and actors would go on talk shows to promote the new film. Nowadays, YouTube gets tens of millions of views of the trailer, people obsess online for any leak of plot information, and fans drive over a thousand miles to witness a Comic-Con panel. When Hollywood finally premieres the film, the stars pull up in limousines, dressed to the nines, and walk into the theater on a red carpet. Of course, it's the fans who go the furthest. Dressing up as their favorite characters, stormtroopers, Boba Fetts, and Princess Leias will push life aside to camp out for a midnight showing. To say the least, there's an electricity in the air as this new cultural event breaks into our lives.

So, here's the point: A year after a new *Star Wars* movie comes out, the red carpet is long rolled up. The movie stars are on new movie sets. The fans are excited about a different blockbuster. All of the buzz is gone. But the movie still exists. People are not as excited about it in the sense that they dress up as Tusken Raiders and Jedi to watch it in their living room, but their excitement has developed into a deeper love for the movie. Not only that, those fans show the movie to their family and friends who haven't seen it and for the rest of their lives sing its praises from the rooftops (okay, maybe not the prequels).

🔭 Disney led an unprecedented merchandise release more than three months before *Episode VII* hit theaters, naming the marketing push "Force Friday."

This is how we should think about speaking in tongues and the other supernatural events in Acts. These happenings were like God's premiere of the age of belief. Something unprecedented was about to happen, and God caused exceptional events to showcase it. Those events were like rolling out the red carpet, dressing up in costumes, putting the movie on the big screen, and everything else that causes the world to turn its focus on *Star Wars*. But just like all of those special movie-related events eventually fade away, Paul says in 1 Corinthians 13 that tongues will fade away, because love, faith, and hope will be the true marks of a Christian.

You might think that there must be something more to being a Christian than the mundane life of reading the Bible, praying, and serving others. Granted, if you spoke a foreign language spontaneously, you would probably feel like God was using you in an extraordinary way. But if you are in Christ, you are being used in extraordinary ways. When you love with a Christ-like love, you are doing so with Spirit-enabled power. This is when the Christian life really glorifies God, because your actions glorify Jesus in front of others. People who try to speak in tongues are hard to relate to. But if those same people, instead of trying to speak in tongues, speak in love, it can make all the difference in the world. "A new command I give you: Love one another. As I have loved you, so you must love one another. By this everyone will know that you are my disciples, if you love one another" (John 13:34–35).

Some Christian circles refer to speaking in tongues as evidence of the "baptism of the Holy Spirit." Moreover, they say this experience is needed to receive additional power to live the Christian life. Again, this misinterprets the sign gifts. The Bible says we have everything needed to live godly lives and do ministry. "His divine power has given us everything we need for a godly life through our knowledge of him who called us by his own glory and goodness" (2 Peter 1:3). If we do not speak in tongues, we should not feel as though we are missing out on what God has for us. To have such a mindset robs us of the joy and the real power he has already bestowed on us through Christ.

Conclusion

If a believer doesn't share the viewpoint of tongues explained above, I don't question his love for God. This isn't a major doctrinal point that we must get right in order to be saved. That being said, the whole issue of speaking in tongues can be a huge distraction for the believer and others around him. Some are even taught that they are not really Christians if they don't speak in tongues, or they are told they're not receiving the full benefits of their walk with God if they don't experience this gift.

It's dangerous when anything diminishes Jesus' work on the cross. God gifts his children with what they need. After all, he gave up his Son for us. Do we really believe he won't also give us everything else we need? The gift of tongues was only a gift, and we cannot demand a gift. We cannot earn a gift. A gift is given. If God does not give us the gift of tongues (and in my many years of being a believer, I haven't seen any Christian speak in tongues in the biblical sense), then we should assume we do not need it.

The Gifts of Healing

The power to heal is another similarity between the Jedi religion and Christianity. But, right after I make that statement, it must be qualified. How do the Jedi and the Sith use the Force to heal? How did Jesus and the apostles heal? Is the healing spiritual, physical, or both? And, most importantly, do we as Christians in the 21st century have the Spirit's gifts of healing that Paul writes about in 1 Corinthians 12:9?

> Now to each one the manifestation of the Spirit is given for the common good. To one there is given through the Spirit a message of wisdom, to another a message of knowledge by means of the same Spirit, to another faith by the same Spirit, to another gifts of healing by that one Spirit. (1 Corinthians 12:7-9)

Force Healing

After Luke is banged up by a Tusken Raider in *Episode IV,* Obi-Wan approaches him, checks what looks to be Luke's pulse, and then places his hand on Luke's forehead. He rests it there for several moments until he hears Artoo beep. Obi-Wan tells the little droid, "Don't worry, he'll be all right." A few seconds later, Luke wakes up and doesn't even have any signs of injury. Consider what happened. The Tusken Raider gets in at least a few good hits with his gaffi stick, and Luke is knocked unconscious, most likely from hitting his head on the rocky ground. How is he able to get up so fast? The only explanation that makes sense is that Obi-Wan uses the Jedi power of Force healing on the young farm boy.

Force healing can be thought of as super intense and effective Reiki technique. When done successfully, a Jedi performing Force healing channels the Force to heal the life energy of the injured or sick person restoring him or her to full health. Like the way Jesus and the apostles healed, a Jedi heals another individual in a matter of moments.

Even though a Jedi often uses Force telekinesis to manipulate objects without touching them, Obi-Wan touches Luke. This is a more intimate encounter and one that Jesus and the apostles opted for often. In Luke 8, the woman who had suffered from bleeding for twelve years reached out, touched Jesus, and was healed instantly. Later that same day, Jesus took a dead girl by the hand and raised her back to life. Touching the ailing person was not always necessary. In fact, even Peter's shadow could heal the sick (Acts 5:15). Jesus also could heal people with just his voice, like when he called for Lazarus to come out of his tomb. Still, there is something affectionate about laying hands on someone in pain that we see in both *Star Wars* and the Bible.

Jesus and the apostles performed miraculous healings, such as restoring paralytics, giving sight to the blind, and curing the sick. They went as far as anyone could go by restoring life to the dead. This is something that the Jedi resist doing, citing that it is "unnatural." When Palpatine tells Anakin that the dark side is "a pathway to many abilities some consider to be unnatural," he alludes to saving people from death. The Jedi do not have the strength to stop death from happening. When Yoda talks of his impending death, Luke says, "Master Yoda, you can't die." To this, Yoda replies, "Strong am

I with the Force, but not that strong." Death is the great equalizer that all life forms must face.

Purpose

Force healing is a special area of study to which certain Jedi choose to devote their lives. For the most part, Jedi heal for one reason: to help the sick and the injured. Jedi healers, being full of compassion, help out at medical facilities and risk their own lives on the battle-field. There doesn't seem to be any spiritual transformation after a healing, only a physical improvement.

Jesus had immense compassion for those he healed. Although, he didn't heal to teach compassion for the ailing. His plan was not to jumpstart the ridding of physical suffering from the world. And the reason he healed wasn't because he wanted to reward the faithful. The primary reasons Jesus healed were twofold: 1) to fulfill prophecy and 2) to prove he has the authority to forgive sin. Jesus needed to heal to fulfill the prophecies of the Messiah in the Old Testament.

> When evening came, many who were demon-possessed were brought to him, and he drove out the spirits with a word and healed all the sick. This was to fulfill what was spoken through the prophet Isaiah: 'He took up our infirmities and bore our diseases.' (Matthew 8:16–17)

Consider this other prophecy from the Prophet Isaiah: "Then will the eyes of the blind be opened and the ears of the deaf unstopped. Then will the lame leap like a deer, and the mute tongue shout for joy" (Isaiah 35:5–6a). When Jesus heals the deaf and mute man in Mark 7, he fulfills prophecy. When he heals a crippled man in Matthew 9, he fulfills prophecy.

Jesus healing the man in Matthew 9 also brings us to the second reason Jesus healed, which was to prove he was who he said he was.

> Some men brought to him a paralyzed man, lying on a mat. When Jesus saw their faith, he said to the man, "Take heart, son; your sins are forgiven." At this, some of the teachers of the law said to themselves, "This fellow is blaspheming!" Knowing their thoughts, Jesus said, "Why do you entertain evil thoughts in your hearts? Which is easier: to say, 'Your sins are forgiven,' or to say, 'Get up and walk'? But I want you to know that the Son of Man has

authority on earth to forgive sins." So he said to the paralyzed man, "Get up, take your mat and go home." Then the man got up and went home. When the crowd saw this, they were filled with awe; and they praised God, who had given such authority to man. (Matthew 9:2–8)

If we watch the *Star Wars* saga starting with *Episode IV,* we meet Obi-Wan for the first time when he scares off the Sand People. We already heard about him through Princess Leia's hologram message, but we don't know too much except that he's powerful enough to help defeat the Empire. When Obi-Wan imitates the hunting cry of the krayt dragon, he frightens the Tusken Raiders away. Shortly after that, he heals Luke in a matter of moments. When this strange new character says that he is, in fact, Obi-Wan Kenobi, we believe him. Why? Because he proves through his actions that he is every bit as powerful as we expected.

This is the same sort of authority that Jesus established with his power early on in his ministry. Jesus' point in the above passage from Matthew is that anyone can say "Your sins are forgiven," because there is no way to prove it. However, only God himself could heal like this.

🔭 The skeleton that C-3PO walks past in *Episode IV* is the greater krayt dragon. The fake skeleton still lies in the Tunisian desert to this day.

Can Christians Heal Today?

To figure out if any Christians have the gifts of healing today, we need to explore why Jesus and the apostles healed. Jesus spent most of his life *not* healing people. Think of all the pain, suffering, and death that he saw around him for thirty years, and he let the people enduring it suffer and die. Of course, he had the power to save them, but he didn't, because the right time in God's plan had not yet arrived. Though we don't know for sure, I doubt Obi-Wan was going around Tatooine healing people, because that would have drawn the Empire's attention towards Tatooine and endangered both him and Luke.

Like Obi-Wan, Jesus kept a low profile in Nazareth. In fact, he was fairly reluctant to perform his first miracle, which was when he turned water into wine. Ponder this verse from that account: "'Woman, why do you involve me?' Jesus replied. 'My hour has not yet come'" (John 2:4). What a strange way to respond to his mom's statement. The reason Jesus said this was that, up to that point, he had never done any miracles, no walking on water, no feeding five thousand, and no healings. The "hour" that Jesus mentions includes a special time of miracles leading all the way up to the ultimate healing at the cross. We need to consider this wedding feast the first bookend in this exceptional time that includes healings. As far as the closing bookend of this era, while the Bible doesn't say when the gifts of the Spirit will come to a close, it does say that they will (1 Corinthians 13:8).

Remember the shift in God's plan of salvation that was happening during this period. This goes back to our movie premiere analogy. Like Disney turning the spotlight on a new *Star Wars* movie, God was turning his spotlight on Jesus and the small group of men in Acts who were given the distinct gifts of healing by the Spirit. The healings we see in Acts were tied to an exceptional time in God's redemptive history, like all the "for a limited time only" promotional events are tied to the upcoming movie.

This is a good time to pause and be clear that I don't think that God is unable to perform miraculous healings in our day. Nor do I think it's a waste of time to pray for people to be healed. Not at all. The question I raise is, should we expect to see miraculous healings like those in the first century (healings that included severed ears being reattached, sight restored to the blind, and people raised from the dead)?

Jesus did not give the authority to heal to everyone who believed in him but limited it to his apostles. Keep Ephesians 2:20 in mind. During the first century, God was building his Church on the foundation of the prophets and the apostles. "When Jesus had called the Twelve together, he gave them power and authority to drive out all demons and to cure diseases, and he sent them out to proclaim the kingdom of God and to heal the sick" (Luke 9:1–2). Since the apostolic age is finished, the gospel has gone out to the Gentiles, and the canon of Scripture is closed, it makes sense that we don't see miraculous healings like this anymore. Still, if this is the case, it doesn't seem to line up with 1 Corinthians 12:9, which says that the Spirit gives some (regular folk in the Church) the gifts of healing.

It's true that the early churches like the one in Corinth seemed to have the gifts of healing, but it also seems that the apostles' ability to heal was fading away as the years clipped by. To illustrate, think about this counsel that Paul gives Timothy. "Stop drinking only water, and use a little wine because of your stomach and your frequent illnesses" (1 Timothy 5:23). Timothy was not only sick, he was sick frequently. And yet Paul doesn't instruct Timothy to request the elders lay hands on him in prayer. In fact, there's not really any spiritual instruction at all. Instead, Paul tells him to use wine as a form of medicine. Likewise, when Obi-Wan's ghost appears to Luke on Hoth, Luke is in bad shape, but Obi-Wan doesn't heal him. On the contrary, he tells him to go to Dagobah. Instead of the mystical experience of Force healing, Luke takes a dip in a bacta tank to mend his wounds.

🔭 Bacta is a synthetic chemical liquid that promotes rapid healing of the patient's wounds. It's known throughout the galaxy as the "miracle fluid."

Let's look at another incident from one of Paul's letters. "Erastus stayed in Corinth, and I left Trophimus sick in Miletus" (2 Timothy 4:20). Paul left Trophimus sick? Isn't this the same Paul who healed people left and right? The same apostle whose handkerchiefs could heal the sick? Paul's second letter to Timothy was written in ad 67. At this point, it seems clear from Scripture that the time of the sign gifts were drawing to a close. If the gifts of healing are in fact gone, how are we to handle our physical woes now?

Physical Suffering

The "health and wealth" false gospel has so permeated our churches and our theology that many believers think something is wrong spiritually if they get a disease. And the odds are, you and I probably will battle some form of life-threatening illness if we live long enough. In much of the world, cancer, multiple sclerosis, autism, asthmas, diabetes, stroke, heart disease, and a host of other health problems are on the rise. Since people, including believers, get sick a lot these days, we need to make sure our theology is solid when it comes to the area of sickness and healing.

Much of Anakin's descent into the dark side stemmed from his longing to prevent his loved ones from suffering and dying. We all can relate to this desire. No one likes to experience pain or have the people close to them go through it. In an effort to alleviate sickness, many gravitate toward James 5:14–15b. "Is anyone among you sick? Let them call the elders of the church to pray over them and anoint them with oil in the name of the Lord. And the prayer offered in faith will make the sick person well." This is a verse that many people who claim a gift of healing quote when performing a healing service. The main problem with this verse is that the promised outcome does not seem to be the case in everyday life. I know plenty of faithful Christians who prayed to be healed and were not.

> When he had gone indoors, the blind men came to him [Jesus], and he asked them, "Do you believe that I am able to do this?" "Yes, Lord," they replied. Then he touched their eyes and said, "According to your faith let it be done to you"; and their sight was restored. (Matthew 9:28–30a)

The faith referred to in James 5 is the faith that Jesus *can* heal, not the faith that he *will* heal. Too many Christians attach a promise to God that he never made. God not healing a person doesn't mean he is unfaithful or that our prayers were not offered in faith. There are all sorts of things that we pray for that God doesn't see fit to bring to pass. Whether or not he heals us falls into this category. He may or he may not. The question should be, will we praise him even if he doesn't? As Job said after being afflicted physically, "Shall we accept good from God, and not trouble?" (Job 2:10).

The reason Palpatine is able to manipulate Anakin in the area of saving Padmé from death is that Palpatine causes Anakin to question the light side of the Force. During *Episode III*, Anakin is ready to turn to anything that will give him temporary, physical relief (in this case, for his wife). He will trade his religion, his future, and even his own soul for this.

Paul knew all about physical suffering. He prayed more than once for God to take away his physical suffering.

> I was given a thorn in my flesh, a messenger of Satan, to torment me. Three times I pleaded with the Lord to take it away from me. But he said to me, 'My grace is sufficient for you, for my power is made perfect in weakness' Therefore I will boast all the more gladly about my weaknesses, so that Christ's power may rest on me. (2 Corinthians 12:7b-9)

Conclusion

In the first century, God chose to glorify himself by healing people either through others or directly through Jesus. It's definitely possible that he may do this today, but I don't think this is the normal way he acts now. Regarding physical suffering, the Bible emphasizes that we have a God-glorifying attitude during it more than it emphasizes we find a way to escape it. God will heal us perfectly one day when he gives us glorified bodies in heaven. Until that happens though, we do well to have the same mindset of Paul when he says,

> Therefore we do not lose heart. Though outwardly we are wasting away, yet inwardly we are being renewed day by day. For our light and momentary troubles are achieving for us an eternal glory that far outweighs them all. So we fix our eyes not on what is seen, but on what is unseen, since what is seen is temporary, but what is unseen is eternal. (2 Corinthians 4:16-18)

The Gift of Prophecy
Clouded, Prophecy Is

Another parallel between Christianity and *Star Wars* is prophecy. This is seen with the Old Testament prophecy of the coming Messiah and the *Star Wars* "Prophecy of the Chosen One." Prophecy is another gift of the Spirit that Paul lists in 1 Corinthians 12. Briefly, prophecy is when God communicated through people (prophets or prophetesses). God chose who would be his messengers and used them to convey information about his character, his laws, and future events. Similar to becoming a Jedi, a person could not strive to have the gift of prophecy.

Like Yoda, Obi-Wan, and Mace struggling to interpret their prophecy, God's people have always struggled to understand not only prophecies but also prophets and the gift of prophecy itself. Mistakes in this area can lead the Church into all sorts of peril. Believers are distracted from living for Christ due to the latest "end of the world" prediction. This section will help explain what the gift of prophecy is and if we should expect to see it at work in churches today.

When false prophets claim they hear from God, it does more than just waste our time. In fact, misleading God's people is such a severe offense that in Deuteronomy 13 and 18, Moses says false prophets should pay with their lives.

> That prophet or dreamer must be put to death for inciting rebellion against the Lord your God, who brought you out of Egypt and redeemed you from the land of slavery. That prophet or dreamer tried to turn you from the way the Lord your God commanded you to follow. You must purge the evil from among you. (Deuteronomy 13:5)

In the New Testament, Jesus warns his followers about falling for a false prophet. "For false messiahs and false prophets will appear and perform great signs and wonders to deceive, if possible, even the elect" (Matthew 24:24). Christ gave true prophets, along with the apostles, pastors, and teachers to equip his people for works of service so that we can avoid being "tossed back and forth by the waves, and blown here and there by every wind of teaching and by the cunning and craftiness of people in their deceitful scheming" (Ephesians 4:14).

Like the early false prophets who claimed Jesus had already come back, the Jedi struggled to know if the Chosen One had come. Sometimes, they thought it was Anakin, at other times, Luke, and Yoda even alluded to Leia to being the One. This caused problems as they tried to figure out the prophecy. This is a lesson for us. God's prophecies were rarely clear until after they are fulfilled. It's usually not until then that the hearers can look back and connect the dots.

For instance, every Israelite thought that the Messiah would be a conquering king who freed them from Roman oppression. Now, we realize that Jesus first came as a suffering servant and will only come as the conquering King at his Second Coming.

Another example is Malachi 4:5. "See, I will send the prophet Elijah to you before that great and dreadful day of the Lord comes." But it's not until Jesus says that John was the "Elijah" to come that we see how this verse is fulfilled. "For all the Prophets and the Law prophesied until John. And if you are willing to accept it, he is the Elijah who was to come" (Matthew 11:13–14). If you only read the prophecy in Malachi, you would be looking for the original Elijah. It's not until Jesus says that John the Baptist fulfilled this that the prophecy can be understood (Matthew 17:13).

The problem with Anakin's nightmares, as with any prophecy, is that they are never crystal clear. Remember how Yoda says that the future is always in motion? Was Anakin seeing Padmé dying or was he seeing the natural pain of bearing a child? His possible misinterpretation may have caused Padmé's death, a self-fulfilling prophecy of sorts. Can prophets still hear from God? The concern is, how can we know for sure? How can we test the validity of their words? The lack of verification doesn't stop false prophets from rising up in our day and saying they have heard from God. Unfortunately, it also doesn't stop people in our day from believing them.

The Delivery Method

Representing God to the people, prophets are like conduits of information from God. Prophecies were always conveyed through words, visions, or dreams. For example, in the book of Amos, Amos uses the phrase, "this is what the Lord says" over and over. "Surely the Sovereign Lord does nothing without revealing his plan to his servants the prophets. The lion has roared—who will not fear? The Sovereign Lord has spoken—who can but prophesy?" (Amos 3:7–8). After God gave Amos a vision, Amos wrote down what the Lord said word for word. Amos' experience was different from the cloudy vision Luke has of Han and Leia. Even though it's through a vision, the Lord communicated to Amos in a way so that every word was written down as the Lord intended.

Dreams (usually unpleasant ones) are another method that God used to send information to his prophets. Similar to Anakin dreaming of Padmé dying, Daniel's dreams caused him great anguish. "I, Daniel, was troubled in spirit, and the visions that passed through my mind disturbed me" (Daniel 7:15). After Daniel's dream, he didn't write down what he thought the dream meant. He wrote down the "substance of his dream" (Daniel 7:1). At first, he could only write down what he saw. It wasn't until he asked the angelic being that he learned what the dream meant. "I approached one of those standing there and asked him the meaning of all this" (Daniel 7:16).

So, how do the Jedi get their prophecies in the first place? Since there is no personal being in the Force, we can assume prophecies must come from sensing the future. The origin of the "Prophecy of the Chosen One" is unknown. Some Jedi think it came from ancient Jedi philosophers. Others speculate that it came from a prophet of the Ophuchi Clan, a group of religious hermits descended from the Jedi. Whoever it was wrote down the prophecy, and the word-for-word record survived generation after generation in the Jedi Archives.

Dreams and visions were not the primary ways God sent messages. Most of the time, God communicated audibly in a way that was unmistakable. "While they were worshiping the Lord and fasting, the Holy Spirit *said,* 'Set apart for me Barnabas and Saul for the work to which I have called them'" (Acts 13:2, emphasis mine). The point here is that Barnabas, Simeon, Lucius, Manaen, and Saul didn't just get a feeling or impression. The Holy Spirit spoke, and Luke wrote down the Spirit's words.

God gave this experience to only these five men in Acts 13:2. Similar to the earlier "casting lots" situation of Acts 1, we're never commanded to listen for the Holy Spirit or given any information about this sort of thing possibly happening to us. When referring to whom receives spiritual gifts, Paul says, "All these are the work of one and the same Spirit, and he distributes them to each one, just as he determines" (1 Corinthians 12:11). If God doesn't give someone the gift of prophecy, he or she will not hear from God in this way. Paul alludes to not everyone receiving this gift with the rhetorical question, "Are all prophets?" (1 Corinthians 12:29). Yoda, at times and at will, shuts his eyes and tries to pick up on future happenings. People in the Bible to whom God spoke didn't need to do this.

God just talked. And God continues to speak to us but through his Word, not through our feelings or dreams.

Prophets in the New Covenant Era?

In the Old Testament, there were less than sixty prophets (including prophetesses). It was never a widespread practice, and sometimes many years went by before God spoke to a prophet. Likewise, while in the past all Jedi could have Force visions, by the time we reach Anakin's era, only certain Jedi and Sith have this power. Unlike the other Jedi practices, the ability to have prophetic visions cannot be taught from Master to apprentice. Jedi prophecy is more like a gift that only some Jedi have.

When the Spirit ushered in the age of belief at Pentecost, what had been limited to a select group within Israel was now open to all kinds of people (Jews, Gentiles, men, women, young, and old). Now, all kinds of people can believe, and all sorts of folks might prophesy. This is relayed when Peter, in Acts 2, quotes the Prophet Joel. Peter uses the prophecy of Joel to show how it is fulfilled in the New Covenant era.

> In the last days, God says, I will pour out my Spirit on all people. Your sons and daughters will prophesy, your young men will see visions, your old men will dream dreams. Even on my servants, both men and women, I will pour out my Spirit in those days, and they will prophesy. (Acts 2:17–18)

It's apparent from Paul's first letter to the church in Corinth that prophecy was still happening in the New Covenant era. To understand if we should still expect to see this, consider again our movie premiere analogy with all of the preliminary arrangements. The early Church was still being established. This is why Paul includes the "apostles and prophets" in Ephesians 2:20. All kinds of signs and wonders were still happening in the Apostolic Age. But now, the foundation has been laid.

> Consequently, you are no longer foreigners and strangers, but fellow citizens with God's people and also members of his household, built on the foundation of the apostles and prophets, with Christ Jesus himself as the chief cornerstone. (Ephesians 2:19–20)

There was a time when all Jedi had Force visions. But in the years leading up to the formation of the Empire, most of the Jedi lost this ability. Similarly, prophecy like some of the other gifts of the Spirit seems to have only occurred during a time when God was building the Church's foundation. The canon of Scripture was closed long ago. Now God says we have all the revelation required to live the Christian life. "All Scripture is God-breathed and is useful for teaching, rebuking, correcting and training in righteousness, so that the servant of God may be thoroughly equipped for *every* good work" (2 Timothy 3:16–17, emphasis mine).

I don't expect there to be any more prophets, but just in case, God provided tests to determine if someone is one. As 1 Corinthians 14:29 reminds us regarding prophets, we should "weigh carefully what is said."

> You may say to yourselves, "How can we know when a message has not been spoken by the Lord?" If what a prophet proclaims in the name of the Lord does not take place or come true, that is a message the Lord has not spoken. That prophet has spoken presumptuously, so do not be alarmed. (Deuteronomy 18:21-22)

It's not until we reach the end of *Episode VI* that we realize the "Prophecy of the Chosen One" and the corresponding prophet (whoever he or she was) were the real deal. At that point, the legitimacy of the prophet can be established. Until then, it would have been illogical to believe every prophecy from this source. Yoda reminds Mace Windu and Obi-Wan that the prophecy could have been misread. They know it's unwise to risk lives on a prophecy before it comes true. It's the same kind of thing in Christianity. We don't blindly follow someone claiming to be a messenger sent from God or trust in his prophecies. We should be skeptical if specific events prophesied haven't occurred.

Even if prophecies do come true, that's still no indication that the prophet is from God. It could be a messenger from Satan disguised as an angel of light (2 Corinthians 11:14). Therefore, God gives another test to determine if a prophet is authentic.

> If a prophet, or one who foretells by dreams, appears among you and announces to you a sign or wonder, and if the sign or wonder

spoken of takes place, and the prophet says, "Let us follow other gods" (gods you have not known) "and let us worship them," you must not listen to the words of that prophet or dreamer. The Lord your God is testing you to find out whether you love him with all your heart and with all your soul. (Deuteronomy 13:1–3)

It's not uncommon for people to pop up from time to time claiming to be prophets from God. God sends these as tests to see if you will be discerning and love Christ by rejecting these charlatans. The above passage commands us to arm ourselves with God's Word, so that we know if we are being led astray by a false prophet who preaches doctrine not in accord with the rest of Scripture.

When Anakin tells Mace that Palpatine is a Sith Lord, Mace responds, "If what you told me is true, you will have gained my trust." That's showing a lot of wisdom. If I didn't know better, I would think he had been reading Deuteronomy.

14

THE LEADING & WILL OF GOD

○○○○○○○○○○○○○●○○○

"Did You Hear That?"

Along the same vein as prophecy, many Christians believe that God speaks through our inner being, and that if a believer learns to tune in on the Spirit's voice, he can, in effect, gain extra insight into God's will for his life. This is usually described as being led by the Spirit. Similar to the Jedi calming their minds so that they can find the will of the Force, many Christians try to hear the Spirit speaking to their hearts. Afterwards, they may say, "God spoke to me." In their defense, they usually don't mean that God spoke audibly to them, but the result is the same, and they perceive the message they received as just as valid.

If God really does communicate by this means, then we all need to learn to listen to what he says in order to obey. But if the Bible does not teach that he does this, then we need to abandon this practice as unprofitable. This is such an important topic that we will spend this entire chapter learning more about the Holy Spirit as well as how to find God's will.

The Knowable and Unknowable Wills of God

If there's anything we should strive to do right, it's God's will. In fact, the Bible commands us to understand the Lord's will. "Therefore do not be foolish, but understand what the Lord's will is" (Ephesians 5:17).

So, it's actually disobedience not to understand God's will. But before we can understand something, we have to at least know it, and therein lies the challenge.

When Darth Vader approaches the Emperor, he asks, "What is thy bidding, my Master?" Immediately, the Emperor starts a conversation. If only it were that easy! What if God would just tell us his will for our lives? There's good news. He has! Remember, 2 Timothy 3:16–17 says that Scripture provides all the knowledge we need to do every good work God has planned for us.

But there's a catch. The key to understanding God's will for your life is to know that God has *two* wills. One is knowable and the other is not. The "knowable will" can be described as his "ethical will." Whenever the Bible speaks of knowing and doing God's will, it refers to that "will" disclosed in Scripture. This will makes a clear distinction between sin and obedience. For example, "Give thanks in all circumstances; for this is God's will for you in Christ Jesus" (1 Thessalonians 5:18). It's not a mystery what God's will is for you in this area of gratitude. You don't have to pray for hours on end to figure out if he wants you to be grateful or ungrateful. He has already told you to be thankful in every situation.

God's other will can be described as his "controlling will." Whatever God wants to happen, it happens, because he controls all things. He planned from eternity past that you would be reading this sentence right now! Right after you finished reading it, you were smack dab in God's will. Congratulations! Pretty easy, huh? It's actually impossible for anyone to avoid being in God's controlling will. Just as Anakin and Luke have destinies that are impossible to escape, we cannot miss our destinies. The encouraging thing for believers versus the Jedi is that we have a loving, rational, wise Father who has already perfectly crafted our past, present, and future for our good.

Led by the Spirit

Along with the filling of the Holy Spirit, the Bible teaches a concept of being "led by the Spirit." Understanding what it means to be led by the Spirit is crucial in so many areas of the Christian life. Is being led by the Spirit like R2-D2's compulsion to search out

Obi-Wan Kenobi? Is it comparable to Qui-Gon telling Jar Jar that the Force will guide them? Does it encompass warning signs like Luke feeling cold and death from the cave on Dagobah? Before we answer these questions, let's start by examining a time when the Holy Spirit's leading was associated with an unusual event in history. Doing so will help us understand the typical way we are led, which is described in the next section.

When Jesus started his ministry, the Holy Spirit led him out into the wilderness to be tempted (Matthew 4:1). The Bible doesn't say exactly what this involved, but the whole experience was quite out of the ordinary. Satan has a conversation with Jesus, and after the devil leaves him, angels come to minister to Jesus. We have no indication that Jesus went into the wilderness because he had some sort of feeling or notion. Even if it did work this way, remember that historical accounts like those found in the Gospels are not meant to be commands for us or examples of how we should expect God to act now. This account is similar to Obi-Wan telling Luke to go to Dagobah. Luke doesn't just feel a strong emotional pull to fly to that system. Instead, Obi-Wan tells Luke specific details of where he is to go and who he is to find.

Paul was forbidden by the Holy Spirit to take certain directions in his missionary journeys.

> Paul and his companions traveled throughout the region of Phrygia and Galatia, having been kept by the Holy Spirit from preaching the word in the province of Asia. When they came to the border of Mysia, they tried to enter Bithynia, but the Spirit of Jesus would not allow them to. (Acts 16:6-7)

Again, the Spirit must have told Paul to refrain from preaching Christ in Asia. Beforehand, Paul used his mind to make decisions and create plans, but the Spirit intervened and changed how events unfolded.

Right before Luke leaves Hoth in *Episode V,* Wedge says, "See you at the rendezvous." That's the plan, but soon after, Luke turns his X-wing towards a new destination. Artoo beeps his concern, and Luke says, "There's nothing wrong, Artoo. I'm just setting a new course... we're not going to regroup with the others... we're going to the Dagobah system." Luke continues to keep the starfighter on manual control rather than let Artoo pilot it. This helps us picture what happened to Paul. Artoo assumes they are going to meet up with the other Rebels, but Luke has a different purpose in mind. Artoo can't do much to stay the course when his master prevents him from doing so.

🔭 Many of the Rebel soldiers during the Battle of Hoth were Norwegian residents, including mountain-rescue skiers. George Lucas made a donation to the Norwegian Red Cross in appreciation for their work.

For us, God is still the pilot in the sense that he has the power to override our control. Sometimes in life, job struggles, relationship conflicts, or health problems can feel like things are knocked off course, leaving us plotting desperately to get back to our previous path. But we can trust our Father in heaven knowing that he places us on each and every course in life to make us more like Christ while we also take part in his unfolding plan.

We've reviewed a couple of historical examples of when the Spirit intervened in an unusual way. But these situations in the Gospels and Acts don't apply to us. They were just experiences that other people had. We can't obey or strive for an experience like theirs hoping to receive what wasn't intended for us. So, how should we interpret what the Bible means when it says the Spirit leads you and me?

For our application, there are only two places in the teaching passages that refer to being led by the Spirit: Romans 8 and Galatians 5. In the first section of Romans 8, Paul explains that there are only two ways to live. Someone lives with his mind set on either what the flesh desires or what the Spirit desires. The mind is governed either by the flesh or by the Spirit. The person is either in Christ or he is not. Paul equates living for Christ as being "led by the Spirit," since it's the Spirit who works in the life of every believer.

So, being led by the Spirit, in the context of this passage, refers to the Spirit leading you into a life that is different from how you were before Christ. Being sanctified is a lifelong process. You aren't set free of sin immediately. You are, however, free from its bondage.

God accepts you immediately and promises that the Holy Spirit will help change your behavior as you mature in Christ. Your new life is characterized by the fact that sin no longer controls you (as Romans 7 describes). "For those who are led by the Spirit of God are the children of God" (Romans 8:14). In this verse, Paul means that the sanctified life (the led-by-the-Spirit life) is the evidence that you really are a believer.

To help understand this concept, think of Anakin and Luke. Anakin is being led by the dark side into a life characterized by fear, anger, and hate, while Luke is being led by the light side into a life characterized by courage, patience, and love. They still make decisions, but the Force acts as a power that seduces Anakin away from living for peace and justice and moves Luke towards it. Even though the Jedi and Sith have clairvoyant powers that can, in a sense, lead them, I use the word "led" in a different manner. I don't mean how Vader is led to the Rebel hidden base or how Luke is led to Cloud City by the Force. I use "led" like Paul uses it in these passages, which relates to leading one into a transformed life.

The other passage that uses the phrase "led by the Spirit" is Galatians 5. Paul makes the same sort of argument as he does in Romans. He contrasts living for God with not living for God. Some other phrases he uses here to describe the Christian's obedience are "walk by the Spirit," "live by the Spirit," and "keep in step with the Spirit." All of these mean the same thing. Basically, this passage commands us to refrain from committing sinful acts of the flesh, such as sexual immorality, hatred, jealousy, fits of rage, and selfish ambition. We are told to put these off and obey God's commands, which produce attributes like love, joy, peace, kindness, and self-control. Like Romans 8, when Galatians 5 talks about being led by the Spirit, it refers only to being led into a more holy life, one in which the believer is being changed by the Holy Spirit to want to live for his or her Lord in a more God-honoring way.

Like the phrase "led by the Spirit" means something different than its ostensible definition, the phrase "May the Force be with you" implies a different concept once we learn more about the seduction of the dark side. It's interesting how only the Jedi, not the Sith, say this phrase to each other. It wouldn't make sense for the Jedi to wish a ubiquitous energy to be with someone. It also wouldn't make sense for the Jedi to say this only to wish a ubiquitous energy to be with someone. Instead, the Jedi say this phrase as an encouragement to their friends to keep faith in the light side and reject the dark. Just as with this illustration, many of us need to redefine our terminology. If you are a believer, it's impossible for you not to be led by the Spirit.

"Always in Motion is the Future"

Believers love God. The challenge for all of us, though, is to make sure we love God in the way he has prescribed in his Word. Those who love God want to honor him with their choices. Sometimes, these decisions are life or death. For instance, should you approve of a dangerous but potentially helpful surgery on your loved one? This is a decision that most would agonize over. Decisions like this are made substantially harder if we think God holds the right choice and it is up to us to determine what he wants us to do.

When Luke has visions of Han and Leia in pain on Cloud City, he can't concentrate on anything else and is soon plagued with the burden of whether or not he should rush to their aid. Making his decision harder, Yoda and Obi-Wan both tell him not to. Talk about a moral dilemma! We know the weight of this decision and feel Luke's conflict.

When Luke asks his new Master if Han and Leia will die, Yoda lowers his head, closes his eyes, and tries to predict the future. "Difficult to see. Always in motion is the future." How true, but only from our perspective. For us, it seems the future is in motion, because we aren't the ones who planned it or control it.

🎬 Harrison Ford was not always the actor Lucas had in mind for Han Solo. Other actors considered for the role include Sylvester Stallone, Christopher Walken, and Billy Dee Williams.

For God, the future is locked in. Not even Satan can thwart God's controlling will. While the devil does wreak havoc on the world, it's not as though God must employ lightning-fast reflexes to clean up the mess. On the contrary, before time began, God choreographed everything, your life and mine, the good and the bad, things that you can set your watch to, and the situations that come out of nowhere. God can't be blamed for the evil that people do, but that doesn't mean it is beyond his control. Future events seem to be in motion only for those who will participate in them. From God's perspective, his plan A happens precisely as he determined it so long ago.

"I Wonder if Your Feelings on This Matter are Clear"

Whenever the Jedi or Sith attempt to sense the future, they usually tread into murkiness and end up at odds with those around them who are also trying to sense what will happen. Consider this exchange between Obi-Wan and Qui-Gon:

Obi-Wan: "It is not disrespect, Master, it is the truth."
Qui-Gon: "From your point of view."
Obi-Wan: "The boy is dangerous. They all sense it.
          Why can't you?"
Qui-Gon: "His fate is uncertain, not dangerous."

It's not just Qui-Gon with whom Obi-Wan disagrees. Obi-Wan rarely sees eye-to-eye with Anakin, prompting Obi-Wan to say, "Your senses aren't that attuned, young apprentice." Only to have Anakin retort, "And yours are?"

When Luke wants to go to the Imperial Academy, his Uncle Owen thinks it's a bad idea. From Luke's perspective, postponing a whole year feels like a lifetime. Uncle Owen doesn't see that much difference considering it's only one more season.

The Emperor and Darth Vader aren't always on the same page either. After Vader tells the Emperor about feeling Luke's presence, the Emperor says, "Strange, that I have not. I wonder if your feelings on this matter are clear, Lord Vader."

Sometimes, Christians say that God is telling them to do this or that but can't find any scriptures to support their claim. For example, if a pastor tells his church that God is calling him to a different church, yet his congregation says that God is telling them he should stay, who's right? You can begin to see how making decisions after attempting to "hear" the Holy Spirit's voice can cause all sorts of confusion and unnecessary conflict. God tells us in the Bible what to do in regards to sin, but beyond that, he gives us the freedom to make choices on our own. It's fine for a pastor to leave a church and go to another one as long as he has good biblical reasons. It's unfounded, though, for him to say that God is directing him specifically to do so.

The Jedi and the Sith are often wrong when predicting future events. Qui-Gon does not foresee Anakin's terrible downfall. Yoda does not see Luke's triumph. And Anakin misunderstands the visions he has regarding Padmé in pain, not realizing that it would be his actions that would cause her to die.

Not only does trying to figure out God's controlling will cause problems with our own walk, it can cause factions in the body of Christ. Most of the day-to-day decisions in life are merely a matter of preference. If we couch these decisions as if God favors one over the other, we will inject legalism into the Church and cause divisions between those who favor one preference and those who favor another.

"Stretch Out With Your Feelings"

"I have a bad feeling about this," "Stretch out with your feelings," "Search your feelings," "Your feelings for them are strong."

What's all this talk about feelings? Are we watching *Star Wars* or a Jane Austen adaptation? For starters, feelings are important for the Jedi, because they help them engage with the Force. Early in Luke's training, Obi-Wan instructs him to, "let go your conscious self and act on instinct." Since many Christians are taught a similar feelings-based doctrine as a way to learn God's will, we need to spend time studying what God's Word says about the role feelings should play in our lives.

Emotions are a gift from God. Feelings are part of what it means to be human. Problems occur, though, when we mistake our feelings for a prompting from the Holy Spirit. Then we risk allowing our feelings to supplement or, worse, overrule what God commands in his Word. To illustrate, we might avoid confronting someone over his sin, because we "don't have peace about it." This is frequently just couching our fear in a wrapper that makes us seem like we're doing the right thing when, in reality, we are in direct disobedience to biblical commands.

Star Wars teaches us how dangerous it is to rely on feelings and, in our case, try to sense God's voice to make decisions. Just like the Jedi have no method of determining if it's the light side or the dark influencing them, a believer has no technique to determine if the internal feeling or voice he senses is from himself, God, or Satan. If you have something Scripture says you need to do, don't be alarmed if you feel sick to your stomach, have butterflies, or maybe, like Han staring at the *Falcon,* just have "a funny feeling." None of that indicates that you shouldn't do it. Oftentimes, obeying what God commands in his Word is hard to do. We don't have peace. But at that point, we ignore our feelings and trust God. Feelings are just that, and we shouldn't assume our emotional response is the Holy Spirit directing us.

The Still Small Voice

Qui-Gon teaches Anakin that midi-chlorians are life forms living inside all living beings that communicate with the Force. Without midi-chlorians, the Jedi would have no knowledge of the Force. Thinking about it this way, it makes complete sense that the Jedi would try to clear their minds of clutter in order to find out from the midi-chlorians what the Force's will is.

I used to do the same sort of thing with the Holy Spirit to try to figure out God's will for my life. Sometimes when I prayed, I'd try to listen to God speaking to my heart. I wouldn't necessarily be thinking about anything in particular, just waiting.

In 2004, a postdoctoral researcher discovered bacteria living in the cells of female ticks. Because of the similarity to midi-chlorians, he received permission from Lucas to name the symbiotic bacteria Midichloria.

Why was I doing this? Why did this seem like it could work? This is a popular method for many Christians to try to find God's will, but is it biblical? Is it taught in God's Word as an acceptable method, or does it just continue generation after generation without much question regarding its biblical basis? I can't do much about midi-chlorians. There's no turning back, as it is now part of *Star Wars* canon. But I hope to help you understand the discipline of trying to hear the Spirit's voice, why this practice evolved, and if this exercise should continue.

Many well-intentioned believers say we need to listen to God's "still small voice" in order to determine what he wants us to do. The "still small voice" is a phrase found in the King James Version of 1 Kings 19. "And after the earthquake a fire; but the Lord was not in the fire: and after the fire a *still small voice*" (1 Kings 19:12, emphasis mine). The NIV translation calls this a "gentle whisper."

This is an especially important passage to understand the context. In it, we find that, fearing for his life, Elijah has fled to Horeb. The following account describes when God appears to Elijah.

> The Lord *said*, "Go out and stand on the mountain in the presence of the Lord, for the Lord is about to pass by." Then a great and powerful wind tore the mountains apart and shattered the rocks before the Lord, but the Lord was not in the wind. After the wind there was an earthquake, but the Lord was not in the earthquake. After the earthquake came a fire, but the Lord was not in the fire. And after the fire came a gentle whisper. When Elijah *heard* it, he pulled his cloak over his face and went out and stood at the mouth of the cave. Then a voice *said* to him, "What are you doing here, Elijah?" He replied, "I have been very zealous for the Lord God Almighty. The Israelites have rejected your covenant, torn down your altars, and put your prophets to death with the sword. I am the only one left, and now they are trying to kill me too." The Lord *said* to him, "Go back the way you came, and go to the Desert of Damascus. When you get there, anoint Hazael king over Aram. (1 Kings 19:11–15, emphasis mine)

Notice that the Lord has already told Elijah that he will show up soon. All the next verses do is describe that, for reasons known only by God, the Lord caused a strong wind, an earthquake, and a fire to occur. Maybe this was just to freak Elijah out a little and get his attention. It certainly seems to have done the trick, because when the Lord speaks again, Elijah pulls his cloak over his face like a frightened child pulls the covers over his head.

The point is that the gentle whisper (the still small voice) was a sound, one that others nearby would have heard, too. The ESV translation says that Elijah heard "the sound of a low whisper." This is one of if not the main proof texts used to defend this belief, and it's not even about God speaking to one's inner being.

There's a certain amount of humility required of the Jedi in their quest to find the Force's will. The Jedi and Sith are some of the most powerful beings in the galaxy, yet they keep silent in order for microscopic life forms to be allowed to speak. Qui-Gon teaches Anakin that he must learn to quiet his mind in order to hear the midi-chlorians speaking to him. When this happens, they will tell him the Force's will. While we shouldn't duplicate this type of meditation to hear from the Holy Spirit, we should imitate the Jedi's humility when we study God's ethical will revealed in his Word.

It's an admirable quality for believers to want to do God's will. It distinguishes God's people from unbelievers who couldn't care less. No Christian would spend the time and effort required to try to listen to the Spirit if he didn't truly believe that this is a way God communicates. But again, if we have no way to distinguish the voices in our head, then how do we know for sure that it's God's voice?

There are other places when the Bible mentions hearing God's voice. Jesus tells us in John 10 that his sheep hear his voice. In the context of this passage, is this an instruction to try to hear God's voice internally, determine his will, and make a correct decision or is this describing something else?

To help understand this passage, John tells us that Jesus used a figure of speech (John 10:6). In other words, Jesus is not literally a shepherd, nor are we literally sheep. These verses do not describe a special spiritual method by which Jesus communicates with believers through impressions. Instead, this passage begins by describing believers being drawn to Christ. When the shepherd "calls," this is the inward call when we first trust in Christ. The verses go on to describe believers obeying God and unbelievers disobeying him. Consistent with the literary device being used, the Lord's "voice" that we "hear" is the one conveyed through his Word. Believers know the truth and, therefore, will not obey a false prophet described as having a "stranger's voice" in verse 5. This section of Scripture also describes Jesus being the only means of salvation and that Jesus will lay down his life for God's people. This passage is packed with a lot of things, but how to find God's individual will for your life is not one of them.

When the Empire destroys Alderaan, Obi-Wan senses that something terrible has happened, but he can't quite put his finger on it. If we try to listen to the Holy Spirit to find God's will, we will be stuck with similar ambiguity. God gave us the absolute truth of his Word so that we would not be tossed around in life enslaved to our own random thoughts and emotions.

"Decide You Must"

Making big decisions in life can be extremely difficult. As we have seen, we can't always take Obi-Wan's advice of just doing what we feel is right. In fact, for the Christian, making the right choice can be especially tough, because we want to please the God of the universe. As a result, we put pressure on ourselves to get things right.

The characters in the *Star Wars* galaxy have it no easier with their big decisions. Should Luke leave Dagobah to try to rescue Han and Leia? Should Queen Amidala trust Qui-Gon's judgment? Should Watto wager Anakin's freedom in a pod race? Should the Jedi Council allow Anakin to be trained? One wrong move could have major ramifications for the entire galaxy!

🔭 The chance cube (used to decide Anakin's fate) is supposed to have three red sides and three blue. Watto rigged his with five red and only one blue and weighted it to land on red.

Our decisions are usually less consequential to the galaxy. For instance, which college should you attend? Should you take this job or that one? Who should you date? Who should you marry? Should you have children? Should you adopt? What about being a missionary or going to seminary? The list goes on, and those are only the decisions we deem especially important. Some believers spiritualize decisions like the color of their shirt or with whom to have lunch. From their perspective, all of life is about doing God's will and they want to do everything possible to be within it.

Realizing that there are all sorts of pitfalls in this area, how are believers to make God-honoring decisions at every turn in the road? The answer is surprisingly simple. Since it's impossible to know God's controlling will until after it happens, we should devote our time and energy towards being in his ethical will. And how do we do that? We dedicate our attention to obeying the commands laid out in the teaching passages of the New Testament. When it involves matters related to his controlling will, we pray not expecting God to pop the answers into our heads. His controlling will is for him alone to know. When it comes to decisions, our prayers should focus on the ethical dilemmas that may be involved in a decision. We pray for insight into his Word, because that's where God reveals his ethical will for us. Now, let's dive deeper into some other decisions we might face.

In a romantic relationship, like every other area in life, we need to strive to honor God by obeying his Word. Paul tells us not only what God's will is regarding sex but accompanies this revelation with a command: "It is God's will that you should be sanctified: that you should avoid sexual immorality; that each of you should learn to control your own body in a way that is holy and honorable, not in passionate lust like the pagans, who do not know God" (1 Thessalonians 4:3–5).

In order to be "in" God's will, it's not enough to simply know it. We must obey the corresponding command. Obedience is what leads us to being in his ethical will. God does not tell us exactly how this will look. Is holding hands allowed? Is kissing forbidden? These are decisions that you have the freedom to make, and only you can determine if you cross the line physically where you are no longer glorifying the Lord.

Before I was married, it would have been fine to pray for the Spirit to sanctify me in this area of sexual immorality, but I would have been mocking God if I asked him whether or not I should date a woman who had no interest in obeying or helping me obey the above commandment. That prayer would not be necessary, because his Word already establishes the answer.

Lots of Christians stress over the decision whether or not to marry, who to marry, or even who, if, and when they should date. In *Episode V,* the love story between Han and Leia makes even the most hardened cynic want to cheer for them. Their romance is not without obstacles, though. Being key players in the middle of a galactic war is not exactly like vacationing in Paris. Plus, he's a scoundrel and she likes nice men. Will they make it? Should they make it?

Han and Leia's relationship aside, how can you know if God wants you to marry a certain person? The answer is not as hard as we make it sometimes. Believers are free to marry someone of the opposite sex, but only if he or she is a believer. "A woman is bound to her husband as long as he lives. But if her husband dies, she is free to marry anyone she wishes, *but he must belong to the Lord"* (1 Corinthians 7:39, emphasis mine).

It's obvious that Anakin fails to make the right decision by marrying Padmé, because the Jedi are forbidden to marry. The Jedi tenet is black and white on this issue, just as the Bible is on believers marrying unbelievers. Unfortunately, sometimes, we can mistake strong romantic feelings as the Holy Spirit's prodding. The situation can become even worse if we think that God's main goal is to make us happy. Anakin's choice reminds us of what not to do. Oftentimes, finding and doing God's will can be distilled down to whether or not we will obey a single biblical command.

Just because the two people involved are believers doesn't mean there aren't other important matters to consider before marrying. Does one have a strong desire to do world missions? Does one want to adopt children and the other does not? Will the man be able to provide for his family? Some of these the Bible may address, and others it may not. In those cases, seeking the counsel of mature believers is always a wise choice.

Sometimes, the decision to take a job can weigh heavily on a believer, especially if there is more than one from which to choose. Again, we can look to the Bible to determine if it would be a sin to take the job. For instance, it's a sin for a man to take a job knowing that he will not be able to provide for his family (1 Timothy 5:8). It's sin if the job forces him to conduct himself in an immoral manner (Philippians 1:27). It's sin if the job is so isolated that fellowship with other believers is impossible (Hebrews 10:25). God gives us a lot of freedom when it comes to deciding on a profession. Would you like to work on droids? Then you are free to take a job in robotics. Does the idea of making the Kessel Run in less than twelve parsecs sound cool? Then a career flying airplanes might be for you. Once you rule out the sin factor, enjoy making your decision!

To summarize, the process of making decisions can be something we do to honor God. However, it can also be a trap Satan uses to distract us with questions that are impossible to answer. Once you know from reading the Bible that you won't be sinning by making a certain choice, you will be in both the ethical will *and* the controlling will of God no matter what decision you make. If you need to wrestle through a decision, look to God's Word and pray for insight, but do not mistake your thoughts as the Holy Spirit telling you what choice to make. We can only know God's ethical will for certain. Commands like "love your enemies," "give generously," "be joyful always," and "do not worry" are all blatant revelations of God's will for our lives. We just need to obey the commands like these that the Bible gives us, make the best decisions we can, and trust that his controlling will is perfect. The encouragement is that everything God orchestrates is for the believer's good. Moreover, he has given us his Holy Spirit to motivate and strengthen us so that we will mature and glorify him with our lives, including our successes as well as our mistakes.

THE JOURNEY CONTINUES

Don't cut in the sublight engines just yet. We've still got more Star Wars and theology to talk about. The title of this last part does not apply to this book only but also to the lifelong journey you're on with Jesus. Chapter 15 will teach you about the role the Church plays in your walk with God. Chapter 16 will help you figure out what your responsibility should be in areas related to government, country, and politics. Finally, in Chapter 17, "The End Times," we'll study what the Bible says about the Second Coming, the last days, and the ultimate destination of your journey.

PART V

THE CHURCH

○○○○○○○○○○○○○○●○○

G od could just take people to heaven as soon as he forgives their sins, but he doesn't. He keeps believers here to be the Church. In this chapter, we'll study the Church in the New Covenant era, comparing and contrasting it with the Jedi equivalent. Like brothers and sisters in Christ, the Jedi often only have each other on which to rely. The Jedi Order acts as a sort of Church in the sense that they are a large body of diverse members whose goal is spiritual growth. We'll consider the "Church" (capital "C"), i.e., the universal body of all believers, as well as the local church (lowercase "c"). Let's start with explaining a major purpose of the Church.

Equipping the Believer

God designed the Church to instruct believers on how to live in a way that honors him. "Christ gave teachers and pastors to equip his people for works of service, so that the body of Christ may be built up" (Ephesians 4:12). Paul goes on to explain that the goal of this is so that believers aren't blown here and there by every wind of teaching.

The Jedi Council shepherds the Jedi as pastors and elders might guide their flock. When this is done correctly, the Jedi grow up in the knowledge of the Force, able to serve as guardians of peace and justice throughout the galaxy. Every wise Jedi knows he must be equipped with a lightsaber, but he also needs to be taught to distinguish from the dark side of the Force and the light, as evidenced by Luke early in his journey when he asks, "But how am I to know the good side from the bad?"

The *Star Wars* saga is broken up into two trilogies. *Episodes I–III* demonstrate the larger corporate body of the Jedi. The scale of this is massive. Therefore, it is difficult for us to appreciate the love and respect one Jedi has for another. The original trilogy gives us a more intimate perspective, first with Luke and Obi-Wan and later with Luke and Yoda. But the goal of equipping the Jedi doesn't change, only the means of reaching that goal.

In the prequels, the Jedi Temple and Council exist to facilitate the teaching, rebuking, correcting, and training of the Jedi Order. After the "Great Jedi Purge," only a handful of Jedi remain. However, sheer numbers do not indicate success or failure for the Jedi. On the contrary, it's during this dark time that our heroes overcome their tribulation to bring balance to the Force.

Let's look at how Obi-Wan plays a pivotal role to equip Luke. When Luke first learns of the Force, he believes in it without question. Obi-Wan doesn't need to argue his point or levitate his belongings around the room. Even though Luke believes right away, he understands very little. He needs a lot of instruction to grow in his new faith. From that point on, Obi-Wan teaches Luke and prepares him for the trials he will face one day. This is a picture of someone trusting in Jesus but then needing to be taught what to do next.

During *Episode IV*, we witness a personal relationship between Obi-Wan and Luke that mirrors the one between Paul and Timothy. By this point in the saga, the Jedi's fire has almost been extinguished. Obi-Wan has lost his friends, his home, and his freedom. He needs to rebuild the Jedi Order, and he starts with a single person.

Obi-Wan begins equipping Luke to become a Jedi, but he does so much more. It's not just the know-how of swinging a lightsaber and performing Jedi mind tricks that Luke needs. He needs a mentor in the faith like Paul was to Timothy. Obi-Wan protects, encourages, trains, admonishes, and loves Luke. It is Obi-Wan's unwavering commitment that helps Luke succeed.

Fulfilling the classic "hero's journey," Obi-Wan, the mentor, dies and Luke, the hero, must finish not only his spiritual journey but also his galactic adventure alone. Likewise, Paul invested his life into Timothy so that Timothy could carry on the ministry once Paul was gone. The Obi-Wan/Luke relationship spurs us on to be either a Paul or a Timothy. If you are mature in the faith, find someone into whom you can pour your life. If you are new to the faith, search out a mentor in your church from whom you can learn.

🔭 Lucas was influenced by Joseph Campbell's *The Hero with a Thousand Faces*, in which Campbell describes how ancient myths followed certain archetypes, such as the hero's journey.

Luke never has more than one or two Jedi from whom to seek counsel or training. He doesn't have any other Jedi to ask if Obi-Wan gave him the truth about the Force and his father. He also doesn't have the Jedi Archives or the Jedi Code to help him glean wisdom or guidance.

For the Christian, this situation is especially dangerous. We can't allow ourselves to become isolated. We need to immerse ourselves in sound doctrine and surround ourselves with mature believers. Luke makes it through his adventure without the Emperor luring him to the dark side, but with few Jedi in the galaxy to whom he could turn, this could have easily been the end of our hero.

Why is it so important to be well equipped in God's Word? The reason is that some churches teach bad doctrine. Some do so out of ignorance, others out of deceit. When this bad theology influences behavior, people get hurt emotionally and spiritually. When you put yourself under the teaching of anyone (including this book), it's your responsibility to be like the Bereans, "for they received the message with great eagerness and examined the Scriptures every day to see if what Paul said was true" (Acts 17:11b). Pastors, elders, and anyone who teaches in a church has an obligation to equip believers to discern the truth. This helps Christians live God-honoring lives while evading the ubiquitous lies of the world.

Anakin has a hopeful beginning, spending his early years learning about the Force from great Jedi Masters like Qui-Gon and Obi-Wan. The entire Jedi Council, including Yoda and Mace Windu, also help to shape his view of the Force. Anakin also has access to the Jedi Library on Coruscant and can discuss the failures and successes of past Jedi with any of his mentors. Anakin lacks little in terms of gifts or resources to become a great Jedi. Unfortunately, he lacks two crucial traits: humility and discernment. Palpatine recognizes these weaknesses in Anakin and swoops in to turn the young Jedi to the dark side.

In our world, charlatans try to deceive ill-equipped people in order to gain money and followers. Their most effective weapon is the "prosperity gospel." You'll find this sort of teaching in churches across the globe, even on major TV channels. We can learn from Anakin's mistakes and not believe the misinterpretations or outright lies that come from many of these popular pastors and teachers. Most leaders in churches are men who love Jesus and want to serve him faithfully, but some are not. We must be on guard 24/7 to ensure our faith is not shipwrecked.

Scripture talks about how people gravitate to false teaching, because that's what their itching ears want (2 Timothy 4:3). Church leaders know that if they teach the hard truths of the Bible, they could drive people away. But the true believers, the folks who hunger for the truth, will search out a church that teaches the Word of God faithfully.

It would have been easy for Yoda to perpetuate the lie that Vader killed Luke's father. This would have served the light side well, because Luke would not have struggled emotionally with destroying Vader. But that would not be the reality. Yoda makes the hard call to tell Luke the truth, and in doing so, puts aside his own needs in order to do the right thing.

With the elegance of a false teacher, Palpatine misleads Anakin with the promise of a better future. He also tells Anakin that he is more powerful than the rest of the Jedi. He appeals to Anakin's pride, giving him exactly what his itching ears want to hear. It's easy for Anakin to fall under Palpatine's influence, but it's not healthy.

When we find a church that teaches sound doctrine, the groundwork is laid for our relationship with God to deepen. As God intends, we are equipped for works of service, given the opportunities to invest in others, and taught to discern true teaching from false, all while building up the body of Christ.

Fellowship

We have tackled a lot of fairly deep theological concepts in this book. The point, though, is not to fill our minds with a bunch of profound, spiritual ideas. The goal of our theology is to help us to love God and others better. 1 John is all about how we should love others in light of God loving us. In fact, John says that we aren't really in love with God if we don't love others.

For the Jedi, it's not only his fellow follower in the faith that he is to love, but also those outside the Jedi ranks. The Jedi are sworn to protect the citizens of the Republic. Thus, they are willing to sacrifice even their lives (the ultimate act of love) for them if necessary. For Anakin, the Jedi represents the Church and the Jedi Council represents church leadership. Meaning, if he loves anyone, it should be his Jedi brothers and sisters (to borrow terms from Christianity). If he can't do that, then even his love for Padmé is not true love, merely a selfish distortion.

Like Anakin's self-absorption, the trouble with many churches today is that people walk through the doors asking what can this church do for me. It's not a bad question in and of itself. We need to ask if the church can equip us to live lives that honor God. It's when we are only looking out for ourselves that we run into trouble. Whenever we are around other believers, we need to strive to build them up in Christ.

Anakin misses the mark badly when it comes to loving others. Luke has many of the same weaknesses, such as impatience, pride, and recklessness. And yet, Luke overcomes those shortcomings and proves that he really is a Jedi. He puts his life on the line for others many times during the films, but the pinnacle of his love for others comes at the end of *Episode VI*. Luke falls into the Emperor's trap of letting his anger and hate overtake him during his duel with Vader. But once Luke confronts the decision to kill his father, he doesn't. Instead, he chooses to take on the wrath of the Emperor by refusing to obey him. When Luke does this, he fulfills Jesus' command found in Matthew 5:44, which teaches us to love our enemies.

Our churches should, likewise, teach us to love so that it spills out not only to our fellow Christians but also to our enemies. It's not difficult to love those who treat us well. It wasn't hard for Han and Leia to love each other. What is challenging is for someone like a Jedi to love a Sith.

"My command is this: Love each other as I have loved you" (John 15:12). Jesus' powerful example is what differentiates church gatherings from other groups. Most people come together and form organizations based on common interests, such as video games, antique cars, or bowling. Churches are the complete opposite. People from different backgrounds, with different personalities and interests, come together for a single reason: to worship Jesus.

Unfortunately, all those dissimilarities form the perfect cauldron for misunderstandings, differing opinions, and egos to stir up. Church is not a place for perfect people to get along perfectly. It's a place for sinners to admit they are imperfect and to look to Christ for the power to reconcile. Since we're all unworthy without Christ's righteousness, the Church levels the playing field and creates an atmosphere where we can build each other up rather than tear each other down.

The Jedi, like the Church, is also comprised of different alien races with their own distinct cultures. Jedi can be men or women who are each shaped by different opinions, preferences, and experiences. This often results in conflict between them. Consider how the Jedi Council disapproves of Qui-Gon's rebelliousness, particularly concerning his desire to train Anakin. As doctrinal issues can cause arguments and divisions in the body of Christ, Qui-Gon's focus on the Living Force causes dissension among the other Jedi, who see more benefit in fulfilling destinies than living in the moment.

🔭 Lucas resigned from the Director's Guild of America after he was fined $250,000 for not including director Irvin Kershner's name at the beginning of *Episode V*.

This book is filled with examples of how one Christian can believe something while another believes the opposite. What we learn from *Star Wars* is how to handle our differences. We don't let bitterness take hold as Anakin does when he says, "It's all Obi-Wan's fault. He's jealous. He's holding me back." Anakin never talked with

Obi-Wan about how their relationship was falling apart until it was too late. If we harbor bad thoughts against others, especially believers, we fail to love them. Our Father never resents us even though we mess up all the time. We should show the same grace and love to others.

Anakin's actions should not surprise us considering human nature. The Jedi have no God who loves unconditionally or provides the supernatural ability to do the same. Even Padmé says at one point that she cannot follow Anakin on his path. This is a common failure in every world religion. Only Christianity boasts a God who can love sinners. If that model is not there, then people are left to try to muster up love for others out of a sinful heart. That superficial affection may work for a while, but when life really gets hard, the relationship will inevitably break down.

Submission

The Bible tells us that Christians must always submit to their pastors and elders in the areas that they have authority over us unless it would be sin to do so. "Have confidence in your leaders and submit to their authority, because they keep watch over you as those who must give an account. Do this so that their work will be a joy, not a burden, for that would be of no benefit to you" (Hebrews 13:17).

All through *Episode II* and *III,* Anakin fails continually to submit joyfully to Obi-Wan and the Jedi Council. He catches himself occasionally, but it's usually only after he has defied them, talked back, or shown disrespect for their authority.

God places us in roles where we must submit to those in authority. Citizens submit to their government. Employees submit to their employers. Wives submit to their husbands. Children submit to their parents and so on. In our local churches, we submit to the pastors and elders whom God has placed over us. We honor God when we show this respect and submission.

Padawans must submit to their Masters. There are many times when Anakin doesn't agree with the Jedi. He doesn't agree that his fear is worth pointing out. He doesn't agree with their views on romantic relationships. And he doesn't agree when they put him on the Council but do not make him a Master. Most of the time, he doesn't submit with a good attitude. Instead, he becomes defensive, hides his marriage, and grows increasingly bitter.

While Luke doesn't have any problems submitting to Obi-Wan, he struggles to submit to Yoda. By the time Luke meets Yoda, Luke thinks pretty highly of himself. He's saved a princess, blown up the Death Star, and single-handedly taken down an Imperial walker. He looks at this pint-sized, wrinkly, green, backward-talking dude who lives in a swamp and assumes he has nothing valuable to offer. Soon, Luke will enter a dangerous time when he is tempted by the dark side. He needs to repent of his pride, submit to Yoda, and learn everything he can from this wise Master.

When Luke faces the decision to leave Dagobah in order to help Han and Leia, he goes against the counsel of his Masters. It's important to submit to the leaders of your church in the areas they have authority over you, but you might have to make a similarly hard decision. For instance, if you feel like you're not receiving good biblical teaching or prudent counsel from your church, schedule a time when you can talk with your pastor(s). Perhaps you differ theologically on something. Discuss the issues and pray together. If your church leaders do not change their stance (and they probably won't), you can either stay, keeping relatively silent about your opinion, or you can attend another church. It's a decision only you can make. The point may be minor and something you can live with. Of course, if your church misrepresents the gospel, then that is definitely a reason *not* to submit to the leaders or their teaching and go elsewhere instead.

Evangelism

In the *Star Wars* galaxy, someone might have a high midi-chlorian count but not know it. Since they're not born with the knowledge of the Force, this information must be shared with them. In the Old Republic, the Jedi try to recruit younglings strong in the Force before they have a chance to develop any sort of fears or attachments. If the Jedi aren't sent out to tell others of the Force, the Jedi Order will die out.

Similar to the Jedi sharing about the Force, Christians have an obligation to share the good news of Jesus with others. Believers follow in the footsteps of the apostles regarding their evangelical outreach. Unlike the Jedi, a blood test can't shed light on whom to share with. Instead, we must do as the "Parable of the Sower" alludes to and scatter our evangelistic message all over the place, to every type of person, because we have no idea who might respond. Sometimes, it's the last person in the world who we would think would be interested in the gospel. Even though God can turn someone into a believer (without our involvement), he created a method in which we can participate. In short, we must preach the Word before someone can believe it (Romans 10:14).

Whose responsibility is it to share Christ with unbelievers? Is it every individual Christian, the local churches, missionaries, evangelistic groups, or a mix of all of this? The *Star Wars* films only give us a couple of instances when a Jedi shares about the Force: Qui-Gon with Anakin and Obi-Wan with Luke. Was this the normal method of Force evangelism, or does the Jedi Order regularly send Jedi throughout the galaxy to find new Force-sensitive recruits? These samples indicate that it's the responsibility of the individual Jedi to share their faith.

🗡 Mos Espa is the city where Qui-Gon meets Anakin. Recently, Tunisian sands began burying the real-life site. A crowd-funding campaign was started in 2014 to help preserve the location.

This brings up the question of how much importance the Church should place on evangelism. Jesus commands his apostles to go out into the world and share the gospel, but he doesn't command us directly to do this. While Paul went on missionary journeys, he doesn't command the churches to do the same. We do read from Paul that we are "sent" to preach the gospel (Romans 10:15). But for most of us, going out into the world, means going to work, to the grocery store, or to school. For those who don't go on missionary trips, we share Christ whenever we can with whomever God has placed in our lives.

Still, we need to reconcile the fact that the majority of the New Testament teaching passages prioritizes believers' sanctification far above unbelievers coming to Christ. So, are churches spending too much time reaching out to the lost? Are they doing too little? Let's keep going and see if we can find the answer.

Seeker-Sensitive Jedi?

Is there anything that we should do to make the gospel more inviting? Luke is resistant at first when hearing Obi-Wan's offer to be trained as a Jedi. The young farmer understands that this means giving up his old life and trusting in the unknown. When presenting this proposal, Obi-Wan doesn't promise anything good for Luke. He doesn't try to emphasize the positives of cool lightsabers, traveling to exciting worlds, or meeting a beautiful princess. Besides Obi-Wan stressing that Leia needs his help, he doesn't try to "sell" Luke on the idea at all.

Qui-Gon goes a step further in "anti-selling" the life of a Jedi. While young Anakin is giddy at the thought of boarding a starship and venturing off into the life of a Jedi, Qui-Gon brings the boy back down to reality by stressing that, "training to be a Jedi will not be an easy challenge, and if you succeed, it will be a hard life."

These are good examples of how believers should share Christ with others. In this present climate of pastors preaching that God wants you to have "your best life now," it's good for us to be honest with others. I don't mean that we should bend over backwards saying all the hard things about being a Christian, but we shouldn't hide them either, thinking that the person will not accept Christ if we disclose the difficult stuff. Jesus was not shy about promising his followers suffering in this life (John 16:33).

This is another area where understanding the doctrines of grace (discussed in Part 3) helps us in our Christian walk. If someone is one of God's elect, nothing will stop him from coming to Christ at the appointed time. The Church doesn't need to water down the gospel so that it is more palatable. That's human thinking. God commands us to preach the truth. It seems counterintuitive to try to get people to obey the command to die to themselves, but Proverbs 3:5 tells us not to lean on our own understanding. "For the message of the cross is foolishness to those who are perishing, but to us who are being saved it is the power of God" (1 Corinthians 1:18).

Many churches strive for the label "seeker-sensitive" to describe their church services. The term is fairly self-evident. These churches design their Sunday mornings to cater to the unbeliever who may visit. The pastor might reference pop culture, deliver a topical rather than expository message, and end the sermon with a call to believe the gospel. The music is more of a rock concert than an attempt to lead believers to praise God with song. The church service is designed with an overarching goal to help unbelievers feel welcome. Some megachurches even offer gyms, shopping, and a Starbucks to get more people in the door.

On the surface, this seems like a very loving, others-centered approach to reaching out to unbelievers. I don't question the hearts of people who might belong to a church like this. There's nothing wrong with having a Starbucks in your church. I like coffee just as much as the next person. My question is, what's the fundamental strategy, and is that strategy something on which the Bible places a premium? Was Paul more concerned with the numbers on the roster or the purity and holiness of the body of Christ? It's great to try to cater to others, but not when it results in a church service that benefits unbelievers at the expense of preaching God's Word.

In the past, pastors would preach messages replete with "fire and brimstone" in order to scare a person into the kingdom. God was not painted as a loving God but an angry God who you better take seriously. The pendulum has swung far the other way. You would be hard pressed to find a church with a large congregation that endorses this sort of preaching. Now, the message is, "come as you are, and you don't have to ever change, because God is loving and accepting." His anger against sin and looming judgment have been written out. To be fair, the gospel does say come as you are. Don't try to clean yourself up before coming to Christ, because that's impossible. But when churches don't include repentance and lordship as a part of accepting Christ, they gut the gospel.

Obi-Wan doesn't allow Anakin to simply do as he wants. When Anakin doesn't act in accord with his position as a Padawan, Obi-Wan says, "We will do as the Council has instructed, and you will learn your place, young one." Church leaders need to have a similar boldness (although with more gentleness) when it comes to preaching about lordship to their congregations. They should not filter the Bible in an effort to avoid offending unbelievers.

✗ The Jedi Temple was first shown in *Episode I*. The Temple was added to the 2004 DVD release of *Episode VI*.

A danger with many seeker-sensitive churches is that the church leadership rarely gets to know everyone in their congregation. Eventually, unbelievers are treated as though they are believers, because they have been so integrated into the church. In a large congregation, who can tell the difference? But Paul says, "Do not be misled: 'Bad company corrupts good character'" (1 Corinthians 15:33). Paul was more concerned that believers have transformed lives than he was with unbelievers feeling comfortable. The Jedi are faithful to protect the purity of their religion. If even the Jedi are this way, why do so many churches see no danger in integrating unbelievers into their fellowship? Seeker-sensitive churches, in an effort to win more souls for Christ, have not only missed the forest for the trees, they have lit a match to that forest.

It's fine to have unbelievers visit our churches. It's a great opportunity for them to hear about Jesus and see how believers love each other. The difference is that they are still outsiders looking in on something special. Therefore, it's okay for them to feel a little left out at times. It's actually the more loving thing for Christians to do. The worst thing is to make people feel like God accepts them when he does not. False assurance of salvation is a very dangerous position, because you fail to see your desperate need for Christ. Most churches are not actually saying to their unbelieving visitors, "You are Christians like us," but the waters get muddied, whether deliberately or not. Today, churches across our land have huge percentages of unbelievers attending services, and many times it's the unbelievers influencing the believers to behave in worldly ways rather than make a biblical stand for Jesus.

Dark Side Allowed in the Jedi Order?

At the end of the day, does all this seeker sensitivity harm believers spiritually? Is this how God intended churches to function? Have we become so worried about offending people and keeping the pews filled that we disobey God? Would you find it strange if the Jedi Council recruited a Force-sensitive individual, brought him into the Jedi Temple, trained him as a Jedi, but did not emphasize the dangers of the dark side or the immediate need to repent of fear, anger, and hate? Should the Jedi Council allow him to influence the other younglings, Padawans, and Jedi? Of course not, and the Jedi Council would give their lives to stop this from ever happening. This illustration is different from a Sith wanting to repent of his allegiance to the dark side and devote himself to the light. The issue is when someone wants a little of both.

Unbelievers need our love, and we should give it freely, because as unworthy as we are, God loves us. However, Paul saw the importance of keeping the Church pure and was not afraid of excluding unbelievers to ensure this purity. In 1 Corinthians 5, the church tolerated a professing believer's sin rather than call him to repentance. Sound familiar? It should, because that is the mark of so many churches today. Paul knew the most loving thing was to treat the man like an unbeliever so that he might repent. When a church does this properly, a soul can be won for Christ. Regardless of whether the person repents, God commands his Church to keep his holy standard.

Later in 2 Corinthians, Paul writes about this same man. This time, Paul tells the Corinthian church to welcome him back, because he repented. This is how God designed our churches to work. Paul says that the man was made sorrowful for a little while, but that it was good, because it caused him to repent. Lots of churches, nowadays, are too worried about upsetting someone to mention sin, let alone call for repentance.

The Jedi Council should not lower their standards to include Anakin. Once he shows even more dark qualities, they should expel him from the Jedi ranks. While they sense immoral qualities in him, they stop short of their responsibility. Because of this, Anakin is lost to the dark side, and most of the Jedi are killed.

All of us will sin until the day we die. This is not about pointing fingers to feel self-righteous. It's about helping others to avoid the road that leads to destruction. If our lives are characterized by a certain sin, like sexual immorality, greed, or laziness, this should alarm not only us but also our local churches. Believers need to be involved in each other's lives so that each of us can identify if another gets dangerously off track. At that point, as Galatians 6:1 commands, the one not trapped in sin needs to come alongside gently and help the brother or sister find the way back.

This is where the Jedi get it right. Obi-Wan loves Anakin so much that he evaluates Anakin's life constantly and cautions him about his wrong choices (like getting too close to Palpatine). Regrettably, Anakin shows his true colors and ends up wanting nothing to do with Obi-Wan. This will happen sometimes. If church leadership puts pressure on someone to repent, the experience might expose the person as an unbeliever. If the person does not repent, it's the responsibility of the church, specifically the church leaders, to expel him.

🔭 In 2015, thousands of Turkish university students signed a petition to build a Jedi Temple on their campus.

The Jedi are extremely careful when it comes to choosing whom they will take in as a Padawan learner or as a member on the Council. In general, they only recruit the very young to begin Jedi training. They are quite rigid in this practice and rarely deviate from it. When evaluating Luke as a potential Jedi, Yoda has grave concerns not only about Luke's age but also regarding his impatience, recklessness, anger, and fear. Moreover, Yoda, Mace Windu, and the rest of the Jedi Council are hesitant to approve Anakin's training because of similar qualities. Is all this too paranoid, too strict, or just plain snobby? After all, who do they think they are playing God with people's lives like this?

Actually, what these wise Jedi do is commendable, and the 21st century Church would do well to make the same sort of judgment calls when evaluating those who call themselves believers. The Jedi guard their religion to keep it pure from the dark side's influence. If the Jedi do not discern a person's inclination to the dark side ahead of time, then it's too late once he or she has been trusted within the Jedi fold. This is why Anakin's betrayal is so devastating. He already has full access to the Jedi Temple. During Order 66, he walks right up to his victims and strikes them down before anyone has a chance to defend himself. Historically, the Jedi are so selective, because there can be terrible consequences if the purity of their Order is diluted with even the slightest dark side influence.

Conclusion

By the end of *Episode IV,* Luke is not ready to share the good news of Jediism with his friends at Tosche Station. He had a lot more learning to do before thinking about doing that. As these sections on evangelism have shown, sometimes churches (even with the best intentions) sacrifice some of the gospel in an attempt to save the lost. Their love for others should be commended. We should be concerned for those in the world who do not know Christ. But our zeal must be combined with the knowledge and truth of the Bible.

Paul starts off Romans 10 with these words: "Brothers and sisters, my heart's desire and prayer to God for the Israelites is that they may be saved. For I can testify about them that they are zealous for God, but their zeal is not based on knowledge" (Romans 10:1–2). Paul says that it doesn't matter how much enthusiasm people have to seek out and serve God. If their idea of God is not true, their faith will not save them. Likewise, if those who evangelize are not biblically grounded, then there is a danger that their message will not reflect God's truth.

Paul spent very little time instructing churches to evangelize. Instead, he equipped them to know Christ. He taught that believers grow in their knowledge of God through his Word. When we study the Bible, our theology deepens. We, in turn, know God better. When we know God better, the Holy Spirit uses that knowledge to increase our love for God. A deeper love for God results in more love for people. A stronger love for people links to wanting to share the gospel!

Not only that, we will have the theology in our minds and hearts to present the gospel boldly, answer their questions, and offer up prayers consistent with Scripture. This approach is why all of Paul's letters start off with chapters on theology and end with how that knowledge manifests in the practical side of living for Christ.

Therefore, we have come full circle back to the primary role of churches, which is to equip believers for good works. It's why Yoda spends so much time training Luke on Dagobah. By the time we reach *Episode VI*, Luke has the proper "doctrinal foundation" to face Vader and point him back to the light side. To thrive as a body of believers, a church's emphasis on evangelism, while perhaps appropriate, should never supersede the foremost purpose of equipping the saints.

Transform Society?

When Obi-Wan enters the cantina at Mos Eisley, his goal is not to transform the scum and villainy around him into good, upstanding citizens. Unlike years before in *Episode II*, when he uses a Jedi mind trick to influence a death stick dealer to go home and rethink his life, he doesn't even waste his breath this time. Why not? Doesn't he care for those poor creatures? Obi-Wan, like the rest of the Jedi, knows it is not his mandate to try to change the morality of those around them. He is a keeper of the peace, no more.

🔭 Anthony Daniels plays a human named Dannl Faytonni in the nightclub where Obi-Wan talks with Elan Sel'Sabagno a.k.a. Sleazebaggano (wanna buy some death sticks).

The characters in *Star Wars* know how hard it is to set others on the right course. Leia knows it's impossible to choose a path for Han. Obi-Wan and Yoda wring their hands after Luke chooses to face Vader prematurely. Even Threepio must let his little counterpart travel a different way when they first land on Tatooine in *Episode IV*. Unlike God's ability to govern everything, we have zero control when it comes to the morality of others. The only lasting change comes with accepting Christ, and we can't choose that for anyone else.

So, how do we find the balance of being salt and light but not put undue pressure on ourselves to change the world? Jesus tells us in Matthew 25 to feed the hungry and look after the sick, but in the very next chapter, he says that there will always be impoverished people (Matthew 26:11). Are we destined to fail? Will the Church end up only discouraged?

Some of the answers are found only by a careful reading of Scripture. In Matthew 25, when Jesus talks about feeding the hungry, caring for the sick, and visiting those in prison, it's all in the context of believers caring for other believers. This is why he says "brothers and sisters of mine" in the following verse, "The King will reply, 'Truly I tell you, whatever you did for one of the least of these brothers and sisters of mine, you did for me'" (Matthew 25:40). Jesus does not tell believers to give drink to every thirsty person or food to every hungry person. The point of the passage is that God's people will care for one another, and this evidence will distinguish them from unbelievers.

I know I'm on thin ice with this one, but please hear me out. Of course we don't turn a blind eye to those in need when we can do something about it. But we need to handle passages like Matthew 25 in context and not think that the Church's main purpose is to rid the world of injustices, poverty, and sickness.

Jesus met the physical needs of many people, but he didn't do it for the majority of the world or emphasize this task for his followers. In fact, when Jesus' disciples are annoyed at the woman pouring expensive perfume on Jesus' head, they ask why the perfume wasn't sold and the money given to the poor. Aware of this, Jesus scolds them, saying that she did the right thing (Matthew 26:6–13).

Admirably, many churches, in an effort to love God and others, set their sights on cleaning up their communities. Actions include boycotting secular movies, planting flowers in public areas, and offering church playgrounds to their communities. This can be wonderful, but it's important to keep in mind that the Church can't eradicate drug use, premarital sex, domestic violence or the dozens of other sin-related problems of an unbelieving society. Referring to the slavery that exists on Tatooine, Anakin asks Qui-Gon, "Have you come to free us?" "No, I'm afraid not," Qui-Gon replies. While that would have been a remarkable show of compassion, it was not Qui-Gon's mission.

Along the same lines, it's fascinating how Paul handles the subject of slavery, a horrible social injustice by most people's standards. In his letter to Philemon, Paul does not tell Philemon to free his slave Onesimus. In Ephesians 6:5–9, he also doesn't push for the church to eradicate slavery. The Holy Spirit who inspired Paul to write his letters knew how ugly slavery was and would become in the future. Why didn't Paul take the opportunity to guide the Church better? Instead of spearheading an end to this terrible practice, Paul gave instructions on how masters and slaves should be masters and slaves to the glory of God.

As despicable as slavery is, God never commanded the Church to clean the world of it or any other sin unbelievers commit, if for no other reason than it would be impossible. Christians in the early 20th century adopted a "Social Gospel" movement, through which the believers vowed to clean the world of everything from bad schools to wars. They believed that the Church was to pave the way for Christ's Second Coming by removing social evils from the world. They thought they were making some progress in this endeavor until a couple of world wars made them reconsider. These believers loved Jesus and wanted to serve him the best they knew how. Unfortunately, they let a misinterpretation of Scripture take them down a long and frustrating path.

Global slavery or wars notwithstanding, is there anything wrong with wanting a nice community in which to live, one where you don't drive past strip joints, liquor stores, and a poor soul asking for spare change? Is it bad to want to help a person get off drugs, reconsider having an abortion, or just receive a cup of hot soup on a cold night? Not at all. These are all wonderful desires. But while we help others, let's be careful that we do not put the cart before the horse. It doesn't help anyone if we are simply trying to change society so that unbelievers live cleaner lives. While this is nice in the short-term, it doesn't meet people's deepest need.

🔭 In 2014, Disney, Lucasfilm, and Bad Robot launched "Star Wars: Force for Change" to raise money to help children around the world.

Churches should make sure that the things God says are most important, like learning his Word, battling sin, and loving other believers, do not take a backseat to trying to transform our fallen world into a better one. When churches put the bulk of their time, energy, and resources toward the goal of transforming society, their dedication to believers' sanctification can fall by the wayside. We don't want to look back years from now and wonder why professing believers don't seem to know or value God's Word, why church leaders let sin run unchecked within the body of Christ, or why some churches are more concerned about feeding the homeless than they are about feeding the body of Christ spiritually.

Final Thoughts

As we study the Bible's marching orders for the Church, we must be on guard not to become legalistic. God leaves many aspects of the Church as a matter of preference. A church doesn't have to meet in a dedicated building, have a youth group, or meet on Wednesday nights. If you favor traditional hymns led by an organ or if you like your worship leader to play contemporary songs with a Les Paul guitar, both are fine. God gives us a tremendous amount of freedom regarding believers coming together. The main point is for churches to fulfill the biblical purpose of gathering. In general, and over the long haul, your church should equip you to study God's Word, encourage you to obey your King, and deepen your love for Jesus and others.

16

REBELS & REPUBLICS

○○○○○○○○○○○○○○○●○

"I'm Not Brave Enough for Politics"

Growing up, many of us were taught not to discuss religion or politics in social situations, because both subjects are too personal. Differing opinions are almost certain to divide people. But just as it's impossible to ignore religion, i.e., Jediism, in *Star Wars,* it's impossible to ignore the politics, especially in the prequels.

For believers, it's our responsibility to make good choices in every area of life. We should strive to make God-honoring decisions even in the realm of politics. Plus, politics is everywhere. Even as I write this, candidates are preparing for a presidential race. As I start this chapter, questioning if I even should include it, I remind myself, along with all believers, that we should discuss politics with love, gentleness, and the mindset that God doesn't love us any more or less because of our political affiliation.

Even though politics can be complicated, we need to understand how the Bible describes the role of government, the Church, and individual believers in a political context. *Star Wars* brings up many themes and situations that can help shape our political views in light of our religion. Just as we study history so as not to repeat mistakes, we can use *Star Wars* to learn how to honor God or not honor him with our political decisions.

We need to go back to God's Word and figure out how a Christian should handle politics. In doing so, we'll answer questions such as: What is the purpose of government? Are some forms of government more "Christian" than others? Is America a Christian nation? Are there ways we can vote so that God's kingdom flourishes? As we unpack the answers to these and other questions, we'll learn that we don't need to treat politics as taboo, but rather, like everything else in life, that we should try to bring God glory through it.

Agents of Wrath

Why does God put governments and other groups in positions of authority? Basically, to keep sinful people from acting out their selfish desires to the point where society breaks down due to the chaos. Whenever God removes his restraint (in the form of human law enforcement) from the masses, riots, theft, and murder break out. Anyone who thinks people are basically good needs only to watch an ensuing riot on the news to see the depravity of humankind in high definition.

God gives governments the means to inflict damage, pain, and even death on their people.

> For the one in authority is God's servant for your good. But if you do wrong, be afraid, for rulers do not bear the sword for no reason. They are God's servants, agents of wrath to bring punishment on the wrongdoer. Therefore, it is necessary to submit to the authorities, not only because of possible punishment but also as a matter of conscience. (Romans 13:4–5)

The Empire in *Star Wars* has consequences to those who break the galaxy's laws. The "wanted man" whom Obi-Wan kills in the Mos Eisley cantina has the death sentence on twelve systems. We can tell by his behavior that his death sentence was undoubtedly deserved.

🏹 The name of the disfigured man in the cantina is Doctor Cornelius Evazan. This insane surgeon searched for the path to immortality by unethically operating on others. His criminal activity earned him the death sentence.

God puts people in power, but they are not supposed to bully those in the weaker position. Sinful people corrupt and pervert what God established as good. Just like everything else on Earth, government, in and of itself, is not an evil entity, but it can become one, as was the case with the Republic when it turned into the Empire.

In a perfect world, all governments would be ethical and only punish the people who break the law. But many evil governments have existed, such as the USSR under Stalin, Nazi Germany under Hitler, and North Korea under Kim Jong-il, where the leader God put into power was not out for the good of people and used the sword as a means to torture, repress, and conquer.

Vader must force people to obey through the constant threat of death, because they are not going to obey out of love or allegiance. He executes the Rebel officer on *Tantive IV* in front of others as a warning to not cross his authority. For those of us who are in a position of authority as a parent or manager, for instance, Vader's example of using fear and intimidation to rule over others may appear effective at times, but it is not the way God commands his people to act. All Christians are to be servant-leaders, just as Christ leads. This means we lead by laying down our preferences for the benefit of others.

You probably don't live under a fascist totalitarian government like the Empire, because if you did, you wouldn't have access to this book. But you most likely live under a government that bears the sword. For example, America has laws against committing murder. The punishment for such a crime, depending on the state, is death. Capital punishment is a biblical concept, because we are made in the image of God.

Problems can occur if the lawmakers don't understand life from God's perspective though. This results in society, including many politicians, regularly attacking, distorting, or destroying the sanctity of life. Public schools teach the theory of evolution. Planned Parenthood profits from aborted babies. Euthanasia proves that people want to end their lives rather than allow God to have a say. If the case can be made that we all evolved from basically nothing, then what's the big deal when that evolved "nothing" ceases to exist? But, Christians know that we're not just a collection of bones, blood, and tissue. There's value to every human life, because God deems each life to be valuable. This is why, when a life is taken, a life must be given in return. God establishes governments to enforce this principle.

When Romans 13:4 mentions the government bearing the sword, it's in the context of punishing its own people rather than enemies of other nations, although that happens, too. When the Empire views Princess Leia as a threat, her life is scheduled for termination. While this is a perversion of God's justice, Leia realizes long before she is captured that her rebellion could result in her death. Therefore, she's not surprised when she is sentenced, especially considering the government she is under.

However severe a government might punish someone on Earth, that is nothing compared to the eternal punishment that awaits everyone who does not repent and trust in Jesus. When authorities punish wrongdoers, this should be a frightening illustration of how God will serve justice to unbelievers.

God-Established Authority

Another purpose for government is to test our submission to God.

> Let everyone be subject to the governing authorities, for there is no authority except that which God has established. The authorities that exist have been established by God. Consequently, whoever rebels against the authority is rebelling against what God has instituted, and those who do so will bring judgment on themselves. (Romans 13:1-2)

Unbelievers hate anything or anyone ruling over them. This attitude was at the root of Adam and Eve disobeying God in the Garden, American colonists revolting against England, and the Rebel Alliance taking up arms against the Empire. Even if we do not retaliate physically against our government, we disobey God if we grumble about who is in the White House or the civil laws we're under.

> This is also why you pay taxes, for the authorities are God's servants, who give their full time to governing. Give to everyone what you owe them: If you owe taxes, pay taxes; if revenue, then revenue; if respect, then respect; if honor, then honor. (Romans 13:6-7)

People in our day often mock authority. They make fun of presidents and other politicians. They don't respect the police. They ridicule teachers. And they disobey their parents. In Romans 1, as Paul lays out a long list of sins that characterize unbelievers, he includes "disobedient to parents" along with others like "haters of God," "inventors of evil," and "ruthless." Not submitting to human authority is a serious offense, because it reveals the unbeliever's ultimate failure to submit to God.

God puts everyone into different groups that require submission to others. In Ephesians 5 and 6, Paul explains how certain groups should submit to others in authority. He begins this section with the command, "Submit to one another out of reverence for Christ" (Ephesians 5:21). Paul sets up the paradigm of people submitting to those in authority to showcase their submission to God.

It's actually sin that causes people to want to be in control of their lives. In their first encounter with each other, Han Solo and Princess Leia argue about who is going to take orders from whom. Leia says, "From now on, you do as I tell you." At which, Han retorts, "I take orders from one person, me!" Even Han's last name, "Solo," advertises that submission is not his strong suit. Incidentally, men are to submit to women who are in charge except when it comes to teaching or having authority in the church (1 Timothy 2:11–12). This is not to say that women, overall, are not as smart or even that a woman cannot understand a complex biblical concept better than a man. It's simply the hierarchy that God, in his perfect wisdom, has set up.

Submitting to others is a gift from God. When people do not submit to those in authority, it often results in disharmony, destruction, or death. If citizens don't submit to the police, there could be riots. If wives don't submit to husbands, there could be divorce. And if people don't submit to governments, there could even be executions.

We've already touched on the fact that, at times, the ones in authority can oppress those under them. The Bible is very careful to command Christian masters to treat their slaves well, for parents not to exasperate their children, and for husbands to love their wives as

Christ loved the Church. While their loving behavior might make it easier to submit, their compassionate conduct is not a prerequisite.

Submit yourselves for the Lord's sake to every human authority: whether to the emperor, as the supreme authority, or to governors, who are sent by him to punish those who do wrong and to commend those who do right. For it is God's will that by doing good you should silence the ignorant talk of foolish people. Live as free people, but do not use your freedom as a cover-up for evil; live as God's slaves. Show proper respect to everyone, love the family of believers, fear God, honor the emperor. (1 Peter 2:13–17)

Peter makes the point in his letter that it's commendable before God to suffer under unjust and painful circumstances. He uses the example of believing slaves submitting to their masters even when their masters are harsh.

In *Episode I,* Anakin obeys and respects his master Watto faithfully. Even though we don't want him to be enslaved, we admire these scenes partly because we know how difficult it is for us to submit to the authority figures in our own lives. There's an echo in most people's hearts of God's design for us to submit to authority.

🔭 While Sebulba talks down to Anakin about being a slave, Sebulba was actually a slave himself at one point and owns at least two Twi'lek slaves.

Peter reminds us that Jesus, not deserving the pain he suffered, did not retaliate. He did not threaten. "Instead, he entrusted himself to him who judges justly" (1 Peter 2:23b). When we complain about those in authority, such as our government, we sin. Through this, we also question the wisdom of God, because he put those men and women in office.

In *Episode IV,* Han is not only resistant to submit to others, he's prone to criticize the choices they make. Consider how he complains about having to wait in the Death Star's command office while Obi-Wan deactivates the tractor beam. This rebellious nature actually makes Han more miserable than the people who willingly accept their weaker positions. When people act in a selfless, Christlike manner and submit to authority, not only does it make circumstances easier, it can also make them more enjoyable for everyone involved.

This submissive attitude helps us receive the good things God intends. Children need loving parents to give structure and guidance to their lives. Wives need a strong, loving husband to protect and care for them. And citizens need the government to protect them from the sinful people and nations who want to steal from them, conquer them, or wipe them off the face of the planet.

Amidala fears the bureaucrats would so oppress her people that there would be nothing left of their cities, her people, or their way of life. Eventually, she trades her diplomacy for a blaster. Usually, we're not tempted to take up arms against those in authority, especially our governments or police force. Our temptation to sin in the area of submission typically has more to do with choosing to have a good attitude regarding whom God has placed over us.

It does make it more difficult to submit if the government is made up of people who care more about advancing their own power than for the welfare of the people. Naturally, people will rebel in these situations, but what does the Bible say? As Christians, we are commanded to submit to our government unless it would be sin to do so, even if it makes our lives miserable. It can be everything from speed limits to tax laws. While in most countries it is not a sin to disagree with your government, try to change a law, or vote different people into office, if we do not submit to the rules or rulers (including the ones we feel are wrong), it's the same as rebelling against God.

We should remember that God is not like an impersonal government. Rather, he is our perfectly loving Father. He is better than even the best parent, teacher, or police officer, because he loves us more than any of those can. Even if our protests against the government never achieve our desired outcome, we must be content that our Father knows what we need.

God Uses Evil People

Both the Empire and the Sith are perfect examples of evil men using their positions of power to hurt others and try to advance their own rule. When Princess Leia is surrounded by Imperials on the Death Star, Governor Tarkin threatens her with the destruction of Alderaan if she doesn't reveal the location of the Rebel secret base. No one listens to her pleas for mercy. The Empire's philosophy is not benevolence towards its subjects. It believes in controlling people through tyranny.

When Tarkin announces that the Senate has been dissolved, Commander Tagge exclaims, "That's impossible! How will the Emperor maintain control without the bureaucracy?" Tarkin's answer? "Fear will keep the local systems in line. Fear of this battle station." There's no doubt that the Empire is a tyrannical government. We've had our own share of evil empires throughout history. The Roman Emperor Caligula, in Tarkin fashion, said, "Let them hate as long as they fear." The Empire punishes people when they fail to submit. The people never profit from their obedience except by having their lives spared.

Despite the fact that evil governments rule through their own sinful choices, God uses them to work out his plan. God is not responsible for the evil, but he uses it to bring about what he wants to accomplish. The book of Habakkuk starts with Habakkuk pleading with the Lord for help. Injustice, destruction, violence, strife, and conflict abound in the kingdom of Judah (where Habakkuk lives), and God doesn't seem to be doing anything to stop it. God tells Habakkuk that he will raise up the Babylonians (a "ruthless and impetuous people") to bring judgment on those who do evil (Habakkuk 1:6). Habakkuk questions how a holy God could tolerate the evil Babylonians. God says that after the Babylonians serve his purpose of executing judgment on the evildoers of Judah, he will wipe the Babylonians out, too (Habakkuk 2:16).

Evil nations and people will never triumph in the end. God topples their regimes and judges them for their sin. Eventually, Habakkuk not only praises God but also learns the valuable lesson of trusting and rejoicing in God despite his circumstances.

Though the fig tree does not bud and there are no grapes on the vines, though the olive crop fails and the fields produce no food, though there are no sheep in the pen and no cattle in the stalls, yet I will rejoice in the Lord, I will be joyful in God my Savior. (Habakkuk 3:17-18)

Is America a Christian Nation?

How we answer the question of whether or not America is a Christian nation might affect how we vote, how we serve as citizens, and how we evangelize, just to name a few. In *Episode III,* both senators and the Jedi evaluate the Republic to figure out if it's still good or if corruption has made it the very evil they are against. If believers view America as a Christian nation, then the conclusion is America should be blessed more than non-Christian nations if we obey. Compared to a country like North Korea, it certainly seems like America is good. We even have songs about God shedding his grace on America, the beautiful. But just because America cares for its citizens, polices the world, and is especially nice to Israel doesn't mean that God loves her any more or less than he does another country.

"We must keep our faith in the Republic. The day we stop believing democracy can work is the day we lose it," says Queen Amidala. For the Rebels, regaining their freedom is of utmost importance. Unlike the Jedi who place their faith in religion, the Rebels put their faith in the Republic. And yet, the Jedi still fight for democracy. The problem occurs when religion and patriotism become so meshed that it's hard to distinguish them. Obi-Wan, who should be devoted to the Jedi and the Force, says in *Episode III,* "My allegiance is to the Republic, to democracy."

The same thing happens today. Some might mix politics with Christianity to the point where it's difficult to distinguish the Church's responsibilities from the government's. Patriotic songs are played at churches on the 4th of July, and red-white-and-blue crosses decorate homes. In fact, many still think that if you're an American and have not professed atheism or some other religion outright, then you're a Christian by default.

✈ Harrison Ford, Samuel L. Jackson, and James Earl Jones star in the 1992 movie, *Patriot Games.* Since Jones was only the voice of Darth Vader, *Patriot Games* was the first time Ford and Jones worked together.

Admittedly, the percentage of American citizens who attend a Christian church exceeds that of most other countries. But what does that mean exactly? The problem begins with even asking if America is a Christian nation, because there is no such thing.

Israel is the only nation that God ever set apart. As we learned earlier, even though God gave special protection and care to Israel, they did not reciprocate his love, and, eventually, God judged them for their wickedness. The Old Covenant is finished, and God's special relationship with the physical nation of Israel is over with, too.

Furthermore, the concept of God blessing a nation physically for obedience is an Old Covenant concept that not only ended two thousand years ago; it was never intended for any other nation except Israel. The term "Christian nation" is confusing for many reasons. Does this mean a country comprised of only Christians? If so, knowing what we know about how one becomes a Christian, how would a government ever successfully legislate its people into Christianity? Sure, laws could be set up forcing people to order their lives based around biblical values. America has certainly done that. But doing this would not change the hearts of the people to want to love God, which is the essence of Christianity. This is no different from the Empire trying to make laws to force people across the galaxy to submit to the Emperor. The Empire could make laws strict enough where it could get outward obedience, but people's hearts would never be swayed.

Israel, in the Old Testament, was a theocracy. Religion and politics where intimately intertwined. How they viewed God and their religious laws heavily influenced everything about their political structure. The Israelites often wanted to take God out of the picture, but they usually left a stripped down version of his law. This was the only way of life they knew. Some people today want America to be a theocracy. They would like to see God's laws woven into every aspect of American society, including politics, courts, and schools. They feel if this is done, through the democratic process, then America will flourish under God's blessings. Again, this is a misunderstanding of the power (or lack thereof) of law in the unbeliever's heart and a misinterpretation of how God blesses people in the

New Covenant era. Sometimes, God blesses people with material wealth and good health, but there is no correlation between the gifts and the recipients' obedience.

The history of early America is beyond the scope of this book, but some key points are helpful to ponder. Even though some of the founding fathers were deists, most were not Christians. And when they penned documents like the Declaration of Independence and the Constitution, there was no mention of Christianity or Jesus. You would think if you wanted your people to worship Jesus Christ, you would state this somewhere in your nation's founding documents. The founding fathers were more concerned with preventing a certain church or religion from dominating the lives of people like the Church of England did. This is why separation of church and state and freedom of religion were given such importance. While these are wonderful liberties, they do not place Christianity in a privileged position.

By *Episode III,* the Republic's constitution is in shreds. For Americans, what does it mean if the Constitution is changed further to push out any mention of God? As citizens, it should alarm us, and we should try to preserve it. But as Christians, we don't need to be worried. It won't matter if our currency no longer says, "In God We Trust." Believers will trust in him regardless, and unbelieving Americans never did. Different laws might make it difficult to worship publicly, but they can never prevent believers from loving God.

Americans, as a whole, do not behave like Christians. Most do not attend church or obey God's laws. These days, people are more concerned with worshipping celebrities than God. Most Americans are basically wrapped up in living for themselves. There are pockets of America where many people do attend church. But even some of these folks only do so because that's the culture.

An American citizen must choose to serve Christ just like those in other countries. Americans are not grandfathered into God's acceptance just because they're Americans. In the Old Covenant era, all a Jew had to do to become part of "God's people" was to be born. The Bible doesn't say that this model applies to any other nation.

Americans are not the only ones who think the United States is a Christian nation. Other countries do it all the time. When America was attacked on 9-11, the terrorists did so because they viewed America as a Christian nation. The Koran, the holy writings of Islam, commands its followers to kill infidels, e.g., Christians, because they do not bow the knee to Allah. Even though many Americans couldn't care less about Jesus, terrorists like these generally think every American deserves to die because they live in a "Christian nation."

Romans 13 supports a government that tries to bring killers like this to justice. But that's the government's role, not ours. We are Christians before we're Americans. Individually as believers, we should love everyone, including our enemies who try to harm us. Thus, we shouldn't rejoice when a terrorist is killed. We should be saddened, because they no longer have any hope of salvation through Christ.

Just so that I'm not misunderstood, allow me to stress that I love America. There's no other country in which I would rather live. I'm very grateful for all of its freedoms and for all the men and women who have sacrificed so much to preserve and protect these freedoms. This chapter is not meant to decrease your patriotism but rather to help you see it within the larger picture of being a Christian. Our viewpoint on this topic shapes not only how we live for God but also how we treat others throughout the world.

Believers and Ballot Boxes

When Padmé moves for a vote of no confidence in Chancellor Valorum's leadership, her beliefs, values, and concerns all crystalize as her political voice is heard. Bail Organa seconds the motion, and it's not long before Valorum is removed from office and replaced with Palpatine. This is the beauty (or the terror) of democracy depending on how you look at it. The Senate sealed their own fate and that of the galaxy when they elected a Sith Lord as Chancellor. What should we learn from their mistake? For what sorts of things should believers vote? Is there such thing as a more "Christian" political party? Should we even vote at all?

🔭 After Padmé moves for a vote of no confidence, a group of "E.T.s" can be seen in the Galactic Senate. This was Lucas' nod to Steven Spielberg, who put a child dressed as Yoda in his 1982 film, *E.T. the Extra-Terrestrial.*

As Christians, we need to make God-honoring choices when we do anything, including politics. "So whether you eat or drink or whatever you do, do it all for the glory of God" (1 Corinthians 10:31). In our quest to right the wrongs of society, we need to look out for various potential pitfalls. For one, believers should never let politics divide the Church. Just as we should not look down on non-Americans, we should not be any less compassionate to those who do not share our political beliefs.

Second, we need to remember God's plan is right on schedule including who gets elected. Meaning, if our preferred candidate is not chosen, we shouldn't feel as though life is unraveling. God's sovereignty will not allow mistakes to happen. Living under a bad government might make our lives harder, but it's still part of God's plan.

Besides, a different government will never take away all our problems. The Senate in *Star Wars* certainly does not take away problems. Usually, their bad decisions only create more. For instance, they vote for Palpatine yet fail to vote against the Trade Federation's blockade. Not only do they give Palpatine the office of Chancellor, they also give him more executive power along the way. In their defense, the Republic's back was up against the wall. Still, that's no excuse to let fear of the Trade Federation and the Separatists guide their decisions. Usually, if we let fear, misinformation, and a desire for a quick fix lead us instead of godly wisdom, we end up in a worse place.

Does the Bible give any guidance regarding how Christians should vote, or is it an issue of preference? By the way, my aim here is not to persuade you toward a certain party but to get you to think biblically about your political choices. To add to some confusion, different Bible verses seem to support voting one way or the complete opposite. For example, Scripture commands us to be generous (2 Corinthians 9), but it also says the one who is unwilling to work shall not eat (2 Thessalonians 3:10). How do we bring the two together?

We need to get back to the fundamental principles of what God's Word says about people, about law, and about government to figure out what to do. This is complicated, and believers are often on opposing sides. We should vote for the candidate who is closest in line with our worldview, but does that automatically mean that unbelievers should be outside of our consideration?

☌ Satirical political T-shirts came out in 2015 with messages such as "Obi-Wan Kenobi 2016—Our Only Hope" and "Chewbacca/Solo 2016—Let the Wookiee Win."

Since a politician's main goal should be to help people have better lives, it's helpful if they have an accurate assessment of human nature at the fundamental level. If they don't, then their plans have little chance of success. Not only that, their solutions could backfire. The Bible teaches that more laws do not make people better. More laws (without Christ) actually make people worse, because their sin and evil passions are stirred up (Romans 7).

Obi-Wan and the rest of the Jedi know it's a bad idea to keep giving Palpatine more power. Padmé and the loyalists know it, too. Unfortunately, they are in the minority, and liberty dies eventually with the majority's thunderous applause. If the senators knew more about the dark side, more about the potential evil of a single person, Palpatine would not have been allowed to take over the Republic. But the people were not discerning, and their shortsightedness cost millions of lives.

As pointed out in the last chapter, the Church's main goal is not to rid the world of evil. Still, that is not to say that we shouldn't try to uphold biblical principles. It doesn't bother me if the candidate who is running for office isn't a believer. At the same time, we shouldn't support policies if they are counter to God's design.

As we think through these issues, it's not only the politicians we need to consider. We also need to understand the ethical nature of everyone being governed, because that will dictate much of what the solutions should be. Some politicians feel that people are basically good and just need help to get out of their economic and social predicaments. However, they fail to factor in what the Bible says about sin. As we studied in Chapter 10, people are not morally good. If they were, a little help could make them better. In the real world, many people, because of their selfish desires, will take advantage of the help government gives. The government's help will only prolong their sinful state. People need to repent and believe the gospel. A byproduct of that is empowerment by the Holy Spirit to live a better life. The government can't help with any of that.

Although it seems like Christians should be in support of a government that promises to help society, the results of this are not always positive. The world needs more than food, shelter, and education. The world needs Christ. When we think a secular organization can step in and solve all of life's problems, then, at best, we'll end up with a bunch of well-fed, well-educated homeowners who will spend their eternity in hell. Historically speaking, when we look at Communist countries where their citizens rely heavily on the state to meet their needs, we see misery, poverty, and little reliance on or worship of God.

Often, it's the one-on-one relationship that sparks lasting change, because that's when the gospel message might be delivered and, hopefully, accepted. It's doubtful that any government will ever help in that endeavor. If the gospel changes a person's heart, then that person will probably look to God for the strength to endure life's problems rather than look to a politician to end them.

Star Wars (Without the Wars)

Let's think through a common polarizing issue in politics. The Rebels in *Star Wars* do not want to fight in a civil war, but they need to in order to regain their way of life. God's people in the Old Testament era made war, yet in the New Testament era, we are called to love our enemies. Ever since the sixties, we have been indoctrinated with the fact that love and war are mutually exclusive. If war is the opposite of love, then we should oppose all conflict and war. Right?

In *Episode II*, the senators struggle while deciding whether to create an army for the Republic. On one side, we have Senator Ask

Aak declaring that an army will prevent deaths. On the other side, Padmé argues that the creation of an army will lead them into the misery of war. By the end of the movie, the Military Creation Act passes, and the Clone Wars begin.

Episode II was released in May 2002. Less than a year later, the Iraq War began, perhaps a form of life imitating art. Much like the debate that goes on between the senators in *Episode II,* believers can be on both sides when it comes to the subject of war. Some will say evil must be stopped, while others say to love our enemies. When we look to the Bible, Jesus tells us wars must happen (Matthew 24:6). He never commands nations to abstain from war. In fact, in the Old Testament, God commands his people to do battle with others and helps them in battle (Deuteronomy 20:1–4).

In the New Covenant era, Jesus focuses our conflicts with enemies down to an individual level commanding us to love them (Matthew 5:44). Paul says, "If it is possible, as far as it depends on you, live at peace with everyone" (Romans 12:18). Our choices to live at peace with one another need to be *our* choices, not the government's. When we vote in a government that we think will obey this command, we may think that God is pleased. But the thought behind Romans 12:2 is different than believers voting in a passive government. The setting in Romans 12 is personal relationships, not relationships on an international scale.

In our world, similar to during the Separatist Crisis, sometimes the government must step in with force to stop an evil nation from hurting others. No one likes war, but Christians should not view supporting a war as anti-Jesus.

Final Thoughts

Christians need to think biblically through many issues before voting. Sometimes, it can get very confusing, and the previous sections will not address everything. Going forward, remember that the commands in the New Testament are for believers to obey. Knowing this, don't expect a government filled with god-haters to support biblical principles. Arguments for or against capital punishment, environmental conservation, same-sex marriage, abortion, and dozens of other issues can all be framed in the perfect political jargon to seem like the right or wrong thing to do. Before you cast your vote, evaluate your conclusions in light of Scripture, and in the end, rest knowing that, "The king's heart is a stream of water in the hand of the Lord; he turns it wherever he will" (Proverbs 21:1, ESV).

If we don't agree with the current president or Congress, we might refer to the good old days of America, sort of like "before the dark times." When we do that, we forget that God's sovereignty over the universe includes Pennsylvania Avenue. God puts kings, presidents, and rulers (even the bad ones) in place to work out his plan. If your candidate doesn't win the election, you don't need to fret that your city, state, or country is going to hell in a hand basket. The results of every political election will turn out exactly how God wants. Once we understand this, it's easier to have contentment even if we feel a "Sith Lord" has been elected.

Politicians can put on such a show that some of us might fail to appreciate that they are still real people. They have families. They have feelings. But most of all, they have the same need for a savior as we do. That's why the Bible tells us to pray for kings and rulers, because they need to be saved from God's judgment.

> I urge, then, first of all, that petitions, prayers, intercession and thanksgiving be made for all people—for kings and all those in authority, that we may live peaceful and quiet lives in all godliness and holiness. This is good, and pleases God our Savior, who wants all people to be saved and to come to a knowledge of the truth. (1 Timothy 2:1-4)

God makes no distinction between poor and rich, black and white, Democrat and Republican, libertarian and independent. He offers his grace to all types of people. Politicians need our prayers not only to govern with godly wisdom but also, more than anything, to come to Christ.

Now that we better understand government as a body of servants that God puts in place to rule over us and serve us, we can begin to see how it is also a picture of how Jesus, the ultimate authority, rules over yet also serves us (Matthew 20:28). This goes back to how we should submit to those over us, because God is behind it all. Whatever pain we might experience because of our leaders, it's still a part of God's plan for our lives.

Padmé does not live very long under the Emperor's rule, but her children do. For Luke, his knowledge of the Force helps the Rebels defeat the Empire and restore freedom to the galaxy. However, this defeat is only temporary. The Sith and the Empire will rise anew, and the fight will begin all over again. For believers, our knowledge of God doesn't help us defeat a government that will only be replaced by another. It does far better than that. Our faith helps us to have joy though we are not in control, peace despite our circumstances, and hope in an eternal future when Jesus will be our King.

17

THE END TIMES

○○○○○○○○○○○○○○○○●

The Amillennial *Falcon*

I n this chapter, we'll dive into some deeper theological terms. Let's start with "eschatology." This is the study of the "end times," which includes topics such as the millennium, God's judgment, the Second Coming, and the afterlife. A correct eschatological view helps not only with your handling of major portions of the Bible, for instance Revelation, that speak of future events, but also determines the best way to live today.

The culmination of the end times is, of course, Jesus' return or "Second Coming." Placing our hope in Jesus' return helps us to have joy when going through the seemingly never-ending grind of living in this fallen world. If Jesus doesn't come back for us, then what's the point of living the Christian life? We might as well eat, drink, and be merry, for tomorrow we die. But God uses prophecy to encourage us that Jesus will come back. And we need to be ready.

In the *Star Wars* prequels, the Jedi have a prophecy about the coming of the Chosen One. While Qui-Gon and Obi-Wan firmly believe Anakin is the "One," Mace, and especially Yoda, think the prophecy could have been misread. In the same way, some Christians can get so wrapped up in biblical prophecy that they are distracted from living for God now, similar to Qui-Gon's warning to be mindful of the living Force in the present. Yoda scolds Luke for taking this sort of approach. "All his life has he looked away to the future, to the horizon. Never his mind on where he was. What he was doing."

There are three major eschatological perspectives in most Christian circles. They are 1) premillennialism 2) postmillennialism and 3) amillennialism. These might be intimidating words, so let's break them down.

We're all familiar with the word "millennium." We've been hearing about it since Y2K. But before that, we can thank Han Solo's bucket-of-bolts freighter for adding the word to our vocabulary. A millennium is a time period of one thousand years. In regards to Christ's rule, we get the idea of a thousand-year period from Revelation 20:1–7. This is supposed to be a time when Satan is bound and Jesus reigns.

Premillennialism

Christians in the premillennialist camp think that Jesus will return before his thousand-year reign. Many popular movies and books build their stories around a premillennial, pre-tribulation Rapture of the Church. The Rapture is when the Lord takes believers from Earth to be with him. Within premillennialism are different views of when this Rapture occurs in reference to a tribulation period. This future tribulation period, referenced in Daniel 9, Matthew 24, and Revelation 7, will last for seven years, during which humanity will experience terrible wars, famines, earthquakes, and other suffering.

Premillennial end-time theology is the dominant belief on the religious channels. Since this view assumes all of this hasn't happened yet, it's easy to speculate. In an attempt to figure out when Jesus will return, this group pays particular attention to news reports about Israel.

During the prequels, the dark side grows, and Yoda, Mace, and Obi-Wan wonder when the Chosen One will bring balance to the Force. This future event is like our Savior coming back to do away with evil once and for all. But after Anakin turns to the dark side and the Empire takes over in *Episode III,* the question becomes will there ever be balance.

To understand premillennialism better, say there are two people (Person A and Person B) who have never seen any *Star Wars* films and know nothing about the story. After you finish feeling terribly sorry for them, you tell them only a little about the storyline. Basically, you only say that there will be a Jedi who restores balance to the Force, and when balance is achieved, the galaxy will experience a "Golden Age" when goodness prevails. You also tell them there will be a time of tribulation. By the way, you don't tell how many movies make up the saga.

Person A watches the movies in episode order. Person B watches them in the order they were released. As they watch, each person comes up with a different idea of not only who will fulfill the prophecy but when. For example, Person A says it will be Anakin. Person B says Luke.

Person A, who starts watching with *Episode I,* thinks that the tribulation period will happen in the future because of the growing dark side. Person B, who starts with *Episode IV,* knows that the "savior" must come after the *current* tribulation period of the Sith-ruled Empire.

Person A, thinking that circumstances will get worse before balance is restored to the Force and the Golden Age ushered in, is like a Christian looking for a future seven-year tribulation. The tribulation will be the sign that the reign of Christ will happen soon. This view is the premillennial interpretation.

Person B's analysis is the amillennial view, which we'll explore a little later.

Postmillennialism

Postmillennialism, resulting from another interpretation of the thousand years, is held by a much smaller percentage of believers. These folks think that Jesus will come back after a thousand years of Christian dominance in the world. They believe the gospel will be widely accepted by the world and that this massive wave of believing in Christ will be marked by peace, prosperity, and a positive moral change in culture.

Similar to what has been said in previous chapters about some churches' goal to transform society, the danger for postmillennialists is to waste time trying to mold secular culture into a Christian culture. Their logic is that if society is cleaned up ethically, then this will qualify Earth for the thousand years when Satan is not doing all his dirty work. This period sets the stage for Christ's return.

Going back to our movie watchers analogy, this is like Person C entering the room right at the end of *Episode IV* when Luke blows up the Death Star and thinking, well, it's good times from here on out. The bad guys are destroyed, and everybody's celebrating.

It's not until they watch *Episode V* that they see the bad times are far from over. There are still a lot of trials and tribulation left before the final victory over evil happens, when the Chosen One destroys the Sith and returns balance to the Force.

Revelation 20

Before we tackle amillennialism, we need to understand Revelation 20 better. To do that, we need to get a better grasp on the entire book of Revelation. This last book of the Bible is probably the most daunting book in Scripture. Revelation either captivates believers, confuses them, or a little of both. The most important principle to appreciate before reading Revelation is to realize the style in which it was written.

The Bible has one author, God. But God used many men to write its content. The Bible also uses different literary styles, including prose, poetry, and history. For starters, problems arise when we interpret hyperbole or figurative language as literal or when we try to read a historical account as law for us.

John wrote Revelation when he was exiled on the island of Patmos. He wrote down the visions that God gave him. Since they are John's visions regarding the end times, Revelation is described as apocalyptic language. This means we should not take things literally. The following verses serve as an example of symbolic language:

> A great sign appeared in heaven: a woman clothed with the sun, with the moon under her feet and a crown of twelve stars on her head. She was pregnant and cried out in pain as she was about to give birth. Then another sign appeared in heaven: an enormous red dragon with seven heads and ten horns and seven crowns on its heads. Its tail swept a third of the stars out of the sky and flung them to the earth. (Revelation 12:1-4)

Similarly to not taking phrases in the above passage literally, another phrase that we should not interpret literally is the one-thousand-year period. It's consistent with the interpretation of the rest of Revelation to not define this number as an exact amount of time. When John says "the thousand years" in Revelation, he basically conveys a very long period of time.

When Jabba the Hutt tells our heroes they will be digested in the Sarlacc's stomach for one thousand years, no one thinks that they are digested precisely after one thousand years. It would be impossible to know this for certain, because how could it be proven? No one could live long enough or be able to return from the Sarlacc's stomach to tell the outcome. Instead, Jabba saying the phrase "a thousand years" is only conveying a really, really, really, long time.

This is the same way we should interpret the thousand years in Revelation 20. Sometimes in the Bible, numbers are literal. In the Gospels, the twelve disciples really are twelve men. The seventh day of the week really is the day you reach when counting up to seven. But because of the type of literature in Revelation, we should view the thousand years as simply a very long period.

🔭 In an effort to make the Sarlacc look more dangerous, Lucas added a tongue and more tentacles to it in the 2011 rerelease of *Episode VI*.

Amillennialism

Amillennialists hold the last major viewpoint on the end times. They believe in a figurative millennium rather than a fixed one thousand years. They also believe this period is happening now. It started at the beginning of the New Covenant era and will end at Jesus' Second Coming. It's the age referred to in Revelation 20:6 as the thousand years, a time when believers who have died in Christ will reign with him in heaven. Taking all Scripture into account, in my view, the eschatological viewpoint that seems to be the most likely is the amillennial stance.

Again, a disclaimer is needed. Whenever we study a topic like the end times, it's important to remember that the truth of the gospel is usually not in jeopardy. I don't doubt any believer's love for God if they happen to hold to premillennialism or postmillennialism. As always, my goal is only that we handle Scripture in the most accurate way possible.

Remembering what we learned in the chapters on covenants, we know that God is finished with his special relationship with Israel as a nation and as a people. He still saves the occasional Jew, but the Israelites are no longer his focus. The whole world (people from every tribe, language, people, and nation) is his focus now. So, that means many of the prophecies that premillennialists use to make their case for Christ's return are faulty from the start.

Many Christians read the phrase "the last days" as the short time right before Christ's Second Coming. However, the phrase "the last days" in the Bible actually refers to the entire time span between Pentecost and Christ's Second Coming. Luke, Timothy, James, Peter, and the author of Hebrews all refer to the last days as something their listeners (approximately 2,000 years ago) experience.

In the past God spoke to our ancestors through the prophets at many times and in various ways, but in these *last days* he *has spoken* to us by his Son, whom he appointed heir of all things, and through whom also he made the universe. (Hebrews 1:1-2, emphasis mine)

The last days in *Star Wars* take place throughout the entire saga, not just at the tail end, because Anakin, the Chosen One, is on the scene from the beginning. We have been experiencing the "last days" for a long time and may have centuries more to go. No one knows except our Father in heaven. Just like we learned in Chapter 14 about sorting out God's will, we should seek to learn God's ethical will revealed through the Bible and not try to discover his controlling will (including his plans for Jesus' return).

Comparable to every other event that will happen in the future, Christ's Second Coming is an event that Paul says will happen like a thief coming in the night (1 Thessalonians 5:2). No one knows the date of his return. So, it's a waste of time to try to figure it out. All this speculation does is get us off track from serving God and others.

Yoda tells Mace Windu that the prophecy concerning Anakin as the Chosen One could have been misread. For the galaxy, so many things hinge on the correct reading of this prophecy. When Qui-Gon first brings Anakin to the Council, should he be trained as a Jedi? When Anakin shows time after time feelings of fear, anger, impatience, and even hatred, what should be done about it? And what about allowing him on the Jedi Council or advancing him to Jedi Master? The Jedi Council answers these questions through a grid constructed with the presumption that Anakin is the Chosen One. If they are wrong, every other justification for their actions falls apart.

The same thing happens to us if we use the wrong biblical grid when interpreting the end times. We all bring theological biases to Scripture. Whether you realize it or not, you probably have a theological system. It's hard not to. You may have either a dispensational background or a covenantal background. You might not even have a name for your system but have most likely adopted the one from the teacher(s) you are under. At any rate, your theological system will have a huge impact on how you read end times prophecy. Moreover, how you view the nation of Israel and God's relationship with it in the New Covenant era will greatly affect how you interpret biblical prophecy.

The theological framework that I think is the most biblically accurate is New Covenant theology, which I touched on in Chapter 9. This theological system allows for the most correct interpretation of the Bible with the fewest discrepancies.

If we're given a deleted scene from a *Star Wars* movie, it's usually not a problem, because we can fit the scene in with the rest of the story. The same holds true for the Bible. When we understand what God is doing in the New Covenant era, we can put the biblical pieces together better, because we know the whole story. If we don't know our Bible well, we won't know where prophecy fits into the rest of God's larger plan.

Yoda, Mace, and Obi-Wan are devoted to their religion. Yes, their religion is false, but they are men (or aliens) of strong faith. They study the ways of the Force like we should study the ways of God. They know the Jedi tenets like we should know the Bible. They sacrifice for their fellow Jedi and others like we should sacrifice for the Church and our fellow man. They are hopeful that the prophecy will be fulfilled one day and balance will be restored to the Force. They keep going even when times get tough. We need to do the same.

If you subscribe to the postmillennial view, be careful that you are not looking for heaven to be on Earth, because it won't ever be. If you agree with premillennial (specifically with a pre-tribulation rapture) doctrine, forget about stockpiling supplies for your loved ones to survive a Great Tribulation to come. Ignore all the noise that says you need to crack the code that shrouds Revelation. All of these are distractions that serve only to take your eyes off living for your King. Jesus promised us suffering. The tribulation of which the Bible speaks is not a time in the future. The time of tribulation started 2,000 years ago, and it will continue until Jesus returns to take us home.

When you read the book of Revelation, don't get caught up in trying to define and interpret all the symbols. You will fail at doing so and miss the whole point of the book, which is that Jesus was and is victorious. He has promised to return and gather up those who love him to be with him forever. This is the climax. This is the part in *Episode VI* toward which the entire saga aims. While it's fine to wrestle with the meaning of the text, don't miss the forest for the trees, and always make sure the interpretation supports the primary message.

Finally, don't avoid reading Revelation altogether. It's the one book of the Bible that promises a blessing for those who take its words to heart (Revelation 1:3). Reading it will encourage you to persevere in your faith, not compromise with the world, and give you a hopeful expectation of your future. If you don't read it, it's like not watching the ending of *Episode VI*. You miss out on the victory and the celebration.

🔭 The Ewok trumpet call at the end of *Episode VI* is the same musical phrase heard in the 1956 film *The Ten Commandments* when the Israelites begin their Exodus from Egypt.

The Afterlife

Regarding religion or spirituality in general, one of the biggest questions anyone has is, what happens when we die? Specifically, where will we go? Will we be turned into nothingness immediately or will we become nameless angels floating around on clouds?

Will Christians be welcomed into the presence of Jesus at the moment of death or will we sleep until Jesus' Second Coming? What about the resurrection of the body or fellowship with others after we die? *Star Wars* and the Bible each provide answers to many of these questions.

In *Episode I,* Qui-Gon admonishes Obi-Wan to "be mindful of the Living Force." The fact that the Force is living is the reason Qui-Gon, Obi-Wan, Yoda, and Anakin can merge with it after their physical deaths. In Taoism, people do not face God's judgment. Instead, their energy becomes unified with the universe's energy, much like what we see happen to the Jedi. Since God created us as separate beings with distinct personalities desiring to live on forever as individuals, the afterlife of these particular Jedi is an appealing concept for general movie watchers. These Jedi escape any sort of final judgment and simply pass to an eternal blissful existence.

While it's tempting to believe that all the "good guys" live on for eternity more powerful than they were in the physical world, this is not reality. A reckoning will happen at the end of everyone's life, and we all need to plead that Jesus' work on the cross would be applied to us. Many religions have a belief in the afterlife, but they differ radically in what the afterlife is and how you are guaranteed a good one.

When Vader strikes down Obi-Wan in *Episode IV,* we only have to wait a minute or two before we realize that his essence has survived somehow. The final scene of the saga shows that Anakin and Yoda also live on. The Jedi are never in danger of punishment for their sin. The worst part of death for most of them is that they are in some sort of oblivion. That is, until Qui-Gon learns how to merge with the Force after death and retain his eternal consciousness. This gives him the "path to immortality," the Jedi version of conquering death.

Qui-Gon not only lives on, he also passes the knowledge of how to do it to Obi-Wan and Yoda. These Jedi do not go to a paradise in the biblical sense, but their souls, i.e., their spiritual essence, remains. This is somewhat like the state that believers are in before we receive glorified bodies.

While our souls will go to be with the Lord immediately at death, we will receive our new physical bodies at the Second Coming (Philippians 3:21). The Jedi never receive their physical bodies back. After they die, they are no more than ghosts. This is why Leia and the others on Endor could not see Yoda, Obi-Wan, or Anakin at the end of *Episode VI*.

Jesus made a point after his resurrection to show that he was not a ghost but had a physical body. He appeared to Mary Magdalene, his disciples, and to many others. "Look at my hands and my feet. It is I myself! Touch me and see; a ghost does not have flesh and bones, as you see I have" (Luke 24:39). Christianity distinguishes itself from so many other religions with the doctrine of a resurrected body. In Taoism, Yang transforms into Yin at the moment of death. Another way of saying it is that existence changes into nonexistence. Before Qui-Gon discovers how to retain his consciousness eternally, the state after death for him is nothingness.

Paul says, "Therefore we are always confident and know that as long as we are at home in the body we are away from the Lord" (2 Corinthians 5:6). For Christians, when we are in our mortal bodies, we are away from the Lord. In a similar way, the Jedi believe that every creature is away from the Force until they die. Yoda comforts Anakin with this belief telling him to rejoice when someone dies and transforms into the Force. The Jedi know that the afterlife is better than the suffering that goes on among the living. Solomon's words hold true here. "But better than both [the dead and the living] is the one who has never been born, who has not seen the evil that is done under the sun" (Ecclesiastes 4:3). It's only the Christian that goes on to a far better place. This can't be said for the Taoist, the Buddhist, the New Ager, or anyone else who doesn't know Jesus. While the unbeliever's life can be full of disease, sadness, and loss, it's still better than an afterlife without God.

The Jedi's belief in the afterlife is not the same as the other characters in *Star Wars*. Most believe in an afterlife where they will live on aware of their experience. While a positive afterlife is never mentioned, Han Solo references hell or at least a hell-like place when he says, "Then I'll see you in hell!" to the deck officer in *Episode V*. In addition, Uncle Owen threatens that Luke will "have hell to pay" if he doesn't have the units in the south range repaired by midday. Those are off-the-cuff expressions, but most likely, they have some basis in reality.

Once a person dies, he has no other chances from God to trust in Christ. "Just as people are destined to die once, and after that to face judgment" (Hebrews 9:27). At death, the souls of believers will go immediately to be with the Lord and the souls of unbelievers will be separated from all of God's benefits, namely his love and grace.

Genesis 1 teaches that God is separate from his creation. Unlike merging with the Force, when Christians die, their souls go to be with but not a part of the Lord. Being "in Christ" refers to Jesus acting as our representative before God. We will not be a part of God or become a god. Paul, in Philippians 1, implies that the "gain" at death is being with his Lord.

> For to me, to live is Christ and to die is gain. If I am to go on living in the body, this will mean fruitful labor for me. Yet what shall I choose? I do not know! I am torn between the two: I desire to depart and be with Christ, which is better by far; but it is more necessary for you that I remain in the body." (Philippians 1:21-24)

In the last scene of *Episode VI,* the Jedi's joy and peace is evident. It's because at long last, they can spend the rest of eternity immersed in the one thing to which they have devoted their lives. The reason we will be full of joy in heaven is not because we won't get sick or fear death. Eternal life with all its benefits is only a byproduct. The main reason for joy will be because we will be with the One we love.

Will We Recognize Others?

Deceased Jedi recognize others in the afterlife. Few religions other than Christianity allow room for this doctrine. Many fans (myself included) do not like how Lucas went back to *Episode VI* and digitally replaced Anakin's Force ghost (originally played by Sebastian Shaw) with Hayden Christensen. This confuses first-time watchers who view the saga in the order in which it was released. But this does teach an important point for believers. Luke still recognizes his father even though he had never seen the young version of him.

In Mark 9, when Elijah and Moses appear with Jesus during the transfiguration, Peter, James, and John recognize them. The disciples had never met the two prophets, but that didn't matter. Likewise, it seems that the Jedi are able to recognize others in their ghostly state. Perhaps the knowledge of the Force gives them this ability. In heaven, we will still have our identity only without sin. We'll be able to recognize not only Jesus but also other believers (past, present, and future), and they will know us.

🎬 Some fans might recognize the man who played Major Bren Derlin in *Episode V* as John Ratzenberger, the actor made famous for his role as Cliff Clavin on the TV show, *Cheers*.

"You Serve Your Master Well. And You Will Be Rewarded."

Let's return to our analogy of Han Solo before he was redeemed at the end of *Episode IV.* This Han Solo is in it for himself. He has little regard for others unless they help him advance his agenda. He reminds Princess Leia of this harsh reality when he says, "I expect to be well paid. I'm in it for the money." I'm afraid that sometimes we are motivated by a desire for comfort and happiness rather than to glorify God. While we may not be as blunt as Solo, the effect can be the same.

Remember the tactics Satan uses. He will go after your weaknesses. Just like analyzing the Death Star for a vulnerability, Satan, his demons, and religious charlatans do the same thing. If you're motivated by the idea of receiving great rewards in heaven (rather than Christ), you, like Anakin, will be susceptible to the seduction of the dark side. I say "the dark side," but I need to qualify that statement. A frequently misquoted verse goes like this, "money is the root of evil." Some of you are already correcting this. It's actually "the love of money is a root of all kinds of evil" (1 Timothy 6:10). Do you see the huge distinction? Just like everything else in life, sinful people turn something God gives us and use it selfishly.

It's not wrong to desire money in certain situations. For instance, if you have a choice between two jobs and one pays more, all things being equal, the better choice is probably the higher-paying job.

This would not only provide better for your family (if you have one), it would also allow you to be more generous to those in need.

The danger arises when we compromise our allegiance to God in exchange for financial gain. This is why Jesus and the teaching passages of the New Testament warn us of the dangers of money and to not become sucked in by its false claim of fulfillment.

Remember in Chapter 8, we saw that the early *"Episode IV"* Han Solo acts as a picture of the Old Covenant Israelite. He is motivated by physical rewards. God is very clear that under this covenant, the blessings are physical in nature (Malachi 3:9–12).

Recall that we are now under a different covenant with God. The old has passed and the new has come. Now our reward is no longer physical but spiritual. "Praise be to the God and Father of our Lord Jesus Christ, who has blessed us in the heavenly realms with every *spiritual* blessing in Christ" (Ephesians 1:3, emphasis mine).

God still blesses us with physical things. Most of us have a place to live, food, maybe a car, clothes in the closet, and even money left over for entertainment. I assume you spend money on food before you spend it on *Star Wars* collectibles, but I can relate to your priorities if that's not the case.

While money shouldn't be the be-all and end-all of our existence, we also shouldn't act like Buddhists and try to dump everything in the physical realm. The Jedi's main goal is to not have any attachments in this life. They view attachments as the root of all evil. By and large, the Bible makes a clear distinction that it's not the physical side that's the problem but the love of the physical side.

So, the Bible mentions several times that we will receive a crown if we persevere to the end and serve God well. But the Bible clarifies itself and describes this crown as a "crown of life" (James 1:12) or a "crown of righteousness" (2 Timothy 4:8). The crown is not gold or some sort of other physical wealth. The crown of life is simply a colorful way of describing our salvation, our glorification, and being with the Lord forever in heaven. The verses above do not imply that only certain Christians receive the crown, nor does it mean that the more faithful believers will receive a better reward than other believers. The crown of life, as 2 Timothy 4:8 says, will be awarded to *all* who have longed for Christ's appearing.

The Jedi would reject material wealth in the afterlife as a reward for their faithful service. That being said, Obi-Wan, Yoda, and Anakin all zealously pursue the crown of eternal life.

A Hopeful Future

The end times is the final chapter in God's astonishing plan of salvation. Before we were in Christ, God saw us walking down the narrow plank over the Sarlacc's mouth and devised the ultimate rescue operation. For unbelievers, the thought of the end times should frighten them. Relying on their own merit, they have no hope when Christ returns. But this is when the gospel can burst through with hope. God pursues his chosen people, gives them new hearts, and predestines a transformed life. Believers are responsible to share this rescue plan with unbelievers who are precariously living out what may be their last days. We must act like Han Solo who sees Lando already being pulled in by the Sarlacc's tentacle. Han lowers a spear towards Lando and yells to him, "Grab it!" The presentation of the gospel is this spear, the instrument that God can use to bring someone to Christ.

We don't know when the Lord will come back. So, the time for believing is today. When you share Jesus with others, God may use you to be a part of his rescue plan. Be bold in sharing your faith. The doctrine of irresistible grace teaches that God is already working in the hearts of people all over the place. He goes before you and softens hearts. Even if your gospel presentation is rough around the edges, God can use it.

We all have loved ones, friends, acquaintances, and strangers in our lives who need Christ desperately. Like the Death Star's garbage compactor, the walls are closing in on them. Death is inevitable. They might try to prolong its arrival, ignore it, or fool themselves into thinking they have earned God's favor. But all of this is like Han and Leia's futile attempt to brace the walls with flimsy objects that can never hold up. They need the power of the gospel to save them.

While Judgment Day should terrify unbelievers, the end times shouldn't alarm believers. We shouldn't worry, because God has already prepared our home.

Do not let your hearts be troubled. You believe in God; believe also in me. My Father's house has many rooms; if that were not so, would I have told you that I am going there to prepare a place for you? And if I go and prepare a place for you, I will come back and take you to be with me that you also may be where I am. (John 14:1-3)

For the Christian, the end is a wonderful thing. It's when Jesus will come back to do away with sin once and for all. More importantly, it's when he'll bring us home to be with him forever. This is why Paul can actually say that it's better by far to depart from this life and be with Christ. Death is no longer the enemy that it's always been, because Jesus has triumphed over the grave.

Anakin never found the way to escape death through the dark side. The only way to eternal life is found in the light.

When Jesus spoke again to the people, he said, "I am the light of the world. Whoever follows me will never walk in darkness, but will have the light of life." (John 8:12)

And giving joyful thanks to the Father, who has qualified you to share in the inheritance of his holy people in the kingdom of light. For he has rescued us from the dominion of darkness and brought us into the kingdom of the Son he loves, in whom we have redemption, the forgiveness of sins. (Colossians 1:12-14)

When studying eschatology, remember one important fact: Jesus has done it all. He has defeated Satan and is just waiting until his appointed time to return. Our responsibility is not to try to figure out when this will be. Our job is only to live for Jesus now.

EPILOGUE

Through this book, you've been on a long journey with Jesus and the Jedi. Along the way, you learned that God pursued you, rescued you, and purchased for you not only an eternity with him in paradise but also a transformed life here on Earth. You've learned how to avoid the dark path of legalism, how to handle your responsibility in the midst of God's sovereignty, and about the gifts and role of the Holy Spirit. You were even brave enough to enter the dangerous asteroid field of politics.

Hopefully, this was a fun journey for you. However, like Luke in his adventure, I'm sure it was not without some bumps along the way. You may have difficulty buying into certain parts of this book, and that's fine. The last thing I want you to do is take my word for it, although I do pray that you will revisit the Bible (your ultimate authority) as you work through any of these doctrines.

As I've stated before, we love God more when we know him better. We know him better through the study of his Word. Don't let everything you've learned serve only as lofty doctrine. Use that knowledge and be transformed by the renewing of your mind (Romans 12:2). If your knowledge doesn't lead to a deeper love of God and others, then, as Paul says in 1 Corinthians 13, you gain nothing.

This book started with the idea of hope. Sometimes, hope is all that a person needs to get out of bed in the morning. Hope that the day won't be too painful. Hope that relationships will not fall apart. Hope that life will have a purpose. Hope that the future will be brighter than the past.

Luke needs hope when he gazes up at the twin suns of Tatooine. And hope is what he receives when he leaves his desolate life on Tatooine to study the ways of the Force. He must battle his own demons along the way, but in the end, his hope is realized. Not stopping there, his life gives hope to the entire galaxy.

If you are in Christ, you can have a hope about which unbelievers can only dream. Hope in the midst of life's severest trials, because God works out everything for your spiritual and eternal benefit.

Hope, because you play a role in God's plan that no one else can do. Hope, because in the gospel, relationships can be healed. Hope, because the future will be brighter (and lighter) than the past. Keep living for God. Keep pressing ahead. Hold on to that living hope he gives. When you do that, like a redeemed Anakin, you will find the true path to light, love, and life.

> Praise be to the God and Father of our Lord Jesus Christ! In his great mercy he has given us new birth into a living hope through the resurrection of Jesus Christ from the dead, and into an inheritance that can never perish, spoil or fade. This inheritance is kept in heaven for you. (1 Peter 1:3–4)

WHAT TO DO NEXT?

Thank you so much for reading my book. I hope that you were encouraged. I'd love to hear if it helped you or if you have any other thoughts about it.

Feel free to email me at **bradley@popredeemed.com** or check out **www.popredeemed.com** where you can subscribe to the mailing list. If you know anyone who you think would like this book, please let them know. It would also be a huge help if you leave a review where you bought this book. Thanks!

ACKNOWLEDGMENTS

I couldn't have written this book if not for all the wonderful theological "Masters" who have gone before me. God has blessed me with countless great teachers of his Word over the last 25 years. Some who have been especially influential on me are Carl Kalberkamp, Jr., Jeff Elliot, John MacArthur, R.C. Sproul, Alistair Begg, and Russell D. Moore. I doubt any of them would agree with every point of my theology, but they all have taught me the importance of the Bible to my Christian life and to not compromise on what Scripture says. I'm sure their inspiration comes across in my writing even if I don't always realize it.

My biggest theological influence for this book is Geoff Volker, director of In-Depth Studies, a Bible-teaching ministry, and pastor of New Covenant Bible Fellowship in Tempe, Arizona. He lives out 1 Corinthians 10:31 every day and has taught me and so many others how to handle the Bible's teachings in a way that honors God. He has been an invaluable resource during my writing, and I attribute much of this book to his teaching. If anyone wants to go further in studying the doctrines brought up in this book, I highly recommend you reach out to Geoff.

Thanks to my awesome editor, Kevin Miller, who not only did a fantastic job at making sure my thoughts were presented clearly and tersely but also knew enough about *Star Wars* to correct me when I spelled Tarkin with an "e." A big thanks to my beta readers, Mike Tinker, Geoff Volker, and Sarah Knaub, who spent many hours helping me see where my manuscript could be improved. Thanks also to Brent Barcena, who helped with various art projects, Bill Sangalli for the interior design, and to Zach Volker for the awesome book cover.

Thanks to my kids Annabelle, Bryson, and Miles for having good attitudes even when their daddy needed to write about *Star Wars* instead of playing *Star Wars*.

Finally, thank you, Samantha, for not only reading every word of this but also for praying and serving me and our family throughout this long project. I am very thankful to have a godly wife who loves Jesus like you do (and it helps that you like *Star Wars* a lot, too).

ENDNOTES

1. Taoism is defined as "a Chinese philosophy based on the writings of Lao-tzu that stresses living simply and honestly and in harmony with nature; a religion developed from Taoist philosophy and folk and Buddhist religion and concerned with obtaining long life and good fortune often by magical means" "Taoism." *Merriam-Webster.com*. 2015. http://www.merriam-webster.com/dictionary/taoism (17 Nov 2015).

2. C. S. Lewis, *God in the Dock* (New York: HarperCollins, 2014), Kindle Edition.

3. I often use the pronouns *he, him,* and *his* only because repeatedly using "he or she," "him or her," and "his or her" gets tiring for the reader. This is a stylistic choice. My intention is not to exclude women. I also use the words *mankind* and *man* not to ignore women but because the Bible uses these terms to refer to all of humanity.

4. I heard this analogy from one of R.C. Sproul's sermons located at www.ligonier.org/learn/sermons/.

5. "conviction." *Merriam-Webster.com*. 2015. http://www.merriam-webster.com/dictionary/conviction (15 Sep 2014).

6. Temple of the Jedi Order: First International Church of Jediism. Retrieved from http://www.templeofthejediorder.org/ (10 Oct 2014).

7. The Thales and Heraclitus comments are from R.C. Sproul. *The Consequences of Ideas* teaching series. www.ligonier.org

8. I am indebted to R.C. Sproul for these two thoughts about energy (how another might describe it in relation to work or as a formula). These thoughts are from *The Consequences of Ideas* teaching series. *Monism and Pluralism* episode. www.ligonier.org

9. Tyler O'Neil. (27 Jan 2014). "Christians Are Following Secular Trends in Premarital Sex, Cohabitation Outside of Marriage, Says Dating Site Survey." Retrieved from http://www. christianpost.com/news/christians-are-following-secular-trends-in-premarital-sex-cohabitation-outside-of-marriage-says-dating-site-survey-113373/

10. Jon Winokur, *The Portable Curmudgeon Redux* (New York: Dutton, 1992), 302.

11. "Asceticism" is defined as "the doctrine that a person can attain a high spiritual and moral state by practicing self-denial, self-mortification, and the like." Dictionary.reference.com. 2015. http://dictionary.reference.com/browse/asceticism. (5 Dec 2015).

12. "antinomian." *Merriam-Webster.com*. 2015. http://www. merriam-webster.com/dictionary/antinomian (12 Jan 2015).

13. James Hibberd. "Anthony Daniels' Deep-Dive 'Star Wars' Interview: C-3PO's Past, Present and Future," *Entertainment Weekly,* 16 Sept. 2014, http://www.ew.com/ article/2014/09/16/star-wars-anthony-daniels-interview/2

14. Worldometers, "Abortions Worldwide This Year," Worldometers. info. http://www.worldometers.info/abortions/ (17 Nov. 2015).

15. Ephesians 4:26

16. "insidious." *Merriam-Webster.com*. 2015. http://www.merriam-webster.com/dictionary/insidious (17 Nov 2015).

17. "foreknow." Merriam-Webster.com. 2015. http://www. merriam-webster.com/dictionary/foreknow (29 Jul 2015).

18. John Calvin, *Calvin's Complete Commentary, Volume 6: Matthew to John.* (Harrington: Delmarva Publications, Inc., 2013).

ABOUT THE AUTHOR

Bradley Hagan grew up watching way too much TV. When his family got cable, he watched way too many movies. After he gave his life to Jesus, he wondered if all those hours spent in front of the tube could be redeemed somehow for his Lord. The answer is, yes! With pop culture as his backdrop, his goal is to equip Christians to know the Bible better so they can love God more. For more than fifteen years, he has been a worship leader at several churches across America.